Liz Hunt and Sam McCarter

# IELTS Introduction

## Teacher's Book

MACMILLAN

Macmillan Education
Between Towns Road, Oxford OX4 3PP
A division of Macmillan Publishers Limited

Companies and representatives throughout the world

ISBN 978-0-230-42575-0

Text, design and illustration © Macmillan Publishers Limited 2012
Written by Liz Hunt and Sam McCarter

First published 2012

Designed by Expo Holdings, Malaysia
Illustrated by Oxford Designers & Illustrators Limited

Authors' acknowledgements
The authors would like to thank Jo Kent for her sterling work and patience.

IELTS band descriptors on page 6 reproduced with permission of Cambridge ESOL.

These materials may contain links for third party websites. We have no control over, and are not
responsible for, the contents of such third party websites. Please use care when accessing them.

Although we have tried to trace and contact copyright holders before publication, in some cases this
has not been possible. If contacted we will be pleased to rectify any errors or omissions at the
earliest opportunity.

Printed and bound in Thailand

2016 2015 2014 2013 2012
10 9 8 7 6 5 4 3 2 1

# Introduction

*IELTS Introduction* caters for the increasing number of students at lower levels (score bands 3–4) who are preparing for the academic version of the International English Language Testing System (IELTS).

*IELTS Introduction* consists of the following components:

- Student's Book
- Class Audio CDs
- Study Skills Book and Audio CD
- Teacher's Book

## Student's Book

The Student's Book, *IELTS Introduction*, is designed to help prepare students for the IELTS Academic Module. The coursebook aims to take students with a global IELTS band score of 3 through to band score 4. The book contains a wide range of activities to introduce students to IELTS in a gentle way and to help them improve their English to take them up to the level of *IELTS Foundation*.

There are 12 units with additional Grammar and Vocabulary exercises related to the units in the main body of the coursebook. There is also a Writing section with examples of model answers and comments, and a copy of the audioscript. The book covers a wide range of simplified versions of the task in all four skills required for the academic version of IELTS. So, for example, the reading texts are shorter than in the exam and the writing tasks in most of the book do not require students to write full IELTS answers, except towards the end of the Student's Book.

In each unit, there is one reading passage, practice either in Task 1 or Task 2 of the IELTS Academic Writing test and one or more practice sections for one of the three parts of the IELTS Speaking test. As well as providing relevant practice in listening, reading, writing and speaking, each unit includes at least one Language focus section together with at least one section on Vocabulary. As part of the vocabulary development, there are sections throughout the coursebook on word building. All of these sections focus on areas that are important for the IELTS exam and are integrated with the skills. At the end of each unit there is a Study skills section to help students improve certain skills. The book also contains advice and tips about strategies for the IELTS exam.

## Listening

The listening practice covers all the sections of the Listening module with examples of the question types in the IELTS exam. There is one listening practice for the Listening module in each unit. The length of each listening section is shorter and simpler than in the exam, but it follows the exam format. The questions also follow the exam format, but again they are much simpler than in the exam itself.

## Reading

Like the listening, the reading passages and questions follow the exam format, but the passages are shorter and simpler than in the IELTS exam. There is one reading passage per unit and most of the passages have a short Glossary.

## Writing

The main question types for Tasks 1 and 2 are covered in the Student's Book. Students are not required to write full exam-type answers as this would be inappropriate at this level. Considerable input is given before students are asked to write themselves.

## Speaking

Each unit contains practice in at least one part of the Speaking module and in some cases all three parts are covered. Speaking practice also forms part of most of the Vocabulary and Language focus sections as a way to activate the language input.

## Grammar

The Grammar section at the back of the Student's Book contains an explanation of the grammar covered in the Language focus sections in the main units. The section can be used for self-study, or to help explain the grammar to the students. In this section, there is also at least one additional grammar exercise per Language focus section. The exercises recycle the grammar covered in the Language focus sections and can be used for additional practice, for further practice for more advanced students who finish the exercises in the Language focus sections, or indeed as extra practice for weaker students.

## Vocabulary

Just like the Grammar section, the Vocabulary section at the back of the Student's Book contains additional exercises that recycle the vocabulary covered in the main units. The exercises can be used in the same ways as those in the Grammar section.

## Writing

At the end of the Student's Book there is a section containing model answers for the writing tasks in the main units, along with comments. For each unit there is at least one model answer. The Student's Book aims to gradually build students' confidence in writing, so for most of the course only partial answers are required rather than full IELTS exam answers. The model answers and comments should be looked at after students have completed the corresponding writing tasks in the units. It is better to look at the model answers and discuss the comments in class rather than leaving it up to the students to do so as self-study.

## Basic techniques for building confidence among low-level students

Some low-level students may require extra input by way of knowledge and language before they do practice in four skills throughout the course. Advice is given about how to deal with this in the teaching notes. However, you may feel that in some classes even more help is required.

## Reading and Listening

- Before doing reading practice, you can give students words or phrases from one or more paragraphs from a reading passage and ask them how the words and phrases fit together to form ideas. This can be done in pairs or groups, followed by whole-class discussion. When they come to read the passage the contents will be more familiar to them. The same technique can be used before any listening practice. Then as you go though the course you can reduce reliance on techniques like this.
- You can give students between five and seven sentences from the reading passage or sentences from another reading passage on the same topic. The sentences can be shuffled, then students put them in order as they think they might occur in the passage. Alternatively, the sentences can be in order

and students build a picture of schema of the text. A variation of this can be used for the Listening.
- Students may often understand the reading passage, but not the questions. As a variation in the class, do not allow students to look at the reading passage. Let them look at the questions and give them the title of the passage. Ask them in groups to study and explain the questions. Check their answers as a whole class. Then let them read the passage and answer the questions. The same technique can be used for each Listening section. As students' confidence increases, reduce the time that you allow them to look at the questions and discuss.
- Encourage students to collect examples of different types of questions, for example True/False/Not Given statements. For example, they can make a list of examples of statements with common language patterns such as comparisons, cause and effect, evaluations, statements with words of quantity (eg, *the majority of/most*, etc) along with paraphrases of these statements. You can use these statements as examples to explain the different types of True/False/Not Given statements in future classes or as a revision tool.
- While the focus of reading in IELTS is often on speed, vary the pace of the reading and focus on 'slow reading', getting students to read the passage aloud, and discuss the contents before answering the questions.

## Speaking and Writing

- Pre-teach ideas before students do tasks relating to Speaking Part 3 and Writing Task 2. This can build students' confidence in these areas of the exam. Pre-teaching ideas can be in the form of pictures as well as sharing ideas. Students can make lists of ideas that they can use in both speaking and writing. Point out that just as words and phrases can be recycled, ideas and concepts can also be recycled. For example, education can be used as a means of reducing crime, poverty and damage to the environment. If necessary, you can write words such as *education, environment, finance, society, training* and *business* on the board as triggers for students before they start preparing for writing or speaking. Alternatively, elicit the words from students.
- If necessary for pronunciation, use whole-class drills or half-class drills for word, phrase, clause and sentence stress patterns. Mature students can benefit from drills, but be aware of students' backgrounds and sensibilities.

## Teacher's Book

The Teacher's Book provides a key for all the exercises, including sample answers for free practice activities, where appropriate. The teaching notes accompanying the key provide additional guidance for inexperienced teachers and also offer suggestions for extra activities. Throughout the Teacher's Book, the audioscript is provided with the answers underlined for ease of reference. At the end of the Teacher's Book, there is a bank of photocopiable materials with a key – one activity for each unit of the Student's Book. Each of these activities relates to one section of the Student's Book and focuses on using the language already introduced in the unit rather than introducing new language. For example, the photocopiable material for Unit 1 relates to Writing Task 1. All 12 activities can be used in class to develop students' skills.

## Study Skills Book

The Study Skills Book contains further practice for students to do as self-study. The content follows the unit themes of the Students' Book, providing further exam practice.

## The Academic version of the IELTS exam

### Listening (approximately 30 minutes)

The Listening module has 40 questions and lasts approximately 30 minutes.

The module contains four sections with ten questions in each section. The first two sections are of a social nature. Section 1 is a conversation between two people and Section 2 is usually a monologue. However, Section 2 can also be a conversation between two people. Sections 3 and 4 are connected with education and training. Section 3 is a conversation involving up to 4 people and Section 4 is a monologue.

Students hear each section once only and answer the questions in the question booklet as they listen. At the end of the test, students have 10 minutes to transfer their answers to the answer sheet.

The types of questions used are: multiple choice, short-answer questions, sentence completion, notes/form/summary/flowchart completion, labelling a diagram/plan/map, classification and matching.

### Academic Reading (1 hour)

In the Academic Reading module, there are three passages which are from various sources such as books,

journals, magazines and newspapers. The passages do not require specialist knowledge for students to understand them and at least one of the three passages contains a detailed logical argument.

The range of question types that are used in the Reading module are: choosing suitable paragraph headings from a list, identification of information using True/False/Not Given questions, identification of writer's views/claims using Yes/No/Not Given questions, multiple choice, short-answer questions, sentence completion, notes/summary/flowchart/table completion, labelling a diagram, classification, matching.

### Academic Writing (1 hour)

The Academic Writing test lasts one hour and there are two tasks. Students are advised to spend 20 minutes on Task 1 and asked to write at least 150 words. For Task 2, students are advised to spend 40 minutes and asked to write at least 250 words.

Assessment for Task 1 is based on students' ability to summarize, organize and compare data where possible, to describe the stages of a process, describe an object or event or explain how something works. Students' range of vocabulary, ability to use a range of grammatical structures, accuracy, the coherence of their writing and their ability to complete the task are assessed.

In Task 2, students are given a point of view, argument or problem. Assessment is based on their ability to write a solution to the problem; present and support their opinion; compare and contrast evidence and opinions; evaluate and challenge ideas, evidence or arguments; and write in an appropriate style.

The rubric or instructions in the questions follow these patterns:

*Discuss the advantages and disadvantages of …*

*Discuss both these views and give your own opinion.*

*To what extent do you agree or disagree?*

Or students may be asked a specific question such as:

*Which do you consider to be the major influence?*

*What do you think are the causes of this problem and what solutions can you suggest?*

In both Tasks 1 and 2, students are assessed on their ability to write in a style that is suitable for the task.

### Speaking (11–14 minutes)

The IELTS Speaking test lasts between 11 and 14 minutes and consists of three parts. The exam is recorded.

The Examiner assesses students' ability to communicate effectively in English and specifically assesses:

- Fluency and coherence: how well students speak without hesitating and the organization of their answers.
- Lexical resource: the range of vocabulary they use.
- Grammatical range and accuracy: the range of grammar they use, for example the range of structures and complex sentences using connecting words, eg, *because, for instance, and so, but* and so on.
- Pronunciation: how clear and intelligible students are when they speak.

**Band 9 – Expert User**
Has fully operational command of the language: appropriate, accurate and fluent with complete understanding.

**Band 8 – Very Good User**
Has fully operational command of the language with only occasional unsystematic inaccuracies and inappropriacies. Misunderstandings may occur in unfamiliar situations. Handles complex detailed argumentation well.

**Band 7 – Good User**
Has operational command of the language, though with occasional inaccuracies, inappropriacies and misunderstandings in some situations. Generally handles complex language well and understands detailed reasoning.

**Band 6 – Competent User**
Has generally effective command of the language despite some inaccuracies, inappropriacies and misunderstandings. Can use and understand fairly complex language, particularly in familiar situations.

**Band 5 – Modest User**
Has partial command of the language, coping with overall meaning in most situations, though is likely to make many mistakes. Should be able to handle basic communication in own field.

**Band 4 – Limited User**
Basic competence is limited to familiar situations. Has frequent problems in understanding and expression. Is not able to use complex language.

**Band 3 – Extremely Limited User**
Conveys and understands only general meaning in very familiar situations. Frequent breakdowns in communication can occur.

**Band 2 – Intermittent User**
No real communication is possible except for the most basic information using isolated words or short formulae in familiar situations and to meet immediate needs. Has great difficulty in understanding spoken and written English.

**Band 1 – Non User**
Essentially has no ability to use the language beyond possibly a few isolated words.

**Band 0 – Did not attempt the test**
No assessable information provided

# Contents of the Teacher's Book

# Contents of the Student's Book

## Content overview

### Themes

This unit acts as an introduction to the different parts of the IELTS exam and is thematically focused on finding out about the world.

### Exam-related activities

#### Reading

Skimming
Matching headings
Identifying information: True/False/Not Given
Choosing items from a list
Short-answer questions

#### Writing

Task 1    Describing a chart

#### Listening

Section 1
Numbers and letters
Multiple choice
Choosing items from a list
Sentence completion

### Speaking

Part 1    Talking about transport
Part 2    Talking about places you like to visit

### Language development

#### Language focus and Vocabulary

Places to visit
Talking about the present
Word building: Adjectives for describing places
Past simple

### Skills development

#### Reading

Skimming

### Study skills

Listening: Numbers and letters
Writing/Describing: rise and fall

---

## Vocabulary 1    page 6

### Places to visit

**Aim**

The aim of this section is to introduce students to vocabulary that will be useful throughout the unit, especially for Speaking Part 2 on page 11.

**Pre-activity**

Before students open the book, put pictures of different places on the board and elicit adjectives to describe these places. Write these in a column down the side of the board and check pronunciation.

**1** Ask students to look at the pictures in the book. Working in pairs, they can use some of the vocabulary on the board and add some of their own if they wish. As you monitor the students, add any useful new words you hear to the list on the board.

### Sample answers

A The place is very green with lots of trees and a river or stream. It is very wild and looks an exciting place.
B There is a beautiful blue sky with a palm tree and a beach with white sand. The sea is blue/green. It looks very relaxing.
C It's really built-up with a very modern building, which might be a museum. It's an exciting-looking building.
D It's got a huge mountain with snow on the top. It's perhaps a volcano.

**2** Check the answers as a whole class and draw students' attention to the additional vocabulary on the board. Check comprehension by asking students to explain their answers.

### Answers

1 C    2 A    3 B    4 D

**3** If necessary, drill the question and different answers. Then students practise in pairs.

**4** Students can do this individually. Tell them not to worry if they don't know all the vocabulary at this point. They should predict the answers using the words they know. If necessary, allow students to use a dictionary.

**Answers**

| | | |
|---|---|---|
| 1 | *garden* | → grass, flowers, plants, birds |
| 2 | *beach* | → sea, waves, shells, sand dunes |
| 3 | *countryside* | → trees, fields, rivers, lakes |
| 4 | *city* | → roads, offices, museums, theatres |
| 5 | *mountain* | → rocks, valley, cave, waterfall |

**5** Before students check their answers in pairs, elicit the meaning of unknown words. Encourage students to keep an electronic or hard copy vocabulary book. You could suggest they make a page headed 'Places' and you might like to show them how to do a spidergram or mind map. Tell them that grouping words under subjects is a more efficient way of recording words than alphabetical lists. Throughout the course, check that students are updating their vocabulary books.

**6** Tell students to do this exercise individually and then check their answers in pairs. Point out that there is more than one answer.

**Answers**

1 beach/sand dunes; waves/sea
2 rocks
3 countryside
4 theatres
5 garden; birds

**7** Ask students to make the questions individually after putting the examples on the board and reviewing question forms. Monitor students and give help where necessary. They can then ask and answer questions in pairs while you monitor and correct any mistakes. Encourage several pairs of students to answer the questions in their own words as a demonstration for the whole class.

**Extension**

As an extra exercise at the end of the section, students can work in pairs or groups. One student describes somewhere famous in the world, eg, New York, Paris or somewhere local that everyone knows, and the other student(s) has(have) to guess where it is.

## Numbers and letters

### Aim

This section aims to give students practice with listening to and saying numbers and the letters of the alphabet, which is useful for the Listening module.

### Suggestion

As a class awareness exercise, put students into groups and ask them to make a list of a maximum of seven difficulties they may have in dealing with numbers or the alphabet in English. For example, there might be confusion between writing the numbers in English for Farsi speakers, eg, a confusion between 6 in English, which is written like a 7 in Farsi. If the class is monolingual, follow the same process.

**1** Go over the instructions, using the first item as an example or eliciting some numbers and letters from students. Let them work out the others in pairs and then get class feedback. Illustrate how *FFF* might be said as *double ef ef*; 66 as *double six*, etc. Ask students to identify sounds that may be ambiguous, eg, W = *double u* not *vee/wee*. You might like to do choral drilling here.

Keep a record of some specific problematic areas of pronunciation and focus on them throughout the course. As a whole class, students can make a list of the alphabet and the pronunciation of the letters. They can do the same for numbers and add the lists to their vocabulary books.

**2** As an example, dictate one or more of the items 1–6 from exercise **1**. Use an appropriate speed for this level. To check comprehension, ask students to dictate sequences of numbers and letters for you to write on the board.

**3** (O) **1.1** Play the recording once and let students fill in the spaces individually. After comparing their answers in pairs, students can listen again to check their answers. To monitor comprehension, ask selected students to read the completed notes.

**Answers**

1 TLM 19772
2 XY331373TV
3 07967 55 33 79
4 49
5 BE5 9KV

**1.1**

0  flight numberTA5557
1  flight numberTLM 19772
2  booking reference XY331373TV
3  mobile number 07967 55 33 79
4  My address is 49 Malory Park.
5  The code is BE5 9KV.

## Listening 2 page 7

### IELTS Listening Section 1

#### Aim
This section aims to introduce students to the first section of the IELTS Listening module.

#### Suggestion
To help students develop their listening skills, encourage them to listen to different types of listening material, not just material that is available for IELTS. If your school has a resource centre, arrange a visit specifically to introduce students to the listening material available. Encourage students to do one listening exercise, no matter how short, each day.
Some students may feel nervous about listening, so it is important to build up their confidence as early as possible in the course.

#### Exam information
In the IELTS Listening module, there are four sections. Sections 1 and 2 are usually about social topics, while Sections 3 and 4 are more academic. There are 10 questions in each section. Students need to use correct spelling in their answers.

1   Go over the Exam information on page 8 carefully and check students understand the format. Regarding the Strategy, they should underline key words in the preparation time given before the dialogue starts.

Explain to students that they will always have 30–40 seconds before the dialogue starts. They should use this time wisely to find key words in the questions and underline them.

#### Questions 1–5: Multiple choice
Use the example to show how to look at the distractors, find the differences between them, and see how they relate to the stem. In this case, the differences are in the tenses and negative/positive words used.

#### Questions 6–8: Choosing items from a list
Ask students to put a box around 'three' in the rubric. Encourage them to box numbers or important information in the rubrics throughout the course and in the exam.

Point out that they will not get extra marks if they tick four items.

#### Questions 9 and 10: Sentence completion
Ask students to look at the gaps and predict the type of word that is missing, eg, noun/verb/number, etc, and the word itself.

Now play the recording all the way through once, monitoring which questions students are having difficulty with. Get them to check their answers with their partner. Play the recording again so they can fill in any questions they missed previously. Again, they check their answers in pairs. Finally, play the recording a final time, stopping at each answer on the CD to check. Make sure students understand the answers and explain the textual clues that help. Ask them to add up their scores and make a note of the question types they found more challenging.

#### Answers

1  B      2  B      3  A      4  C      5  B
6–8  A, B, D
9  3/three
10  ZB7334921G

**1.2**

(A = Ann; J = John)
A: Hi, John, is that you?
J: Yes. Ann?
A: Yes, it's me. Did you pack everything last night?
J: Yes, I did. But I'm just putting the last few things in my suitcase here at work, like books and things.
A: It's really exciting. I can't wait to get there.
J: Me neither.
A: I had a look at the weather forecast for the holiday and it looks as if it's going to be wonderful. It's going to be <u>30 degrees Celsius and sunny with no clouds at all</u>.
J: That's fantastic!
A: Yeah! The beaches there are marvellous with white sand, large sand dunes and blue sea and no offices or skyscrapers. We can spend some time on the beach. It's very relaxing.
J: Definitely. So don't forget your sun cream. When I'm on holiday I always lie on the beach and read books and listen to music. Then I do some shopping and I eat a lot; in fact, I do all the things that I don't really have time to do here.
A: Me too, but I want to visit a few historical sites as well.
J: As you know, <u>you'll have to do that on your own! I just lie around and do nothing</u>.
A: No problem. I find it difficult just sitting or lying around all day doing nothing at all.
J: Yeah. OK. So where shall we meet and when?
A: I think it's best at the airport itself. Let's meet on the departure level.
J: But where?
A: Well, there's a shopping area just on the left as you come to the departure level.
J: Yeah. I think I know it.
A: And the first restaurant as you go in on the left is Chinese. <u>It's got this map of China with one big star on it</u>.
J: Are you sure I won't miss it?

A: You won't. I can't remember the name, but anyway, we'll have our mobile phones.

J: Yes, so no need to worry.

A: OK. What time then?

J: Say 5 pm?

A: But the plane doesn't depart until 8 o'clock.

J: Yes, but we are supposed to be there two hours before check-in and baggage checks. That can take a good hour at least.

A: Yeah. I suppose so.

J: One thing. Do you think that they're strict about the baggage allowance?

A: Yes, I think so. We're only allowed 25 kilograms each.

J: I thought it was more.

A: Try putting some heavy things in your hand luggage, but don't overdo it!

J: Yeah; that's an idea.

...

A: Remember not to forget your passport and currency. You know what you're like about things like that.

J: I won't. I've already packed them!

A: Don't forget the mmm ... the guidebook!

J: Oh yes. It's still in the drawer here at work. I'm getting it out now as we're talking. Just as well you reminded me.

A: I knew you'd forget something!

J: So what time are you leaving the flat?

A: Mmm ... I think I'd better leave about three.

J: Yeah, that'll give you plenty of time. I can leave work at three if I want, but as we're not that far from the airport, it won't take me as long. So, I'll leave the office at about four.

A: Are you sure that's going to give you enough time?

J: Yeah, plenty.

A: OK. And what's the ticket reference?

J: Yes, we need the ticket reference to collect the tickets from the machine. Here it is, in my diary. It's ZB7334921G.

A: I think I'll write it down too just in case. ZB7334921G. Is that right?

J: Yes, that's it.

### Review

Play the recording again so students can listen to check comprehension. Weaker students can listen and read the script at the same time, if necessary. To help students practise for the exam, they can transfer their answers to a sheet of paper. Check that the spelling is correct. Write the answers on the board.

## Speaking 1    page 8

### IELTS Speaking Part 1

### Aim

This section introduces students to the first part of the Speaking module.

### Suggestion

Point out to students that they do not have to give long answers for this section, perhaps no more than one or two sentences. To help students to get used to answering questions rather than just describing things, you can elicit two or three extra questions about transport or places, write them on the board and ask students to ask each other the questions. Take feedback on the answers students give.

### Exam information

Part 1 takes between four and five minutes. Both the students and the examiner introduce themselves. The examiner will check some basic information (name/nationality) and then he/she asks the students about themselves, their family, their job/studies, their interests and a variety of familiar topics.

**1** Go over the Exam information with students, giving some examples of the types of questions the examiner will use to find out basic information.
Students can also do the exercise individually and check their answers in pairs before whole-class checking. Ask individual students the questions. Monitor their answers for pronunciation and intonation.

### Answers

| | | | | | |
|---|---|---|---|---|---|
| 1 | name | 3 | country | 5 | transport |
| 2 | Where | 4 | types/methods | | |

**2** You can ask students to use their own answers for the questions. Monitor their answers and elect some stronger students to model good responses to the class.

## Language focus 1    page 8

### Talking about the present

**1/2** Go through the questions as a class and ensure students understand the differences between the form and function of the two tenses here. For more information, refer them to the Grammar on page 150.

### Answers

**1**
1 present continuous
2 present simple

**2** The present simple relates to habit and the present continuous relates to a temporary action.

**3** Check the answers as a class. Ask students to explain the answers to you to check comprehension.

### Answers

| | | | | | |
|---|---|---|---|---|---|
| 1 d | 2 e | 3 a | 4 b | 5 c | 6 f |

**4** Check the answers with the whole class, eliciting the reasons for the correct alternatives.

**Answers**

| | | | |
|---|---|---|---|
| 1 | do people get | 4 | is touring |
| 2 | departs | 5 | don't swim |
| 3 | is happening | 6 | are having |

**5/6** If necessary, go over the Grammar on page 150 again before students do the rest of the Language focus exercises.

Monitor students as they complete these exercises and ensure their justifications for their decisions are logical.

**Answers**

1 reads; read (a a habit/repeated action)
2 eat (a a habit/repeated action); is becoming (e a temporary action (happening at this moment))
3 do not fly; travel (a a habit/repeated action)
4 Do you watch (a a habit/repeated action)
5 study (a a habit/repeated action); am/'m taking (f a temporary action happening around now)

**7/8** Monitor students for pronunciation and intonation in **7**. If necessary, do the additional exercise on page 150. To review this section, read the statements 1–6 in exercise **3** aloud and ask students to name the tense and explain why it is used.

**Answers**

1 What <u>are</u> you studying at the moment?
2 Where do <u>you</u> spend your time in the holidays?
3 <u>Are</u> you learning a language at the moment?
4 Do you lie on the beach when you <u>are</u> on holiday or do you go to museums?
5 <u>How</u> do you travel to class each day?

## Vocabulary 2 page 10

### Word building: Adjectives for describing places

**Aim**

The aim of this vocabulary section is to prepare students for the next section, Speaking Part 2, so that students can describe how they feel about a place as well as describing it physically.

**1/2** Give students time to look at the picture and come up with adjectives, which you can write on the board. During feedback, add new adjectives to the list already on the board.

**Sample answer**

The place is relaxing and pleasant. It is exciting because it is very wild. It is also very beautiful.

**3** Before students complete the table in pairs, ensure they are familiar with the column headings. Monitor for spelling at this point and check the meaning of the words.

**Answers**

| | | | |
|---|---|---|---|
| 1 | excitement | 7 | relaxation |
| 2 | appealing | 8 | attractive |
| 3 | appeal | 9 | attraction |
| 4 | boredom | 10 | impressive |
| 5 | interesting | 11 | impression |
| 6 | interest | | |

**4/5** Students can do exercise **4** individually and then check in pairs before whole-class checking. As students do the pairwork in exercise **5**, monitor for accuracy and give feedback.

**Answers**

1 relaxing/peaceful
2 excitement
3 impressive/thrilling/interesting
4 appeal/attraction
5 interest
6 relax
7 boring/dull

**Review**

To review the section, give students an adjective and ask them to tell you a related noun or verb. Remind them to add any new words to their vocabulary books, with examples of the context. Point out how word forms can help in guessing the meaning of new words.

**Extension**

To check comprehension at the end of the section, write a list of short sentences on the board with a mixture of adjectives, some from the table in exercise **3** and some adjectives describing physical attributes. Ask students to distinguish between the two types of adjectives.

## Speaking 2 page 11

### IELTS Speaking Part 2

**Exam information**

In Part 2 of the Speaking module the examiner gives students a card with some prompts. They are usually asked to talk about a person, an event, a place or an object. They have **1** minute to make notes and then speak for **1–2** minutes. The examiner does not ask them any questions.

**1** Go over the Exam information and explain the procedure. Look at the sample Task Card and point out the question words used. These are typical and each one needs to be answered. Encourage students to talk about each prompt in order. Ask them to do the activity in pairs, then check as a class.

**Answers**

| Describe somewhere that you like to visit. | *lake* |
|---|---|
| where the place is | *countryside* |
| when you visit the place | *weekends* |
| who you visit the place with | *friends* |
| why you like the place. | *relax, study, impressive, appeal, attractive, peaceful* |

**2/3** Students complete the gaps individually and check their answers in pairs and then as a whole class. Elicit the meaning of any unknown words. Students do the underlining in **3** as a pairwork activity. Check the answers as a whole class.

**Answers**

**2**

| 1 | lake | 6 | relax |
|---|---|---|---|
| 2 | countryside | 7 | study |
| 3 | weekends | 8 | appeal |
| 4 | friends | 9 | attractive |
| 5 | peaceful | 10 | impressive |

**3**

**Sample answers**

1 I'd like to describe
2 Some people find
3 it is a good place to
4 appeal to me a lot
5 Another reason I find the place attractive

**4** The words to stress here are *brief notes*. Remind them they only have a minute. Time students as they write and ask them to count their words.

**5/6** Before students start, elicit what they need to listen for and give feedback on. Ask one or two students to talk about the card to the class. Then give your own example.

## Reading    page 12

### Aim

The purpose of this section is to introduce students to the Academic Reading module. The reading passage is considerably shorter than passages students will encounter in the IELTS exam. The vocabulary has been simplified, but the text structure has not been changed and the format of the exam questions remains the same.

### Suggestion

To help build students' awareness of the exam, focus on one type of question that has been introduced, eg, paragraph or section headings. Elicit the structure of the headings, the types of words used, whether they are like newspaper headings, whether they use sentences or phrases, what types of phrases (usually noun phrases) are used, and why these phrases are used.

### Exam information

In the Reading module there are three reading passages, with a maximum of about 2,700 words in total. Each passage has 12–14 questions.

## Pre-reading

**1** When explaining the Exam information, show students a sample text so they can see what the length looks like. Discuss the exam Strategy. Stress that they may not have time to read the whole passage in detail in the exam, so they need to learn to skim. Point out that the title and the questions 1–13 are a summary of the reading passage. They can also skim the questions before they skim the passage.

These pre-reading strategies are extremely important to develop efficient reading skills. Go over them one by one and ask students to justify their answers.

**Answers**

**Section A**
1 Yes. Africa.
2 Yes. Yes.

**Section B**
1 Yes.
2 Yes. No.

**Section C**
1 The people.
2 Because rock art was made so long ago, <u>we do not know who the earliest artists</u> were. However, there are some exceptions to this. <u>We know that most of southern Africa's rock art was made by ancestors of modern San people.</u> In North Africa, we know that the earlier art, dating from more than 7,000 years ago, <u>was made by people who hunted and gathered wild food.</u> Paintings, including those of cattle dating from between 7,000 and 4,500 years ago, may have been made by <u>ancestors of Black West Africans.</u> Much of the art of the last 3,500 years, particularly the engravings of Niger and Mali, was produced by <u>ancestors of the Amazie people.</u>

**Section D**
1 Possible explanations.
2 Rock art is the only way we can tell how our ancestors thought and how they saw their world. However, because most rock art belonged to cultures that disappeared long ago, it is now difficult to understand why the artists painted and carved, or what their art meant to them. <u>Many</u>

researchers believe that the art had religious connections, expressing the artist's thoughts of reality and their position in the world around them.

It must have been a means of communication, but with whom? Bushmen artists showed their visions of a combined natural and spiritual world. Did they do this to tell others what they saw during dream-like states or was it a means to contact the earth's spirit and control nature? During the 20th century in eastern and central Africa, people used and still use rock paintings to bring rain, strengthen themselves and assist their souls through those difficult moments of birth, becoming adults, sickness and death. Perhaps our modern beliefs have ancient origins.

## Reading

**2** As in the Listening module, encourage students to underline key words in the questions. Introduce each question type separately before moving onto the next one so they get an introduction to the different skills necessary. Refer students to the Glossary.

### Questions 1–4: Matching headings
Ask students to underline words like *how* and nouns such as *overview* and *extent*. These give them some idea of the general information in the paragraph. They can then underline the words relating to content, such as *rock art* and *preserved*, which will help them scan.

### Questions 5–8: Identifying information – True/False/Not Given
Indicate the differences between these and point out that they have to be careful with False and Not Given. During checking, ensure students understand the reasons why answers are given and where to find them in the text.

### Questions 9–11: Choosing items from a list
Note the number of letters needed and key words in the items.

### Question 12 and 13: Short-answer questions
Note the word limit. Tell students they can use the answers to the matching headings section to help them locate these answers in the text.

When students have finished answering the questions, ask them to select 7–10 words from the reading passage that they think are useful to remember. Write them on the board with some context to help them to remember the words. They can then write them in their vocabulary books.

### Answers

| | | | |
|---|---|---|---|
| 1 | Section A iv | 7 | Not Given |
| 2 | Section B v | 8 | True |
| 3 | Section C vi | 10–12 | A, C, D |
| 4 | Section D iii | 13 | religious connections |
| 5 | False | 14 | ancient origins |
| 6 | False | | |

## Language focus 2    page 14

## Past simple

**1** After students have answered these questions, put the form on the board, or, if they seem quite familiar with the past simple, get one or two students to write it on the board. For further information, refer students to the Grammar on page 150.

### Answers

1 both irregular
2 You use *did you/he/she/it we/they* before the infinitive without *to*:
*Did you pack everything?*
With question words:
*What/When/Where/How/did you …?*
With *who* as the subject of the verb:
*Who packed (your suitcase)?*
3 you use the *did + not/n't +* the infinitive without *to*
*I did not/didn't (pack my suitcase).*

**2** This exercise can be completed in pairs, followed by class feedback.

### Answers

**Section A**
… were over 8 metres high …
… were very well made …
… people who had no knowledge …
… were made …

**Section C**
… who the earliest artists were …
… by people who hunted and gathered …

**Section D**
… thought and how they saw their world …
… belonged to cultures that disappeared …
… why the artists painted and carved, or what their art meant …
… the art had religious connections …
… showed their visions …
… Did they do this …
… was it a means …
… people used …

**3** Once students have finished this exercise and checked their answers in pairs, ask them to identify regular and irregular verb forms.

### Answers

| | | | |
|---|---|---|---|
| 1 | made; went | 5 | wrote; went |
| 2 | Did (you) have; were | 6 | did (you) visit; stayed |
| 3 | did (the air fare) cost | 7 | didn't fly; caught |
| 4 | grew | | |

**4/5** Once students have done exercise **4**, to check comprehension, select several students to answer the questions. Alternatively, students can ask you the questions. If necessary, chain drill the questions around the class to check for intonation and linking, before students do the pairwork in **5**.

### Answers

1 What were your favourite games when you <u>were</u> young?
2 <u>How</u> did you spend your weekends when you were at secondary school?
3 Why <u>did</u> you start to learn English?
4 Did you live in a town or the countryside <u>when</u> you were a child?
5 Who did <u>you</u> most admire when you were young?
6 What hobbies did you <u>have</u> as a child?

## Writing   page 14

### IELTS Writing Task 1

#### Aim
This section introduces students to their first attempt at interpreting data. At this level, do not expect students to write an exam-length answer.

#### Suggestion
To help familiarize students with using data, you can use information gap activities as in the pairwork exercises in the photocopiable activity on page 110.

#### Exam information
In Task 1, students are asked to describe a graph, a chart, a map, a diagram of how something works, or a process. Sometimes there is more than one set of data, but the different sets are always connected in some way. Students need to write a minimum of 150 words and write in paragraphs. If they do not, it will affect their score. The introduction needs to paraphrase the description in the instructions.

**1** Go over the Exam information with students. Show examples of the different types of data that are common in the exam: line graphs, bar charts, pie charts and tables.

Students could be encouraged to write new words in their vocabulary books under a new heading of 'Task 1'.

Go through the Strategy box with students, stressing the importance of not writing about everything, just the most significant points. Draw their attention to the Tip and point out that numbering, circling and drawing arrows on the diagram can help them plan their answers.

Students can do this exercise in pairs. Check the answers as a whole class and ask them questions about

the exam rubric or instructions and the graph using statements 1–8. Point out that the rubric is typical of rubrics they will see in the IELTS exam. Emphasize the words *summarize, main features* and *comparisons*.

### Answers

1 a graph
2 percentages
3 Europe, North America and All other countries
4 1993 to 2007
5 illustrates
6 summarize the information
7 main characteristics
8 more

**2** Ask students to match the phrases under each heading to the graph and to justify their answers. Check the answers as a whole class.

Ask students to write columns headed *rise, fall, go up and down* in their vocabulary books. As they work through the next seven activities, they can add words to the appropriate columns.

### Answers

1 b    2 c    3 a

**3/4** Go through these carefully when students have done the activities, and stress how this is essential vocabulary for Task 1.

### Answers

rise: peak, increase, climb, go up, hit a peak, grow
fall: drop, dip, became less popular, hit a low, decrease, decline, go down
go up and down: fluctuate, rise and fall, vary, be erratic

**5** Point out to students the importance of learning the nouns that can be made from verbs and vice versa. Encourage them to use both in writing and speaking. Stress that using synonyms accurately, and different forms of the same root, is a good writing strategy.

### Answers

rise, peak, increase, fall, drop, dip, decrease, decline

**6** Elicit the examples from students and ask them to explain their answers.

#### Sample answer

peaked at about 62 per cent around 1998
fell significantly between 1999 and 2007
fluctuated between 30 per cent and 40 per cent

**7** When you have checked the answers, match the description to the graph in exercise **1**. Ask a student to read the completed text aloud.

**Answers**

1 provides information about
2 became less popular
3 fell significantly
4 55% to just under 40%

**8** Elicit from students how to transform this into a verb phrase: *... dipped ...*

**Answer**

there was a dip in ...

**9** When students have done this, select some students with good examples to write them on the board.

## Photocopiable activity  page 110

### Spot the differences

If your students are less able, you can let them look at each other's graph to check the differences. Encourage students to ask each other questions rather than just describing. You can also ask students to write a description of one of the graphs as additional writing practice.

**Answers**

see page 123

## Study skills  page 17

### Listening: Numbers and letters

**1** Explain that certain numbers can cause confusion when hearing them. Sometimes, it is easy to know from the context. Say some examples ending in *-teen* and *-ty* – *13/30; 14/40*, etc, and get students to identify them. Then put some numbers on the board and get them to say them clearly as you point to them. They can then practise this in pairs.

**2/3** As a follow-up, ask students to dictate numbers and letters for you to write on the board.

**4** Review the sounds of the alphabet. If you have students whose language does not use the Roman alphabet, they may have pronunciation problems. There may also be some 'false friends' for students whose first language uses the Roman script. Monitor students and give feedback on errors.

**5**  After checking the answers, allow students to listen again to the recording. Ask one or more students to read the items aloud.

**Answers**

| 1 GV976 | 5 PB3379132F |
|---|---|
| 2 907776; 22 | 6 27 |
| 3 07551 66 63 33 | 7 17.40 |
| 4 24 | |

**◉ 1.3**

1 Flight number GV976 to Baghdad will depart from gate ...
2 The 907776 flight to Paris will depart from gate 22.
3 07551 66 63 33 is my mobile number.
4 Catch the bus number 24.
5 The booking reference is PB3379132F.
6 The flight will depart from gate number 27.
7 That will cost £17.40.

### Writing/Describing: rise and fall

**1/2** Emphasize how useful this vocabulary is, particularly for Writing Task 1.

**Answers**

**1**

1 F   2 R   3 F   4 R   5 F   6 R   7 R   8 F

**2**

ticked verbs: plunge, jump, dive, leap

**3** If students do this in class, get them to write their sentences on the board. Draw their attention to the tense.

Alternatively, you can use the final section of each unit as a self-study task if you feel your students are able to cope with this. You can advise them to do this in their own time as a review activity for the skills learnt in the unit. Give students a time limit for self-study at the beginning of the course and encourage them to make study plans and record their achievements and areas where they need to do some extra practice.

You can check this either as a whole class the next time you meet, or you can provide an answer key for them to self-check. The latter gives more learner autonomy, but for the first two or three units, students may need some guidance if they are not used to this method of learning.

# Content overview

## Themes

This unit focuses on the themes of time, calendars and exhibitions.

## Exam-related activities

### Reading

Scanning
Sentence completion
Identifying information – True/False/Not Given
Matching – classifying

### Writing

Task 2
Introductions
Organization
Writing a paragraph

### Listening

Section 2
Multiple choice
Completing a table
Matching

## Speaking

Part 1 Sentence stress
Part 2 Talking about an electronic device
Part 3 Developing answers

## Language development

### Language focus and Vocabulary

Collocations with *time*
Present perfect
Synonyms

## Skills development

### Reading

Skimming

### Study skills

Reading: Skimming and scanning
Writing: Speaking and writing

---

## Collocations with *time*

**1** Before students open their books, ask them to work in pairs to think of as many ways to tell the time and date as they can.

Ask them to and look at the pictures and match the vocabulary. Elicit whether the pictures show any of their ideas.

### Answers

A a sundial      C a calendar
B a watch       D a diary

**2/3** Ask students to work through the descriptions and statements in these activities in pairs. Monitor pronunciation and appropriate language. Elicit the meaning of *advantages* and *disadvantages* and point out how the words often come up in Writing Task 2, speaking and reading.

### Sample answers

**2**

B The watch is small and the face/dial is old-fashioned. It has a leather strap. We use it to tell the time.
C The calendar is very bright. It hangs on the wall. We use it to see the days of the month.
D The diary is empty. It has spaces to write in. We use it to write appointments in.

**3**

Advantages: watch, diary and calendar for planning one's life, meetings and appointments; diary can help people to remember things
Disadvantages: controls one's life too much and easy to lose, forget to fill in diary

**4** Elicit the meaning of the word *collocation* in the title of the Vocabulary section. Point out how certain words commonly go with the word *time*. Ask students to do this exercise individually and then check their answers in pairs. Elicit feedback from the class.

| 2 | spend | 4 | have | 6 | take |
|---|-------|---|------|---|------|
| 3 | kill | 5 | save | 7 | fly |

**5** When students have finished the pairwork, ask them the questions in exercise **4** without the students looking at their books.

**6/7** Students do the matching activity in pairs, developing the answers in their own way. Follow this with a general concept-checking of the collocations in exercise **4**, eg, *Which verb do you use when time passes slowly?* (*drag*)

Encourage students to enter the collocations in their vocabulary books under the heading 'Common collocations' and a sub-heading 'Time'. Encourage them to add words to help them remember the context.

**Answers**

| a | 7 | b | 3 | c | 2 | d | 6 | e | 5 | f | 4 | g | 1 |
|---|---|---|---|---|---|---|---|---|---|---|---|---|---|

## Speaking 1    page 19

### IELTS Speaking Part 1: Sentence stress

**Aim**

This section aims to help raise awareness of sentence stress to increase students' understanding of the examiner's questions and to increase fluency in their response to questions.

**Suggestion**

As extra practice, ask students to work in pairs and write a short dialogue (about three questions and three answers) about how they spend their free time. They can write it on large sheets of paper for display. Monitor the students' dialogues. When they have finished, ask them to swap their dialogues with another pair of students, who read the dialogue together. They can then work in groups and roleplay each other's dialogues, giving feedback on sentence stress.

**1/2** Read through the Strategy box with students and demonstrate stress in a sentence. For example, put these words on the board, leaving spaces between them: *ship sank sea night*. Read the words aloud. Now add: *the in the at*. Read the first four words again. Then read the whole sentence (*The ship sank in the sea at night.*), putting a stress mark over the stressed words as you say them. Elicit from students which types of words are stressed.

Read the example in 1 to the students. After they have marked the stress in items 1–4, ask them to read the sentences aloud. They can mark the stress in the same way in their vocabulary books.

**Answers**

```
        o            O
1  What are you studying?
         o        o     o       O  O          o
2  Describe how people spend their free time in your home
   o
   country.
   o O    O                  o    O    o
3  Do young people have the same leisure activities as in the
   o
   past?
   o         o          O  O
4  How do you spend your free time?
```

**3** (O) **1.4** Ask students to read out the sentences when they have checked their answers.

**4/5** Monitor students as they do exercise **4**, making sure they read the words aloud before they write. Listen for the correct use of stress as students do exercise **5**. Try to encourage natural rhythm and check that it is not exaggerated. Drill the sentences, if necessary.

**Answers**

1  I'm studying English.
2  I watch TV, go to the cinema or the theatre or I visit my friends and family.
3  I think I spend a lot of time on the Internet playing computer games.
4  I use an iPad to surf the net, chat to friends and read books.

## Listening    page 20

### IELTS Listening Section 2

**Aim**

This section aims to familiarize students with Section 2 of the Listening module. The recording is shorter than in the exam and the vocabulary and grammar are not as difficult as students will encounter in the IELTS exam. The format of the questions follows the IELTS exam, but the questions themselves are simpler.

**Suggestion**

Some students may have difficulty listening to a monologue, even one that has been simplified. Do not feel that students have to answer all the questions in one go. Break the recording into the three sets of questions, if necessary. As an additional practice, play the recording while students follow the audioscript.

**Exam information**

In Section 2, there is usually a monologue (one person speaking). The content is usually of a general nature, such as a radio programme or information about a place. There will be a short break at the beginning and in the middle to give students time to read the questions.

## Pre-listening

**1** Go over the Exam information. Read through the Strategy and stress the technique of underlining words. Point out to students the importance of using the context to help them with listening. For example, write the word *time* on the board and ask them to think of words or phrases which go with this word. Use prompts such as: *Does 'cash' go with this? Does 'clock' … ?*, etc. Check answers as a whole class.

### Answers

1 exhibition, (history/time), opened
2 display/show/fair
3 began/commenced/started
4 a few days ago/a week ago. No.

**2/3** Repeat this procedure for questions 2 and 3 in the Listening section. This time students should create their own questions. They may need help at first, so you could elicit question 2 questions first, and ask them to think of questions for 3 themselves.

### Sample answers

**2**

2 Which words do you listen for in the stem? Is there a synonym for the word *exhibition/entry*? Which words can you use instead of *expensive*? What does *fairly cheap* mean?

3 Which words do you listen for in the stem? Is there a synonym for the word *appealing*? Which words can you use instead of *a range of*? What does *can play with* mean?

**3**

4 a number
5 a noun phrase

**4** Students can do this in pairs, followed by collation of the synonyms on the board. Remind them to enter new words into their vocabulary books.

### Sample answers

A peaceful – calm/relaxing
B modern – up-to-date/trendy
C exciting – thrilling
D fascinating – interesting
E unforgettable – memorable
F attractive – pretty
G boring – dull
H cheap – not expensive

## Listening

**5**  Check students understand the instructions for each section of the listening and elicit the meaning of words in the questions. When students have listened once, they can check their answers in pairs. Replay the recording and check the answers as a class. Analyse any sections students found problematic.

### Answers

| | | | |
|---|---|---|---|
| 1 | A | 6 | C |
| 2 | C | 7 | F |
| 3 | A | 8 | H |
| 4 | 20/twenty (minutes) | 9 | D |
| 5 | car park | 10 | E |

Good morning, and welcome to today's programme. As it's the beginning of the school holidays we are focusing on events and activities to occupy the kids and to give them a memorable day out. Yesterday, we checked out the new exhibition on the history of time which has just started at the restored house at the Observatory by the river. In fact, it started three days ago. A visit is well worthwhile and something to do for a special occasion like a birthday.

And what has made the house and the exhibition so popular? Well, first of all, entry to all the Observatory facilities and the exhibition is free. And what's more, it is suitable for people of all ages catering for both children and adults. It is an unforgettable day out for the whole family, especially the children. What makes it interesting for children is that there are loads of activities that have some kind of interactive element, while at the same time there are lots of seats throughout the area in case people get tired, and the organizers have provided places for people to have snacks.

As for transport, there is also a bus to and from the local station, which leaves 20 and 40 past the hour from the entrance, until 6 pm. The train station is very close so those of you feeling energetic might want to walk – it takes about 20 minutes. All you have to do is follow the signposts along the way. It is a very pleasant walk through a park with lots of trees and open spaces. The bus back to the station leaves from the car park and departs at 15 and 45 minutes past the hour.

…

The local newspaper, *The Clarion*, has reviewed all the facilities. And I can read you what it has said about the top six facilities that they mentioned. First of all, it says the exhibition on the history of time at the restored house is really thrilling with lots of activities for children. There are examples of early English and European clocks and also early examples of clocks from the Arab world and China and India. There are also exhibits on the history of watches from around the world.

The restaurant has been given a very good rating indeed. People generally found it really beautiful, as it had many of the old features. People said they wanted to sit there for ages, but they couldn't as there is so much to see.

The shop was not considered very expensive; with lots of interesting toys and souvenirs for people of all ages that were all good value.

The gardens are very relaxing. There are many different types of gardens and lots of open places to sit and relax and have a picnic and lots of lawns for the children to run around and burn up some energy.

Another facility which received a good rating was the 3D cinema which people found thoroughly interesting. It fascinated them a lot.

As regards the Observatory building itself, people felt it was really a place to remember. They said they wouldn't forget it.

It is very old and very ornate and filled with old instruments which were modern gadgets in their day. Special events like public celebrations are held there as the rooms are spacious and very impressive.

# Language focus   page 21

## Present perfect

**1** Ask students to do this exercise in pairs. Refer them back to Unit 1 and the past simple tense and make comparisons with the present perfect tense using the sample sentence from the Listening. Write the tenses on the board so students can see the form and function clearly. If necessary, refer them to the Grammar on pages 150–151.

### Answers

a   to describe a recent action/event with a present result

**2** This exercise can be done in pairs. Ensure they all understand why the present perfect is used in each case, pointing out the time adverbials. Read a sentence aloud and ask students to explain the purpose with or without looking at their books.

### Answers

1  c     2  a     3  d     4  b

**3** Once students have completed this exercise in pairs, put them in groups to check their answers. Go through the answers as a class and ask them to justify their answers to ensure they all understand why each tense is used. Refer back to the board presentation, if necessary.

### Answers

1  have already been; did (you) go
2  announced; have bought
3  started; have (you) worked
4  have had; went
5  haven't seen; Did (you) have

**4** When students have made their decisions, ask them to tell you why both options are correct for some answers. You can concept-check their understanding by giving them some erroneous answers. Encourage them to give extra information of their own here as you go round and monitor.

### Answers

1  b     2  a and b   3  a and b

**5/6** If you have a group of students that needs extra help, you can go through the verbs and decide which ones need an object depending on the question stem, eg,

*Where have you visited? Have you ever visited … ?* To check comprehension, invite students to ask you the questions they made in exercise **5**.

### Sample answers

1  Have you ever visited a museum?
2  How long have you lived here?
3  Why have you come to this country?
4  Where have you spent your holidays?
5  What have you read in English?

### Extension

At the end of this section, read sentences from exercises **2** and **3**, some with verbs in the correct tense and some with verbs in the wrong tense. Ask students to decide if the tense is correct. If you have time, ask students to do the Grammar exercise on page 151.

# Vocabulary 2   page 22

## Synonyms

### Aim

The aim of this section is to build on the vocabulary for describing (and evaluation) in Unit 1, page 10, and to make students aware that it is possible to use different words to express the same meaning.

### Suggestion

Point out to students how useful adjectives are. Elicit synonyms not just for new words, but for words that students already know, to increase their flexibility. Elicit a range of activities that students participate in, eg, studying in the library, meeting friends, spending time on networking sites, travelling. Ask students to work in groups and comment on the activities listed. Encourage them to use at least two adjectives per activity, possibly also recycling the adjectives from Unit 1, page 10.

**1** Before the class, find as many images of the items in the box as possible. Ask the students to identify the items. When they have finished, ask them to explain their decisions to the whole class.

**2/3** Ask students to do these exercises in pairs, then check answers as a whole class. Identify any collocations, eg, *surf the net*. Check any problem vocabulary. Remind them to enter new words onto a new page in their vocabulary books.

### Answers

**2**
| 1 | iPad | 4 | electronic smart-board |
| 2 | 3DTVs | 5 | digital camera |
| 3 | electronic games | 6 | computers |

**3**

dangerous

**4** As an additional consolidation exercise, divide the class into six groups. Ask students to take one pair of adjectives each and write sentences. Collate the sentences on the board as examples.

**Answers**

1 satisfying/enjoyable
2 fascinating/interesting
3 practical/useful
4 important/invaluable
5 harmful/dangerous
6 effective/efficient

**5/6** In exercise **5**, point out to students how they can use the synonyms to show they know the meaning of both words. It also helps to avoid repetition. Point out that they don't need to use all of the items in **5**. Encourage them to use devices that are not in exercise **1** as well. Monitor each pair for pronunciation and sentence stress as they complete this activity. After giving feedback, students can ask you the questions. Alternatively, a student can ask a question and then choose someone in the class to answer it.

## Speaking 2    page 23

### IELTS Speaking Part 2

**Aim**

The aim here is to focus on the organization of descriptions and the use of adjectives for evaluation.

**Suggestion**

If your students are confident enough, ask them to demonstrate their descriptions to the rest of the class. Give positive feedback and suggest one or two improvements. In this way, you might encourage other students to volunteer to speak.

**1** Before looking at the Strategy box, ask students questions to see what they can remember, eg, *How long do you have to prepare in Speaking Part 2? What sorts of questions are asked? How many people speak here? How much should you write for your notes?*

Time students as they do the exercise and monitor them carefully. Get them to count their words – if they are over the limit, ask them to reduce the number of words.

**2**  Give students time to read the phrases before playing the recording. They can check their answers in pairs before the recording is played again.

---

**Answers**

a 7   b 4   c 3   d 5   e 1   f 6   g 2

---

**⊙ 1.6**

I'm going to describe an e-book reader which I saw for the first time when I was at an airport about a year ago. I bought it just three months ago, before I started this course. And it has been brilliant. It is very convenient because it is very light. I can carry it everywhere with me. I don't have to carry lots of books. It is important to me because it has helped me study. At first it was difficult to pass exams. Since I bought it I have downloaded lots of books. It is really useful as it has also saved me a lot of time and money. In the past I carried three or four books with me everywhere I went and I had to go out and search for books. Now I just download them when I want them. I have read more books since I bought the e-book reader, including real books, and my English has improved.

Some of my friends don't like it, but I think it is a very effective device and I recommend it.

**3** Point out that there might not be an adjective in every phrase. Elicit the meaning of any words students do not know. Ask them why they think using adjectives is useful.

**Answers**

b convenient      f useful
d important       g first

**4** Check the length of time several of the students speak for and check any difficulties. Discuss how useful it is to write notes, and how easy/difficult it is to speak for one to two minutes. Write words that students used while speaking on the board. Tell students who are not speaking to time and check the vocabulary used.

## Photocopiable activity    page 111

### How did you ...?

**1** The sequence of the exercise builds up to exercise **3**.

**2** Encourage students to talk as fully as possible about the phrases.

**3** Use the exercise again during the course as students will not talk about all the items. Next time set a time limit of 2 or 2.5 minutes for each student.

**Answers**

see page 123

### Aim

The purpose of the reading is to introduce students to different types of questions in the Academic Reading module.

### Suggestion

To encourage students to read for reading's sake, give them a text on current affairs of about 300 words from a newspaper or a magazine. Give them two minutes to skim the text and then work in groups to list as much information as they can about the text without looking at it. Elicit as much information as you can about the text from the students, writing notes on the board. Then ask students to read the text again to see how much they understand. Do this activity for about 10 minutes before you ask students to answer questions on a reading passage. In future, you can gradually reduce the skimming time to 90 seconds.

## Pre-reading

**1/2** Elicit from students why they are doing the pre-reading activities. Explain that they are practising strategies: Exercise **1** practises predicting; **2** practises skimming and **3** practises scanning. Give students two minutes for each exercise and time them. Discuss how the techniques help: they help them to find information from a passage quickly and accurately; they help to build a picture of the passage before reading.

### Answers

**1**

1 Yes.    2 Yes.    3 Yes.
(the title, words and phrases in exercise 2 are related to time)

**2**

### Sample answers

measure the passage of time throughout our existence
ancient civilizations
to determine seasons, months and years
timekeeping in prehistoric times
interested in measuring and recording the passage of time
counting the days between cycles of the moon
had a calendar that divided the year into 30-day months

**3** Give students two minutes to find the words and underline them. You can give them more time to match the words to meanings, if necessary.

### Answers

| | | | |
|---|---|---|---|
| 1 | human life | 4 | created |
| 2 | cut | 5 | made up for |
| 3 | phases | 6 | able to be carried |

## Reading

**4** Students can answer each of the three sets of questions in turn. Give them about five to eight minutes for each set. Go over each section and explain the necessary strategies for completing the different section types. Draw their attention to the Tip for questions 1–5 and the Strategy box regarding classification.

When students have finished, get them to add up their scores and make a note of sections they found particularly challenging for further practice in self-study.

### Answers

| | | | |
|---|---|---|---|
| 1 | prehistoric times | 8 | False |
| 2 | sticks and bones | 9 | B |
| 3 | 12 periods | 10 | A |
| 4 | Moon's cycles | 11 | B |
| 5 | Dog Star | 12 | A |
| 6 | Not Given | 13 | C |
| 7 | True | | |

## Reading discussion

**5** Put students into groups to discuss the questions. Give them 15 minutes. Ask a spokesperson from each group to give feedback to the class. Focus on comprehensibility rather than accuracy here. To review the reading passage, elicit between seven and nine words or phrases that are useful to remember. Write the words and phrases on the board and ask students to add them to their vocabulary books.

## IELTS Writing Task 2

### Aim

This section aims to help students to write a paragraph with guidance.

### Suggestion

Avoid pushing students to write full Task 2 answers at this stage. Use the model answers on page 162 to help students appreciate what they should aim for. Ask students to match the comments to the various parts of the model answer.

### Exam information

In Writing Task 2, students have to write an essay on a general academic subject. They do not need to have any specialist knowledge. They are often asked to discuss other people's ideas and give their own opinion.

**1** Elicit what students already know about Writing Task 2 and write notes on the board. Read through the Exam information and Strategy boxes. After students have finished, check the answers with the whole class. Impress upon them how important it is to spend 3–4 minutes analysing the question and making a plan.

### Answers

1 3
2 Give reasons for your answer and include any relevant examples from your own knowledge and experience.
3 About 25–30 words is enough. There is no fixed number of words.
4 Yes.
5 4/5
6 About 60–85 words. But note there is no fixed number of words.
7 about 3

**2/3** To orient the students, elicit several ideas for each part of the essay, eg, convenient and time saving, but also problems like laziness and eye problems. Students can do these two exercises in the same groups, and again feed back to the whole class.

Point out the general statement in the first sentence. Explain how the second statement shows the direction for the whole of their essay and how they need to keep referring back to it to ensure continuity in their essay.

### Answers

**2**
2

**3**
1 It uses different words/synonyms.
3 It mentions all three parts of the question.
4 It uses different grammatical structures.
5 It doesn't copy the words in the rubric.
6 It shows the structure of the rest of the answer clearly: positive, negative, opinion.

**4** First use the table to describe the different parts of a paragraph. After completing the table, students can work in pairs, describing the contents of the paragraph using the notes. Elicit an explanation of the contents of the table from students.

### Answers

2 a    4 c    6 b

**5/6** Ask students to explain their answers in 6. Elicit the difference between adverbs and conjunctions and ask them to explain why they are important (to show links between the information in the text). Point out that 'so' can be included in both categories.

### Answers

**5**

Adverbs: for example, as a result, moreover (… can …), so
Conjunctions: because, so

**6**

Reason: because
Example 1 and 2: for example
Example 2: moreover ( … can …)
Result: as a result
Conclusion: so

**7/8** Point out to students that working out the word form for each blank space is a useful strategy when doing gap-fill activities in the reading and listening modules. After checking their answers in pairs, students give whole-class feedback.

### Answers

**7**
1 noun            6 adverb
2 verb            7 adverb
3 conjunction     8 adverb
4 adverb          9 adverb
5 (modal) verb

**8**
1 advantage       6 like
2 save            7 Moreover
3 because         8 As a result
4 For example     9 So
5 can

**9** Remind students of the essay question in exercise **1**. Draw the diagrams on the board or on a large sheet of paper. Depending on the level of your students, you may have to give them some words to choose from for physical and emotional problems.

After the students have completed the diagrams, elicit answers to fill in the spaces on the diagram. Remind them that this is one way of recording word groups in their vocabulary books, and keeping records of ideas.

### Sample answers

Physical: hand, back, weight gain, tiredness
Emotional: only talk to machines, don't develop real friendships, family 'breakdown', loneliness

**10** After students have completed the exercise, elicit an explanation of their ideas from one or more students. Ask students to explain why the organization is important.

**11** Elicit the meaning of the word *drawback*. Students can work on this exercise in pairs. Get them to write the paragraph in pairs. Monitor their writing and give guidance. Then elicit a paragraph from the students and write it on the whiteboard. They can then copy it down as a model in their books.

Depending on how much experience your students have had in writing, you may like to provide some guidance with discourse markers. *However* is already provided, but you might like to add one or two more for the framework of the paragraph. Tell students to look at the model on page 162 and use this as a framework if they are having difficulties.

## Speaking 3   page 28

### IELTS Speaking Part 3

#### Exam information

In Speaking Part 3, Students will have a discussion with the examiner that lasts between **4** and **5** minutes. Note that this is a two-way discussion and the examiner will ask students questions about what they say. The discussion is about abstract ideas. Students should not use personal information, examples, etc.

**1** After students have read the Exam information and Strategy boxes, ask them questions about the content.

Ask students to make brief notes about one of the topics. Allow them to use dictionaries and to ask you questions.

**2** Explain to students how they can develop their answers in Part 3 by giving reasons, examples and results, as in exercise 4 on page 27. Stress the importance of expanding on answers as much as possible in this section. Some of the topics will be similar to writing and reading topics, so the more practice students are exposed to in these modules, the more ideas they will be able to collect. However, they shouldn't expect the same topics in writing and in speaking in the same exam.

If this is the first time students have done any practice for IELTS Speaking Part 3, choose the first topic and elicit answers to the questions from the class. Encourage discussion and exploration of ideas. Provide any key vocabulary they might need. Then have them discuss the second topic in groups of four and come up with answers for these questions.

After students have finished, allow them to ask you questions from exercise **1** and then ask several questions to students.

**3** Ask students to conduct a mini-interview, choosing one student from each group to answer the questions.

## Study skills   page 29

### Reading: Skimming and scanning

**1** Give students two minutes to discuss in pairs. Elicit some text types that you might scan: mobile contacts list, catalogues, menus; and skim: newspaper article, magazine, academic article.

**Answers**

a  scan     b  skim

**2** Monitor students as they underline the words they would skim in the text, and ask them to compare their answers in pairs. Elicit 'content words', eg, nouns, and 'function words', eg, articles, prepositions and determiners. Elicit which words give the meaning, ie, the content words. If necessary, dictate a list of function words such as *at, in, by, this, the, for* to show they do not convey meaning. Compare these with the words *ancient Greeks, mapmakers, surface, Earth* and so on.

**Sample answer**

Since the <u>time</u> of the <u>ancient Greeks</u>, <u>mapmakers</u> have <u>divided</u> the <u>surface</u> of the <u>Earth</u> into an <u>imaginary fixed grid</u> of <u>equally spaced horizontal</u> and <u>vertical lines called</u> a <u>graticule</u>. This <u>allows</u> any <u>place in the world</u> to be <u>pinpointed using</u> just <u>two coordinates</u>. The <u>horizontal lines</u> of the <u>grid</u>, <u>running parallel</u> to the <u>equator</u>, are <u>called lines of latitude</u>. The <u>vertical lines</u>, each <u>running between</u> the <u>north and south poles</u>, are <u>called meridians of longitude</u>.

**3/4** Give students 30 seconds or less to find and highlight the four words. Discuss why the words were easy or difficult to find. The words are long so it makes it easy to find them even if they are words students do not know.

**5/6** Give students a time limit of 5 minutes for these exercises. Point out that when they scan, they don't need to move through the text in a linear fashion, but that their eyes can jump around the page. Suggest that when they next scan in their first language they note how they do so.

**7** Tell students that this is only one way to scan. They may find it odd at first, but it illustrates how words can be more noticeable to the eye when they are not focusing on meaning. Show them how to scan for information going backwards through a text and going in a zigzag from left to right or right to left.

**8** This gives students further practice. You can ask them to time each other as to how long it takes to find the word. Tell them to reduce the time for searching gradually. After or before students work on a reading passage in future, spend a few minutes doing either scanning, skimming or prediction practice.

## Writing: Speaking and writing

**1** Brainstorming ideas and planning in pairs and groups is something that can be encouraged in and outside the classroom. Students need to have as many ideas on as wide a range of topics as possible.

**2** Students should practise speaking with someone from another group so they can increase their ideas pool.

**3/4** Ideas for writing can come from the discussion. Get students to make a plan before they write and monitor them at this stage. Then get them to write the paragraph and compare with another pair. Give them pointers about what to look for when peer-correcting.

Point out that error correction goes in three stages: self-correction, peer-correction, and finally teacher-correction. Particularly with self-study, self- and peer-correction are invaluable.

## Content overview

### Themes

This unit is focused on the structure and organization in the world around us.

### Exam-related activities

#### Reading

Matching information
Identifying information – True/False/Not Given
Short-answer questions

#### Writing

Task 2
Planning
Choosing ideas
Writing a paragraph

#### Listening

Section 3
Multiple choice
Completing a table
Matching

### Speaking

Part 2
Making notes
Talking about a school subject
Word stress
Talking about an event
Part 3    Beginning an answer
Sentence stress

### Language development

#### Language focus and Vocabulary

Likes/dislikes and preferences
Collocations: Words related to organizing
Comparative and superlative adjectives
Collocations: General nouns

### Skills development

#### Reading

Scanning

#### Study skills

Speaking: Talking about games and team sports
Reading: Nouns

---

## Listening    page 30

### IELTS Listening Section 3

**Aim**
This section aims to introduce the type of test students can expect in Section 3 of the Listening module, ie, it usually contains a dialogue of at least two people talking about a subject of an academic nature. The people can be students and a tutor.

**Suggestion**
As an awareness-raising exercise, put students into groups and ask them to brainstorm the type of conversations students might have together or with a tutor in Section 3. To give hints you can ask: *Will they talk about personal matters/ about their families/their hobbies/an essay/a project/an academic problem/changing course?* Collate the information on the board and discuss.

**Exam information**
In Listening Section 3, students will hear a dialogue between at least two people about an academic subject. This dialogue can be two students talking about a project or an essay. It can also be a tutorial between a tutor and (a) student(s). In the exam, they will hear the recording once only.

### Pre-listening

1   Elicit the kinds of occasions when people have ceremonies. Choose some ceremonies students are all familiar with and discuss the kinds of preparations needed to make a ceremony a success. Write the answers on the board.

Explain *awards ceremony* and look at the pictures as a class. Compare the similarities and differences between the three choices, eliciting vocabulary and putting it on the board. Students can discuss their preferences in groups, giving reasons using the prompts provided in the box.

**2** After the pairwork, get students to refer to the vocabulary on the board, and if necessary, add more.

**3** Elicit vocabulary around the topic of a fashion event and get students to predict what topics the dialogue will include. Decide, as a class, which three ideas from the list they think are most likely to be included in the discussion.

**4** (O) **1.7** Students listen and check their predictions.

**Answers**

providing food, flowers, invitations, presenters, the time of the event, booking the venue

## Listening

**5** (O) **1.7** Go through the listening Strategy box and remind students about the importance of reading the questions beforehand and underlining and circling key words. Elicit what they need to look for in multiple-choice questions, table completion questions and matching questions. For the table completion section, show them they have to listen for information about three people – they should identify which names are male and which are female, and think about the importance of recognising the difference between, for example, two female speakers. Point out to students that they will hear instructions about the theme of the listening test and they will have time to read the questions. If necessary, increase the pauses in the recording.

Go over the Exam information. Play the recording section by section, getting the students to compare answers before playing the test a second time. Play the recording a third time, if necessary, to ensure all the students know where the correct answers are in the recording and why. Have them make a note of the section they had most difficulty with.

**Answers**

| | | | | | |
|---|---|---|---|---|---|
| 1 | A | 5 | (funny) stories | 8 | B |
| 2 | B | 6 | popular | 9 | E |
| 3 | C | 7 | awards | 10 | D |
| 4 | A | | | | |

(O) **1.7**

(H = Harry; C = Christine)

H: Christine, hi. How are you?

C: Oh, Harry, hi. I'm OK, thanks. Just trying to get together the plan for this fashion event I'm helping to organize as part of my work placement. And you?

H: I'm very well. I've just finished writing my essay on the various things that help give structure to our lives like transport, education and different buildings.

C: Sounds very interesting.

H: I managed to get it in earlier than expected. And Dr Ahmed said it looked better than my last essay as <u>the structure was good</u>.

C: Great! Well, if you've got time, you can perhaps give me some advice here.

H: Well, yes. So, where are you now with the plan?

C: Well, mmm, we've done most of the preparation, <u>but I'm feeling a bit worried as there are so many details</u>.

H: Organizing people and events is not easy. I don't like organizing people, even if it's just for an evening out.

C: Oh, I enjoy planning events and parties and dealing with people.

H: Why don't we make a checklist and then <u>you can see how much you've done</u>?

C: Ah, OK. That sounds like a good idea.

H: First of all, I see you've got the date and the venue.

C: Yes. It's in six months' time, in June, right in the middle of the fashion season and it's at the local college of fashion in Chelsea Avenue. We've got the venue for three days, Wednesday to Friday. On the Wednesday we have the day to set everything up and then <u>the event itself is on the next two days</u>.

H: You seem to have a lot arranged already.

C: Mmm, it doesn't feel like it.

H: So what about presenters?

C: We've got two for the show and then one for the awards on Friday evening.

H: Who are they?

C: Well, they're on this table here on the computer. Yes, ... here they are. We've managed to get the designer, Debbie Maine.

H: She'll be very good.

C: Yes. I've seen her at events before and the public love listening to her. <u>She enjoys telling funny stories about the fashion world.</u> Then there's Barry Stockport. Barry's ... mmm ... a very good presenter and <u>is really popular</u>.

H: I don't know him.

C: Barry hasn't been involved in the fashion world for long. But he enjoys organizing and he presented at the Global Fashion event.

H: Yes. That went very well. And the third person?

C: Well, we've managed to get an actress, Marilyn Tiny, which is very exciting.

H: Great.

C: She's presenting the <u>awards</u> on the Friday evening.

H: She'll attract a lot of people to the event. Are the invitations ready?

...

C: And the seating, the flowers, they're all done. But it's the caterers for the award dinner I'm worried about. I've got three firms, all of whom are willing to do it.

H: OK, so what's the problem?

C: The price.

H: Ah.

C: <u>Master Caterer costs the most</u>, but they are very professional and will provide all the equipment, waiters and waitresses. They want an advance of 50 per cent of the cost and the balance at the end of the event.

H: And the others?

C: <u>Silver Service costs less than the other two companies</u>, and will provide the same service. I found them on the Internet, but I don't know much about them.

H: And the other one? What's their name?

C: Foodwise.

H: Ah yes.

C: <u>They are more well known that the other two.</u> They are good, but I prefer Master Caterer. What do you think?

H: Well to be on the safe side, I'd go for Master Caterer.

## Language focus 1 page 31

### Likes/dislikes and preferences

**1/2** Check students understand the difference between the infinitive and the gerund. Refer students to the Grammar on page 151.

**Answers**

**1**

1 I <u>enjoy planning</u> events and parties.
2 I <u>don't like organizing</u> people ...

**2**

Verbs that are followed by an –*ing* form: enjoy
Verbs that take both: like
Positive verbs: fancy, love, prefer, like
Negative verbs: dislike, detest, can't bear/stand, hate

**3/4** Students can do both exercises in pairs. Check their answers as a whole class. After completing exercise 4, read several questions to the students, giving some wrong answers. Students then decide if they are correct.

**Answers**

**3**

| | |
|---|---|
| 1 to watch/watching | 4 to build/building |
| 2 planning | 5 to read/reading |
| 3 going | 6 to arrange/arranging |

**4**

words are not necessary in 1 and 5

**5** If necessary, drill stress and intonation in the questions and monitor students carefully as they do this in pairs. Ask several pairs to demonstrate to the whole class and give feedback.

**6** Students do this exercise individually. Ensure they use both structures. When they have finished, they can talk to other students about their sentences. Monitor for accuracy.

**Sample answers**

**5**

1 Yes, I like surfing a lot, because you can find lots of interesting things such as places to visit.
2 No, I don't, because I think it's a boring game. Football is better.
3 They like going to the museums because they have many old statues from around the world.

4 I prefer hot countries like Spain because I like the sun.
5 Yes. I organized a birthday party for my mother. I really enjoyed doing it.
6 Yes, I think they really like doing volunteer work like building and teaching, because they are helping people to improve their lives.

**6**

I like walking because it is relaxing and you can see the buildings or the countryside better.
I dislike watching TV, especially programmes about sport, because it makes me lazy.
I enjoy visiting friends in different cities because it gives me a chance see new places and visit new museums.

## Speaking 1 page 32

### IELTS Speaking Part 2

**Aim**

The aim of this section is to focus on basic language for organization and writing simple notes for IELTS Speaking Part 2.

**Suggestion**

Elicit phrases from exercise **1** that students think would be useful to learn and to recycle in the future. Point out phrases like *I'm going to describe .../What I really like doing ...* which they can collect for an IELTS Part 2 revision card. As they go through the course, they can be encouraged to update the card.

**1** Elicit what happens in Part 2 of the Speaking module. Ask students questions about the prompts on the Task Card, eliciting the item to describe and the '*Wh-*' question words and the order they occur in. Students work in pairs and put the phrases from the box into the gaps in the text. Check the answers as a whole class. Tell them this is a good sample answer for this topic. Show how the talk is organized and the subject is expanded upon following the order of the prompts.

**Answers**

1 I'm going to describe a subject
2 didn't enjoy studying
3 I thought it was for boys rather than girls
4 I loved doing different experiments
5 what I really liked doing
6 you don't like doing it
7 you might love doing it

**2/3** Once students have located the words in the text, ask them to practise talking about the Task Card, using only the notes. Monitor students' answers and give feedback.

## Answers

**2**

The words match the items on the Task Card.
Describe a subject you liked or disliked at school.
Explain
what the subject was *chemistry*
when you first studied the subject *14*
where you studied the subject *secondary*
and explain why you liked or disliked the subject. *first
didn't enjoy experiments, myself, achievement, try ... first*

**3**

Students' own answers.

**4** Stress that students should use their own ideas here,
but can construct a similar answer to the model.

## Answers

Students' own answers.

# Vocabulary 1   page 33

## Collocations: Words related to organizing

**1/2** Remind students of the meaning of the word
*collocation*. Ask students to explain what a collocation
is using the examples given. Encourage them to
write collocations in their vocabulary books, with
the context. Introduce some dictionary work here.
Encourage them to use a mono-lingual learner's
dictionary. Bring in a set to class if you can. Show them
the features: headwords, pronunciation, part of speech,
meanings, sample sentences, etc. Set them a couple
of tasks to familiarize them with the layout. Show
students a collocations dictionary if they are confident
with using a regular dictionary.

## Sample answers

**2**

trip/event/journey/wedding/ceremony/career/meeting,
etc
*Organize* and *trip* go with many words because they are
both common words.

**3** Go over the phrases in the box to check for meaning.
Ask students to fill in the gaps in pairs. Check as a
whole class.

## Answers

1  organizing trips
2  a large party for
3  a meeting with my tutor
4  my essays on
5  sorting out papers and notes

6  for any trips
7  my room

**4** Go through each of the sentences, eliciting the
opposite viewpoint, eg, *6 I never/seldom get ready for
trips several days in advance. I do it the night before because
I always work better this way.* Students can select one
sentence and give reasons why they agree/disagree
with it. Monitor and choose two or three students to
demonstrate to the whole class. Stress the importance
of justifying statements and opinions.

## Answers

Students' own answers.

# Speaking 2   page 33

## IELTS Speaking Part 2

**1** (O) **1.8**  Elicit information about the Task Card to
orient the students. Review the reasons why certain
words in sentences are stressed and ask students to
mark the words in the phrases. If necessary, use the
recording to get them listening intently to the sounds.

## Answers

1  I, like, talk, party, organized
2  I, school
3  party, parent's, house
4  asked, friends, help, (me)
5  bought, lots, food
6  played, lots, games, listened, music
7  party, very, entertaining

(O) **1.8**

1  I'd like to talk about a party I organized ...
2  ... when I was at school.
3  The party was at my parent's house.
4  I asked friends to help me.
5  I bought lots of food.
6  We played lots of games and listened to music.
7  The party was very entertaining.

**2** Time students strictly here. Also monitor the number
of words in the notes and ensure that they do not write
continuous sentences.

**3** Go through the feedback form and ensure students
understand what is expected in each section. You might
give an example for each section. Encourage them to
give constructive feedback.

Students' own answers.

## Reading   page 34

### Aim

The reading passage introduces students to a type of text that they might encounter in the IELTS academic reading module. The text is shorter than in the exam and the vocabulary has been simplified. The questions are in the exam format, but simplified.

### Suggestion

Point out to students that they don't need to understand everything in the reading passage to answer the questions. Also point out that one purpose of reading academic texts is to extract information without studying them in detail. To help build students' confidence in reading, give them a short text of 200-300 words from the Internet or a textbook on any subject with no questions. Allow them two minutes to look at the text. They then list what they remember without looking at the text again. This process can be repeated as an introduction to reading. You can gradually shorten exposure to the text (to one minute) as students' confidence increases.

### Exam information

Another type of question that is introduced here is matching statements to paragraphs. Sometimes the statements refer to a whole paragraph or one piece of information or part of a paragraph. The statements are similar to paragraph headings. There is often a noun + prepositional phrase or a clause. In most cases, but not all, the words in the statements are paraphrased in the text.

## Pre-reading

**1** Ask students to look at the picture and check and drill pronunciation of the words given. Ask them what they know about beavers. When they have described the picture in groups, get one person from each group to give their description to the class.

### Sample answer

The picture shows a mound in a river, which is made from branches. The branches are cut by the beaver to build the mound, dam and chamber. The beaver uses the rocks in the river to help build the structure. The dam creates a pond.

**2** Remind students what *scanning* means. Refer students to Study skills on page 29. Give them a five-minute time limit to do this exercise. They can compare their answers in pairs when they have finished.

| 1 | dwellings | 6 | pit |
|---|---|---|---|
| 2 | tunnel | 7 | threaten |
| 3 | dispose of | 8 | options |
| 4 | strategy | 9 | species |
| 5 | watertight | 10 | manipulate |

**3** You can encourage students to choose words that are part of a collocation and write the words and the context in their vocabulary books.

Go over the Exam information. Explain *prepositional phrase or clause* and what *paraphrase* means.

## Reading

**4** Ask students what they are going to do first: skim the text and then the questions or skim the questions first. Remind them they should underline key words in both cases. Explain you are going to give them 20 minutes to do this exercise. If necessary, give them extra time. Get them to mark where they reached after the 20 minutes. As they answer the questions, encourage them to write their answers in a notebook or on a sheet of paper to practise writing on an answer sheet as in the exam. Discuss the issue of time and emphasize the need to increase their speed by skimming and scanning followed by close reading of the text when they answer the questions.

Put students into groups of four to compare their answers. If they have different answers, they should discuss and justify their own answer by referring back to the text. If they change their mind, they should put the new answer in a different colour. When the students have finished, go over the answers as a class. Make sure that they all know where to find the correct answer in the text and understand the answer.

Check how many answers they got correct and ask them to keep a record.

### Answers

| 1 | C | 6 | False | 10 | Not Given |
|---|---|---|---|---|---|
| 2 | B | 7 | True | 11 | 10/ten feet |
| 3 | D | 8 | Not Given | 12 | dam |
| 4 | A | 9 | True | 13 | food and habitat |
| 5 | A | | | | |

## Language focus 2   page 36

### Comparative and superlative adjectives

**1** Look at the question and elicit the answer. You might like to use the Grammar on page 151 to do a mini-presentation/review of the rules of comparatives and superlatives on the board.

**Answers**

1  superlative (*largest*)
2  comparative (*thicker, higher*)

**2/3** Students can do these two exercises as individual practice and then compare answers with a partner. Check as a whole class and refer to the presentation and/or grammar reference on page 151 if there are still problems.

**Answers**

**2**

| | | | |
|---|---|---|---|
| 1 | bigger | 5 | earlier |
| 2 | taller | 6 | more common |
| 3 | more exciting | 7 | better |
| 4 | larger | 8 | more popular |

**3**

1  the latest electronic gadgets
2  the longest river
3  the most interesting documentary
4  the best in the world
5  the most difficult type of event
6  the largest mountain range

**4/5** Elicit some sample questions and write them on the board, eg, *Is Shanghai bigger/more exciting than Beijing? Is the food in Athens better than the food in Delphi? Which is the most historical town in your country?* Alternatively for exercise **5**, after students have written their questions, divide the class in half and give each person in each half a number. Tell them to stand up and find the person with the same number to give their questions to. The new pairs then ask and answer each other's questions, giving additional reasons and examples.

**Sample answers**

**4**

Is your home town/city bigger than London?
Do you think living here is more exciting than in your home town?
What is the most exciting thing you have done here?

**5**

Yes, because [ ] is almost double the size and there are lots of new industries like technology companies there.
No, because my home town has lots of entertainment for young people, such as a leisure centres and theatres.
I went to a musical which was very expensive but very exciting.

## Collocations: General nouns

### Aim
This vocabulary section introduces students to a category of nouns that are important in all four skills.

### Suggestion
Each time general nouns come up in the course, point them out to students. They can keep a list or just focus on noticing them. Such nouns occur frequently in all areas of the IELTS exam, eg, paragraph/section headings, matching information, sentence matching, Speaking Part 3 questions, Listening, and especially note completion and essay questions. Common general nouns to look out for are: *advantages and disadvantages, cause/effect, connection, argument, problem, solution, method, way, measure, comparison*. This list is not exhaustive.

**1/2** When students have completed the exercises, clarify the differences between any words that might be close in meaning. Remind students that these words can occur in paragraph headings, in sentence matching in the reading, in speaking and in Writing Task 2.

**Answers**

**1**

1  strategy: way, measure, method, (solution)
2  options: choices

**2**

| | | | | | |
|---|---|---|---|---|---|
| 1 | way | 3 | part | 5 | connection |
| 2 | reason | 4 | advantage | 6 | impact |

**3/4** These activities should consolidate the meaning of the vocabulary for students. Suggest they copy the sentence stems from exercise **3** into their vocabulary books for self-study and encourage them to use them as soon as possible in any practice writing and speaking they may do.

**Answers**

**3**

| | | | | | |
|---|---|---|---|---|---|
| 1 | benefit | 3 | strategy | 5 | effect |
| 2 | link | 4 | factor | 6 | role |

**4**

1  d   2  a   3  c   4  g   5  b   6  e

## IELTS Writing Task 2

### Aim
This section aims to help students write a paragraph about a benefit, recycling the general nouns in Vocabulary 2 on page 37.

### Suggestion
Keep examples of students' paragraphs for use in future classes. Ask students' permission to do so.

Discuss the importance of getting the right interpretation of the essay title as suggested in the Strategy box. Emphasize that it is not possible to take an essay they have already written and use it for another essay if the focus of the title is different.

**1** After students have discussed the pictures in pairs, write their answers on the board. Ask them if either of these activities relate to the school experience in their own countries.

### Sample answer

In picture A, people, including young people, are visiting a museum and looking at exhibits. In picture B, young people are looking at rocks and water at the seaside. Young people are learning outside the classroom.

**2** To introduce the essay task, ask students questions about the general topic and the structure. Elicit one advantage and one disadvantage and write them on the board. Then go over the 10 items in the left-hand column of the table. Look at the essay title with them and elicit a paraphrase of the essay question. Now get them to fill in the right-hand column in pairs. Check the answers as a whole class. Explain that there are different ways to plan their answers, and that organization is important. When students have finished, ask them to work in pairs and use the table to describe the structure of the essay. Encourage them to add information such as examples and reasons, if possible. Then select several students to describe the essay structure to the class.

### Sample answers

3  disadvantages
4  5
5  zoo/concerts/abroad/outside school/common/past
6  advantages
8  benefit/advantage
9  disadvantages

**3** Elicit answers from the class and give feedback on their justifications.

### Sample answer

**2**  Introduction 2 is better organized. It has a general statement about the topic and then the second sentence shows the organization. 1 is not suitable as it is like spoken English. 3 would be better if it had a general statement at the beginning.

**4**  At this stage don't expect students to come up with lots of ideas. As their confidence in writing increases, you can stop giving them information and ask them to brainstorm their own ideas. When students have sorted the ideas, ask them to link them using numbers, letters or lines.

### Answers

Advantages: 1, 4, 6, 7, 8
Disadvantages: 2, 3, 5

**5/6** Students can put ticks next to the ideas that are mentioned in the text and compare their answers with a partner. Ask them to look through the phrases in **6** and put the text numbers next to the phrases. After checking their answers, students write out the text inserting the phrases they want to add. Point out that they do not have to use all the phrases.

### Answers

**5**

4, 2, 1, 6

**6**

1  g                          5  e (also possibly f)
2  f (also possibly e)        6  c
3  d                          7  b
4  a

**7/8** Discuss with the whole class the benefit of using the phrases (they help make the information more precise). Also discuss any phrases students wanted to leave out. When students write or redraft a paragraph or an essay, encourage them to aim to include two or three specific pieces of information like the phrases in exercise **6**. Check the answers to **7** and in exercise **8**, ask them to look back at exercise **4**. Tell them to choose another advantage or disadvantage and think up one or two supporting ideas. They can then write the paragraph and give it to a partner to check. Students can write the paragraph in pairs or groups as an alternative. They can also write them on large sheets of paper, or if you have access to computers they can type and display them on the Interactive Whiteboard (IWB), if available.

### Answers

**7**

2

**8**

Refer students to the model answer on page 162 and ask students to compare it with their own.

## Photocopiable activity  page 112

### Completing a text

Students can ask themselves questions like Student A's first task when they are writing or after they have written an essay. After students have written a paragraph or essay in class, ask them to share their work with a partner and discuss, as in exercise **3**. You can also select a paragraph to do this as a whole class. When students discuss how the text has been improved, you can encourage them to make their essays more specific.

**Answers**

see page 123

## Speaking 3  page 40

### IELTS Speaking Part 3

**Aim**
This section aims to help students understand the examiner's questions by focusing on sentence stress.

**Suggestion**
Give students several minutes to work by themselves before they do exercise **4**, repeating the stressed words only and then repeating the full question. This can be done briefly before students do similar roleplays for Part 3 in the future.

**Exam information**
The third part of the Speaking module is a two-way discussion with the examiner about abstract topics. This means that the content is not about personal information. This part of the speaking test lasts about **4–5** minutes.

**1** Ask students to read the Strategy box and the Exam information. Elicit the format of Speaking Part 3 from the students. Ask them why it is important to use synonyms where possible when responding to the questions.

Get them to do the exercise in pairs, then check their choices as a whole class.

**Answers**

1 b    2 c    3 d    4 a

**2/3**  Students should mark where they think the stress will be in each question. Play the recording to check.

**Answers**

See the audioscript.

1 Do you <u>think</u> it's <u>important</u> for <u>students</u> to <u>like</u> the <u>subjects</u> they <u>study</u>? Why/Why not?
2 <u>What</u> are the <u>main factors</u> that <u>influence young</u> people's <u>choice</u> of <u>subjects</u> at <u>university</u>?
3 <u>What</u> are the <u>advantages</u> of <u>studying</u> at <u>university</u>?
4 <u>How</u> can <u>education</u> at <u>secondary</u> school be <u>made interesting</u> for <u>pupils</u>?

**4** Encourage full development of the answers as you go round. Select four good answers to demonstrate to the class.

Abstract ideas can be more challenging for students. Give them time at the end of this section to note down some of the ideas from other students to add to their own.

**Sample answer**

1 Yes, because if students enjoy the subjects they study and find them interesting, they will learn faster. For example, if students are learning languages like Chinese or French and they are not interested in them, they will not learn quickly. Also if students are fascinated by a language, they will want to visit the country and develop their knowledge generally.

## Study skills  page 41

### Speaking

**1/2** Alternatively, divide the class into two for this, one group for Task Card A and one for Task Card B. Time students as they write their notes. They can check their notes with a partner and adapt them if they wish. They then find a student from the other group and talk about their Task Card, timing each other as they speak and giving feedback.

**Sample answers**

**2**

A chess, 8, cousin, garden, anywhere, summer, competition, friends, interesting/different sport
B rugby, 11, secondary (school), exciting, team, outside, fun, friends, energy, fit

**3** Students should compare their notes with at least two students.

**4** After students have finished, ask two students to talk about the cards and to say whether they followed their notes.

## Reading

**1/2** This can be done as self-study and checked in class, or as part of self-assessment. The latter depends on how autonomous your class can be at this stage. Some classes will have had more experience with this type of learning than others. Whatever you decide, encourage students to work together and discuss their answers in pairs or small groups. Point out and discuss the Tip.

**Answers**

**1**

| | | |
|---|---|---|
| 1 | benefits | 3 options |
| 2 | factors | 4 effects |

**2**

Students' own answers.

# 4 The land

## Content overview

### Themes

The main themes of this unit are the land, the physical environment and change.

### Exam-related activities

#### Reading

Prediction
Skimming and scanning
Matching information
Matching – classifying
Short-answer questions
Multiple choice

#### Writing

Task 1    Describing changes in maps

#### Listening

Section 4
Multiple choice
Completing notes
Map labelling

### Speaking

Part 1    Talking about changes
Part 2    Talking about a person who changed your life
Part 3    Talking about the physical environment

## Language development

### Language focus and Vocabulary

The passive
Nouns and verbs
Locations on maps

### Study skills

Reading: Summarizing and classifying
Writing: Map language

---

## Speaking 1    page 42

### IELTS Speaking Part 1

**Aim**
The aim of this section is to focus students on the concept of change in the physical world.

**1** Ask students to look at the title and predict what the unit might cover. Elicit some adjectives about the pictures and review comparatives. Check the answers with the class. Write any adjectives they think of on the board.

**Sample answer**

Adjectives to describe the pictures: A rural, peaceful, calm, green; B still green, more built-up, urban, suburban

**2** After choosing and discussing in pairs, students can discuss the answer as a whole class.

**Answer**

2

**3** Give students a few minutes to look at the pictures and think about the answers to the questions. Students then ask the questions to a partner. Get some more confident students to give answers to the whole class. Correct and help as necessary.

**Sample answers**

1    Over time the place has changed. The trees have disappeared and there are now more buildings. As well as low buildings there are three tall tower blocks or skyscrapers. The landscape in picture B is divided into fields with fences. In picture A, the fields are divided by trees and bushes.
2    Picture A is more pleasant because it is more peaceful and greener. I prefer picture A, because it more attractive, pleasant and restful.
3    B is more built-up.

**4** If possible, ask students to pair up with someone from a different country, or at least a different town.

Tell them they should give as much information as possible. Give feedback on the extent of their answers, the use of comparatives and vocabulary use in general.

### Review

At the end of this section, ask students to work in groups and list the main causes or factors behind change in modern life. You can elicit a few, such as the Internet, technology in general and globalization. Alternatively, you can elicit a list of about seven factors from the class and write them on the board under the heading *Factors/Causes* (point out the general nouns here). Ask them to choose the top three, rank them and give reasons.

## Listening   page 43

## IELTS Listening Section 4

### Aim

The listening practice introduces students to Section 4 in the Listening module. The length of the recording is shorter than in the exam and the vocabulary and structures are much simpler, but the format is the same. Labelling a map is the main feature of the listening practice.

### Suggestion

As extra practice, make your own map with about seven items on it. Describe the map and ask students to label the items on the map. See the photocopiable material on pages 113–114 for an example.

## Pre-listening

**1/2** Students can do the two activities in pairs. Follow this with a class discussion on markets and different places to shop. Write vocabulary on the board.

### Answers

1

a street market

2

Students' own answers.

**3** Students can do this exercise in pairs. Don't answer questions on meaning yet. Check if they can understand the meaning from the context.

### Answers

| | |
|---|---|
| Question 2 | aims |
| Question 3 | conducted |
| Questions 4–6 | advantages |
| Question 4 | beneficial |
| Question 5 | creating |
| Question 6 | disadvantage |
| Question 6 | as a result of |

**4** Suggest students write the words and their synonyms in their vocabulary books. Point out that it is useful to think of a synonym of the words they know and all new words. Explain how important this is in the Listening and Reading modules.

### Answers

| | | | |
|---|---|---|---|
| 1 | conducted | 5 | advantages |
| 2 | disadvantage | 6 | creating |
| 3 | beneficial | 7 | aims |
| 4 | as a result of | | |

**5** As students look at the map, ask them to look at the compass points and check they know what they are. Look at the direction of the arrows. Try to give some information regarding location, eg, *The flower market is behind the main restaurant area*. Elicit prepositions of location: *next to, opposite, between, to the north of*, etc. Note: this language does come up again later on page 49, so it is up to you how much input they may need at this point.

Go through the Exam information about Section 4 of the listening test. Make sure students understand the academic nature of the recording and the fact that there is only a 5-second pause in the middle. Check the instructions and the strategies for the different question types.

### Answers

All are likely except 4 and 6.

## Listening

**6**  Play the recording, stopping at the end of each section to allow students to check their answers with a partner. Play the recording completely a second time and check the answers as a whole class. Play the recording again as students read the audioscript.

### Answers

| | | | |
|---|---|---|---|
| 1 | B | 6 | tourist numbers (tourists) |
| 2 | A | 7 | restaurant |
| 3 | C | 8 | information centre |
| 4 | local area | 9 | seats/tables |
| 5 | regeneration | 10 | fish market |

Good afternoon, my name is Dr Deacon and today I am going to give you a short presentation on my research so far into developments that are taking place in street markets in London. I am going to examine different markets around London to show the main advantages of street markets to local communities, an example of a market undergoing change and the factors driving change in the markets.

So what are the main advantages of street markets in cities? Well, I did a survey where I asked over a hundred people in a day at Tabard Market in south London to rank the main advantages that street markets brought to local areas and if there were any disadvantages.

The main advantages given were that they were <u>good for the local area</u> and that they were not just about businesses from outside the area making money. Also they were not just for commercial purposes but they also benefited the local community by providing jobs and <u>encouraging regeneration</u>. Seventy-three per cent of people thought this was the main benefit. A large proportion of people thought that providing fresh produce was also a key advantage, despite the fact that sometimes the food on sale was quite expensive. The proportion of people who cited this was sixty-nine per cent. This was followed by an advantage which concerns us all nowadays, a reduction in waste. Sixty-three per cent of people thought that generally street markets were good because they reduced packaging and so they had a positive impact on the environment, despite the transport costs. Fifty-six per cent of people thought that street markets encouraged good health by providing fresh fruit and vegetables, and fifty-five per cent thought that it was good for cultural benefits such as promoting the local area. But some people thought that <u>the main drawback was local people would not come to the market because of the tourist numbers.</u>

...

Before going on to other studies into this very interesting area, I would like to look at part of Tabard market and show how it has been transformed. This plan on this new slide here shows part of the transformation that is taking place. You can see that a railway goes through the market – that is this double line going from the bottom right to the top left. If we go into the market from Tennis Street at this arrow here at the bottom we can see that on the left is a row of shops. <u>At the end of this row of shops there is a house that was knocked down and replaced with a restaurant</u>. If we look opposite the row of shops we can see a large block where there are many market stalls and in the middle of this block <u>a new information centre for visitors</u> has been built.

If we move above the railway line to the northern part of the market, we can see a large area which is the main food market. This area was enlarged. To the west of this there are <u>seats and tables</u> for people to have a rest. Then down here in the southeast corner of the plan is a <u>fish market</u> next to the main restaurant area. And then finally just north of the restaurant area is the flower market.

## Listening discussion

**7** Students can discuss these questions in groups of three or four. Encourage them to use any new vocabulary they have picked up from the recording and questions. Discuss the questions as a whole class and get the students to ask you the questions.

## Language focus 1  page 44

### The passive

**Aim**

This section teaches the passive and the verbs necessary for describing changes in a map. Students are also introduced to intransitive verbs which cannot be used in the passive.

**Suggestion**

Students need a small pool of verbs that are necessary to describe changes on maps. Encourage them to make a class master list of verbs, categorized into transitive or intransitive or both. They can refer to the list each time they describe maps. Use the photocopiable material on pages 113–114 to revise descriptions of changes in maps at a later date.

**1** Use this activity as a diagnostic exercise to see how much students already know about passive forms. Then decide whether you need to give a mini-presentation about the passive, using the Grammar on page 151.

**Answers**

a   1 and 3 are in the passive
b   the focus is on the action
c   *transform* and *knock down* are transitive, *take place* is intransitive

**2/3** Check students' understanding of *transitive* and *intransitive* forms. Elicit from students what topic the verbs in exercise **2** are connected with (changes to the physical environment). Elicit the meaning of unknown words.

**Answers**

**2**

| | | | |
|---|---|---|---|
| 1 | become I | 7 | lie I |
| 2 | construct T | 8 | help T |
| 3 | build T | 9 | demolish T |
| 4 | change T/I | 10 | happen I |
| 5 | replace T | 11 | grow I/T |
| 6 | open I/T | 12 | add T |

**3**

| | | | |
|---|---|---|---|
| 1 | was demolished | 5 | has been added |
| 2 | grew | 6 | has become/became |
| 3 | was constructed | 7 | changed/was changed |
| 4 | was/has been replaced | | |

**4/5** Monitor students as they write sentences. Depending on their level, you may have to elicit and write more questions on the board, like the examples in **5**. Ask several pairs to demonstrate for the whole class. Then ask them to ask you questions about a place you know that has changed.

## Speaking 2  page 45

### IELTS Speaking Part 2

**1/2** Ask students questions about the Task Card, eg, relating to the theme and the organization. Time students as they make their notes. By now, they should be able to make efficient notes within the required time.

Give them a couple more minutes to compare notes and advise each other.

**3** Students might need guidance about the correct way to structure some of these phrases, eg, *The person I'm going to talk about is/lives; I'd like to tell you about how/what he/she did.* Explain *transformed, opened, played a key role in.*

**4** Monitor students as they do the exercise, and ask several students to talk about the Task Card to the whole class. When they have finished, collate any useful words and phrases students used on the board. Ask them to select between seven and nine items to write in their vocabulary books with information about the context.

### Sample answer

Notes: aunt child visit 5 transformed role education music languages special

The person I'm going to talk about is my aunt, who I've known since I was a child. I first met her when she came to visit my mother when I was about five or six years old. She transformed my life in many ways because she played a key role in my education. She encouraged my mother to send us to the best schools and made sure we studied music and different languages. She opened up the world to us and took us travelling with her. My aunt started teaching me English when I was about ten years old and now I am studying it here in London. My aunt is a very special person to me and my sister.

## Reading    page 46

### Aim
This reading passage aims to give students practice in answering questions about a text that provides factual information. The text is used to practise scanning and prediction, which are essential reading techniques for the exam. The text is shorter than in the exam and the vocabulary has been simplified. The questions, though simpler than in the IELTS exam, are in the exam format.

### Suggestion
Train students to practise scanning as a self-study exercise. Students can work in pairs or groups. They can select any text such as a newspaper or a magazine article and ask their partner to find a word or a phrase in the text. They can time each other to see who is faster.

### Pre-reading

**1/2** Elicit where the Andes are and what students know about the culture there. Ask students to describe what the picture shows and ask if such terraces occur elsewhere in the world. Ask what the terraces are

for. Stress how prediction can help prepare them for reading. Let them find the answer to the question themselves by skimming the text within a 5-minute time limit.

### Answers

1, 2, 4, 5

**3** Remind students of scanning skills. Give them a 5-minute time limit again and check how many words they can find in this time. After students check their answer in pairs, elicit the answers from the whole class.

### Answers

| | | | |
|---|---|---|---|
| 1 | climate | 6 | altitude |
| 2 | currents | 7 | zones |
| 3 | moisture | 8 | unpredictable |
| 4 | distinct | 9 | drought |
| 5 | strip | | |

## Reading

**4** Follow the same procedure as before on page 16 regarding preparing to read. Give students 20 minutes to answer the questions. You can give them extra time if necessary. After students have finished, students can discuss their answers in pairs or groups before going over the answers carefully as a whole class. Encourage them to keep a record of their marks so they can chart progress through the course.

Point out the Tip relating to questions 6–9 and ask them to explain why the strategy described will help them.

### Answers

| | | | | | | | | | |
|---|---|---|---|---|---|---|---|---|---|
| 1 | D | 3 | B | 5 | A | 7 | A | 9 | C |
| 2 | E | 4 | C | 6 | C | 8 | B | | |

10 transport
11 (the) temperate zone
12/13 A, D

## Vocabulary    page 48

### Nouns and verbs

**1** Ask students to find the phrases in the reading passage on pages 46 and 47. Discuss the two forms of the word and look at the information in the Tip. Ask them to transfer this information to a page in their vocabulary books headed 'Word families'. Explain how useful it is to know these as it helps in predicting the meaning of unknown words in a text.

**2** When students have filled in the table, elicit what the general context of the verbs and nouns is, eg, *construction, building, change, development*. Indicate that many words have different meanings, eg, *convert/ conversion*, and the context will dictate the meaning of such words.

**Answers**

| | | | |
|---|---|---|---|
| 1 | replace | 5 | extension |
| 2 | growth | 6 | development |
| 3 | transform | 7 | construct |
| 4 | conversion | | |

**3** Students can either do this on their own and check their answers in pairs or complete the task on their own. Help them with words they do not know or allow them to use a dictionary. Check the answers as a whole class. Encourage them to write any new vocabulary and synonyms in their vocabulary books.

**Sample answers**

1 The city has expanded along the coast to the east and west.
2 There were many new developments in the village.
3 The construction of the skyscraper began last year.
4 There has been rapid growth in my home town since I was a child.
5 The swimming pool was replaced with a supermarket because people stopped using it.
6 My home country has changed dramatically in recent years.
7 The bank was converted into a restaurant.
8 The area has undergone a complete transformation

**4/5** Give two or three examples here to ensure students know how to form the questions accurately. Tell them to use the whole range of question stems provided. Monitor the question forms and give class feedback on accuracy. Tell them they can use the sentences in **3** for the answers and advise them not to ask the questions in order so their partner has to listen carefully to the question.

**Sample answers**

1 How has the city spread/changed?
2 What happened in the village?
3 When did the building of the skyscraper begin?
4 What has happened in your home town since you were a child?
5 What replaced the swimming pool?
6 What happened in your home country?
7 What was the bank converted into?
8 What happened in the area?

**6** Elicit the kinds of adjectives needed to make these sentences and collate them on the board. Monitor students as they write and give help where necessary. Try to ensure they are paired up with someone who is from a different area.

**Answers**

Students' own answers.

## Language focus 2    page 49

## Locations on maps

**1** Ask students to look at the map of the market on page 44. Elicit some sample sentences about the map, using the examples given, and write them on the board.

**2/3** Get the students to identify the buildings in the diagrams. Get them to write the sentence in the example in another way: *The car park lies to the west of the railway station.* After checking the answers, get students to do exercise **3**. When you check the answers, elicit more than one alternative, using different verbs, as in the prompts in exercise **1**, and write them on the board.

**Answers**

**2**

1 The lake lies to the west of the tower block.
2 The supermarket is located north of the cinema.
3 The leisure centre is situated to the south of the factory.
4 The school is located east of the houses and west of the flats.

**3**

Students' own answers.

**4** Ask several questions around the class. Then get students to ask you questions. Point out that they can also answer the questions by just giving the location: *Where is the railway station? (It's located) (to the) east of the car park.* Students can also do the exercise on page 152. As an additional exercise, students can work in pairs (A and B). Student A draws a map with simple boxes for buildings or places and describes where the buildings, etc are, giving the location of one building to start with. Student B draws the map and then checks it against Student A's map. Then Student B repeats the process. You can demonstrate this exercise on the board first, if necessary.

**Sample answers**

Where is the lake situated? Where is the leisure centre? Where are the flats located? What is situated north of the cinema?

## My town

Students will need to tear or cut out the images so they can place them on the map. They will need something to stick the images on to the map. Alternatively, they can draw boxes on the map and write the names of the places in the boxes.

You can also draw the maps on the board and ask students to describe the maps to you.

When they have finished, students can describe the differences orally or in writing.

**Answers**

see page 123

# Writing page 50

## IELTS Writing Task 1: Describing changes in maps

**Aim**

The exercises in this section give students the opportunity to practise describing changes in maps.

**Exam information**

In Task 1, students sometimes have maps to compare and contrast. There may be one or two maps to describe.

**1** Go over the Exam information. Some students may not have described maps before. To help orient them, elicit the names of the places in the town, the street names, the date, the directions north and south, etc, and check for pronunciation.

**Sample answers**

The open space is situated north of/to the north of the houses.
There is a woodland west of/to the west of the school.
The bus station is located south of/to the south of the detached houses.

**2/3** Exercise 2 helps students examine a map closely. They can write the answers to the questions on their own or just prepare answers without writing. After checking their answers, they can ask you a few of the questions before doing exercise 3. Give help with any vocabulary in the questions, eg, *runs along*.

**Answers**

1 An/The open space (is situated north of the houses in the west of Westerling).
2 A/the woodland (is located to the west of the school and north the houses in the east of Westerling).
3 North Road (runs along the north of Westerling).
4 Factories (lie to the west of the shops).
5 A/the street market and a/the bus station (are located to the east side of Green Street opposite the shops).
6 The car park is located east of/to the east of the street market.
7 It is situated north of/to the north of the street market and the car park.

**4** Students can do this as an individual activity. They can peer-correct before you check their answers as a whole class. They can then dictate their sentences for you to write on the board.

**Sample answers**

1 The woodland lies west of the school.
2 The detached houses are to the north of the bus station.
3 The street market is located west of the car park.
4 The factories are situated south of the houses.
5 The woodland lies east of the open space.

**5** Give students several minutes to compare the maps on their own before asking them to work in pairs. Elicit the names of the places which have changed and write numbers next to them. Write the names on the board. Elicit sentences as a whole-class activity.

**Answers**

Eight changes: a motorway has replaced North Road, a block of flats has replaced the open space, a multi-storey car park has replaced the factories, the woodland has become smaller, a golf club has been built, a hotel has replaced the detached houses, a technopark has been built, the bus station has become a bus and railway station

**6/7** Give students several minutes to read the Strategy and ask them questions about the contents. Point out that an overview is a general statement. It can be written at the beginning of the description of a map after the introduction, or at the end.

**Answers**

6

1 is the best introduction. 2 and 3 use too many words from and copy the structure of the rubric. Point out that students should always try to paraphrase the rubric.

7

2. This gives the best general information including transformation and additions. It uses nouns rather than verbs. It is formal.

**8** Students have used these verbs before, on pages 45 and 48, so they will be familiar with them. After doing the exercise individually, students can check their answers in pairs.

**Answers**

| | | | |
|---|---|---|---|
| 1 | development | 4 | was replaced with |
| 2 | was converted | 5 | were demolished |
| 3 | occurred | 6 | a multi-storey car park |

**9** Monitor students as they do this exercise to ensure they are using the target language accurately. Choose one or two good answers to read out to the class as examples. Encourage them to write out the two sentences in Exercises **6** and **7** and then write the full text after them.

**Sample answers**

1 was cut down
2 were converted
3 the school (east of the woodland)
4 the street market and the car park
5 (by 2011) is the technopark

## Speaking 3   page 52

### IELTS Speaking Part 3

**1/2** Elicit the form that Part 3 of the speaking test takes. After deciding what the questions might be, they can do exercise **2**. Ask some students to read the questions aloud to the whole class and other students to read the answers. Check for stress and intonation.

**Answers**

1 b   2 c   3 a

**3** Emphasize to students that they need to expand on the answers as much as they can by giving examples and reasons as in the answers in exercise **1**. At this level, do not expect more than one or two reasons and examples. Elicit some more ideas and examples and write them on the board.

## Study skills   page 53

### Reading: Summarizing and classifying

**1** Use the example and elicit how we could classify these activites. Draw a mind map on the board with the word *social* in the centre in a circle and around it the activities

in circles. Go over the vocabulary in the box, ensuring they understand what the words mean. Look at the lists of ideas one by one and elicit suitable adjectives from the box. Discuss the reasons for their choices.

**Sample answers**

1 financial/economic
2 urban/physical/environmental
3 rural
4 environmental/physical
5 educational
6 developmental/environmental

**2** Tell students they can choose an adjective from those in activity **1**. Check their choices. Check how they are organizing their vocabulary books. Show them how using classification is a very effective way to order the words for easy recall.

**Sample answers**

1 environmental/physical
2 educational

## Writing: Map language

**1/2** Ask students questions about the Tip. After checking the answers in exercise **1**, give students a verb and then ask them to give you at least one synonym.

**Answers**

**1**
1 change/modernize
2 build/erect
3 modify/alter
4 develop/spread
5 demolish/tear down
6 turn into/make into
8 lengthen/make bigger
9 become bigger/spread

**2**

**Sample answers**
1 changed/been transformed
2 expanded
3 demolished
4 transformed
5 constructed
6 turned into

# 5  The processes in life

## Content overview

### Themes

The main themes of this unit are making things and the processes in life.

### Exam-related activities

#### Reading

Finding your way around a text
Summary completion
Choosing items from a list
Completing a flowchart

#### Writing

Task 2   Writing a paragraph for an essay
Task 1   Describing a process

#### Listening

Section 1
Completing notes

### Speaking

Part 2   Talking about making things
Part 3   Stress and rhythm

### Language development

#### Language focus and Vocabulary

Word building: Adjectives and nouns
Cause and effect
Intransitive/transitive verbs
Process language: Nouns and verbs

#### Study skills

Writing: Making a revision card for process language
Speaking: Cause and effect chains

---

## Vocabulary 1   page 54

### Word building: Adjectives and nouns

**Aim**
The section introduces the theme of making things and reactions to being involved in making things.

**1** Introduce the questions by showing pictures of different sports and hobbies and asking students to identify them. This can be done using images on the IWB, if possible. Write the activities on the board and get them to classify them, eg, *sports, hobbies, group, individual, creative, active, passive*, etc. Monitor students as they answer the questions and get feedback from the whole class, selecting several students to answer the questions. The vocabulary and activities introduced here prepare students for the Listening section on page 55 and Speaking 1 on page 56.

**Answers**

Students' own answers.

**2** Elicit the names of the objects. When students have finished, get them in pairs to underline only the stressed words in speech bubble (a) as an example: *satisfying, make, meant, tidy up, room, put, all, books, one place*. Students then read the text, practising the stress. They can then in pairs take turns to answer the question: *What did you make?* Elicit the responses a–e from the class and check pronunciation and intonation as students reply.

**Answers**

a 2   b 4   c 1   d 5   e 3

**3** Remind students of the importance of building word families. After they have filled in the table, give students an adjective and ask them to supply the noun and vice versa. If necessary, they can do this in pairs, so you can check pronunciation.

**Answers**

| 1 | relaxation | 5 | amazed |
| 2 | satisfied | 6 | bored |
| 3 | excitement | 7 | disappointment |
| 4 | surprised | | |

**4** Monitor students as they complete their questionnaires, checking spelling, etc.

## Answers

Students' own answers.

**5** Elicit possible questions including words from both columns and write them on the board, eg, *Does running make you feel relaxed? Are you bored when you read a book? Do you feel excited when you watch movies?* Ask students to work with different partners and tell them they have to ask five different people the five questions, write their name and tick if they say yes. Monitor the activity and encourage students to expand their answers. When they have finished, ask them to report back to the class, eg, *Samir feels relaxed when he goes running. Rosie doesn't feel bored when she reads a book.* Write some examples on the board first so they are aware of the verb/subject agreement/negative forms, etc.

### Review

At the end of the vocabulary section, ask students to work in groups. Ask them to decide what are the five most important skills for young people to have in today's world. Collate the skills on the board and elicit reasons and examples.

# Listening    page 55

## IELTS Listening Section 1

### Pre-listening

**1/2** Elicit the format of the Section 1 Listening test and what students need to do before they listen. They can do these exercises individually and check in pairs. Stress the usefulness of analysing the blank spaces in the test. Check comprehension of the vocabulary in the questions and elicit any synonyms. If necessary, revise the numbers and refer students to Study skills on page 17. Point out that it is important to predict answers based on the context. Also point out the pattern of the UK post code for familiarity.

### Answers

**1**
1  number
2  number
3  adjective
4  number
5  number
6  noun
7  date: number/noun
8  number
9  number
10  mixture of numbers and letters

**2**
1  Afternoon classes/Monday and Wednesday
2  Monday and Wednesday
3  level(s)
4  Age
5  Cost
6  Including
7  begin (or synonym)
8  number of students (this is a paraphrase in the audioscript)
9  Telephone
10  Postcode

## Listening

**3**  To help orient students, ask them questions about the picture: where it is, what is happening, what might be considered unusual about this. Using the questions and the picture, ask them to tell you what the conversation in the listening test is about. Play the recording all the way through once. Get them to check their answers with a partner and compare. Play the recording again so they can check.

### Answers

| | | | |
|---|---|---|---|
| 1 | 3, 6 | 6 | materials |
| 2 | 5, 8 | 7 | 1st October |
| 3 | intermediate | 8 | 15 |
| 4 | 18/eighteen | 9 | 0321 875 987722 |
| 5 | 135 | 10 | OD7 4PT |

**(O) 1.11**

(J = Janet; R = Receptionist)

J: Good morning. I don't know if I'm in the right building, but I'm looking for information about the carpentry classes.

R: Yes, you are. How can I help you?

J: Well ... I'm looking for classes ... in the evening or late afternoon.

R: Yes, we have classes in the morning, afternoon, evening and at weekends.

J: What're the times for the afternoon classes?

R: Well, let's see. Here we are. Monday and Wednesday ... afternoons <u>three to six</u>.

J: Mmm I can't do that as I finish work at four. I can make it here by 4.30.

R: Well, there're two evening classes, one is Tuesday and Thursday from six to nine and the other is Monday and Wednesday <u>five to eight</u>.

J: Both of those would suit me. Are they both beginners level?

R: The Tuesday/Thursday class is <u>intermediate</u> level. The other one is more advanced. We don't have any classes for beginners.

J: I'll go for that Tuesday/Thursday class.

R: Have you done carpentry before?

J: Yes, I've done a little, but not a lot.

R: It's very relaxing.

J: Yes. I always felt relaxed after carpentry classes. Things like that always give you enormous satisfaction. I was amazed at how much I learnt. I even made a small box which I've still got.

R: Are you sure the intermediate class won't be too simple for you?

J: Oh no. It'll be perfect.

R: We get a lot of women doing the carpentry class. It's usually a good mix of men and women of all different ages.

J: What is the age range?

R: It can be anything, but the minimum age for the evening classes is 18 ... there's no upper limit.

...

J: Oh, I see. And how much is it?

R: The prices this year are not going up, which is surprising. It's ... mm ... £135 for ten weeks.

J: Oh, that's quite reasonable.

R: And ... that includes materials.

J: Do I have to bring tools or anything?

R: No, everything like that is supplied.

J: When do the classes start?

R: The 1st of October.

J: The class is three hours ... is there a break?

R: There's a 15-minute break in the middle, around 7.30.

J: That sounds really reasonable. In fact, very reasonable.

R: So would you like to register now or would you like to come on the main registration day?

J: Is the course generally booked up?

R: Sometimes. We only take 15 students on each course so it might be wise to book now. We already have eight people booked and paid.

J: OK.

R: I'll send you details by email, if you want.

J: I can take the brochure now. Can I just leave my name and address now and pay a deposit?

R: Yes.

J: My name is Janet Blake. My telephone number is 0321 875 987722.

R: OK. And your address?

J: It's 23C Oldham Way, that's O-L-D-H-A-M and then W-A-Y.

R: OK. And your postcode?

J: It's OD7 4PT.

R: And how much do you want to pay by way of deposit?

J: I can pay £50 now and the balance when I come to complete the registration. Oh, and do I get a certificate at the end of the class?

## Speaking 1 page 56

### IELTS Speaking Part 2

**1** To introduce the Speaking section, point out to students that they are now going to talk about making something using the vocabulary from Vocabulary 1 on page 54. Ask them to read the Tip and the Task Card. Then ask them questions about both the notes and the question words in the Task Card.

After students have finished the exercise, ask them to give you reasons for their choices, encouraging them to match the words to the prompts in the Task Card.

**Answer**

2; 1 is too short and doesn't relate to the last part of the card

**2** Students can do this exercise in pairs. Explain the example. If you have a class that might struggle with this exercise, put the words on card and cut them out. Stick each set of words randomly on the board and, if possible, call students out to put them in the correct order. The class can then copy them down into their books.

Check the answers as a whole class, getting one student to read the completed text.

**Answers**

1 it was cheaper than buying a bookcase

2 I felt very satisfied when I looked at the final product

3 it was such an achievement

4 I also saved a lot of time

5 unfortunately they now want me to make one for them

**3** Let students try this exercise on their own first and before they compare their answers with a partner. You could make a copy of the whole extract in 2, leaving blank spaces for the numbered text, eg, **0** ............ *I made at home last month. I made it myself, because* **1** ........... . Students could practise reading the extract in pairs, adding the phrases in exercises **2** and **3** or using their own words, eg, *I'm going to describe a bookcase I made on my own* ... .

**Answers**

| | | | |
|---|---|---|---|
| 1 | myself | 5 | amazed |
| 2 | quite | 6 | tidy up |
| 3 | making | 7 | convenient |
| 4 | attached | | |

**4/5** After students have finished the exercises, ask them to find another partner they have not worked with before and talk about the Task Card again. Refer them to the feedback grid on page 33 they made in the previous unit. Monitor the activities and give feedback on content, adjectives and pronunciation.

## Vocabulary 2 page 57

### Cause and effect

#### Aim

This section aims to introduce students to cause and effect, which are important functions in all four skills in IELTS. This section prepares students for the next two sections, IELTS Speaking Part 3 and the subsequent Writing Task 2. It also prepares students for the writing in the next unit.

**1** Check students understand the meaning of the word *wealth* in the box and go over the example with them. After finishing the exercise, they can check their answers with another pair. Some students may find this more challenging than others, so give them time.

**Answers**

1 It <u>can</u> harm the environment and people's health.
2 We can make sure <u>everyone</u> in the world is educated.
3 It has a <u>huge</u> impact on young people by giving them new skills and opportunities.
4 It <u>transforms</u> their lives by giving them opportunities in life.
5 They make people's lives <u>easier</u>.
6 It improves <u>people's</u> health.
7 People generate <u>wealth</u>.

**2** Refer students to the introductory activity and ask them to identify the cause and the effect in each question and answer and label each point C/E. Point out that in texts, a cause can come after an effect and vice versa, eg, in passive constructions: *Too many cars create air pollution /Air pollution comes from too many cars./Air pollution is created by too many cars.*

**Answers**

1 What are the main <u>influences</u> in our lives? I think that TV and the Internet <u>affect</u> us considerably.
2 It can <u>harm</u> the environment and people's health.
3 How can we <u>improve</u> the world that we live in?
4 What <u>role</u> does technology <u>play</u> in young people's lives? It <u>has a huge impact</u> on young people by giving them new skills and opportunities.
5 What is the <u>benefit</u> of education for children? It <u>transforms</u> their lives by giving them opportunities in life.
6 They <u>make</u> people's lives easier.
7 It <u>improves</u> people's health.
8 What <u>happens</u> when we have a healthy, productive population? People <u>generate</u> wealth.

**3** As students answer the questions, encourage them to expand their answers as much as possible.

## Speaking 2 page 57

### IELTS Speaking Part 3

**1** When students have completed the exercise, ask them to identify the cause, effect, reasons and examples in the answers. Ask the questions to selected students around the class. Alternatively, you can write notes about the answers on the board, eg, 1A: *technology affecting way live work lot benefits has drawbacks people find stressful difficult deal like everything solutions* and ask students to give the answer using the notes. After the first student answers, rub out some words from the notes, eg, *technology way live work*, before the next student answers. Repeat the process for subsequent students.

**Answers**

1 A    2 B
Both answers are fuller and connected to the question.

**2** Elicit ideas about how students could answer the question, including cause and effect relationships. Write their ideas in note form on the board, eg, *art/ sculpture classes help relax people evening classes learn skills meet other people not think work problems removes stress.*

**3** Before students practise the answers in pairs, draw their attention to the Tip and the Strategy. Give them a few minutes to use their notes to formulate their own answers for the question.

**4** **(O)1.12** Ask students to predict where they think the stress comes before listening to the recording. Write the words from the answer below on the board. Read the words related to the questions and the answer aloud yourself. Ask selected students to do the same.

**Answers**

E: Do you <u>think</u> <u>change</u> is <u>happening</u> more <u>rapidly</u> <u>nowadays</u> than in the <u>past</u>? (main stress – change)
C: <u>Yes</u>, I <u>do</u>, because <u>technology</u> is <u>affecting</u> the <u>way</u> we <u>live</u> and <u>work</u>. (main stress – affecting)

**5** Before and after the exercise, elicit the stressed words to check comprehension. Write the stressed words on the board.

**6** Ask students to ask and answer all three questions again. Tell them this time to make sure that they include cause and effect statements, that they develop the answers enough and that they are aware of word stress. Monitor students for content and stress patterns. Give feedback at the end.

### IELTS Writing Task 2: Speaking into writing

**1** Elicit the meaning of any unknown words and ask students to do the exercise on their own and check their answers in pairs.

**Answer**

1 because it gives them new skills and opportunities
2 having computer skills
3 young people's chances of gaining employment
4 joining social networking sites
5 the lives of the young by helping them make new friends from all over the world

**2/3** Elicit several ideas and write them on the board, eg, *makes them lazy, stops contact, creates health problems.* Ask students the difference between this essay question and the question in exercise **1**. Give them 2 minutes to write down some ideas. Then give students 10 minutes to write the paragraph and check it. Tell students to swap their paragraph with a partner and peer-correct. Elicit what they need to look for: *cause and effect relationships, basic sentence structure, answering the question, reasons, examples and any mistakes.* Choose two or three paragraphs to be read out. Compare the answers with the model answer on page 163. Ask students to identify the causes and effects, etc, in the model answer.

**Extension**
If you want students to have extra practice, ask them to answer the following question in the same way for self-study: *What role does the mobile phone play in people's lives?*

## Reading   page 58

**Aim**
The reading passage aims to introduce students to completing flowcharts.

### Pre-reading: Finding your way around a text

**1** Tell students to look at the picture and title and ask them what they think the text will be about. Write their ideas on the board. Draw their attention to the Glossary; you could ask students to scan the reading passage for these words if there is time. Look at the Exam information and ask if they know what a flowchart is. Ask them what kind of information such a

chart gives. Point out the flowchart on page 60. Go over the items a–f to help with any problem vocabulary. Give them a time limit of 5 minutes to find the information. After students have checked their answers in pairs, ask them to explain the contents of the reading passage using items a–f, adding any specific details they can remember.

**Answers**

a Paragraphs 6, 7, 8
b Paragraph 2
c Paragraph 3
d Paragraph 2
e Paragraph 1
f Paragraphs 4 and 5

**2** Write several suggested word lists for one paragraph on the board and ask students to choose five words for the paragraph. Do this with several paragraphs, if necessary. Point out that they don't have to read every word in a paragraph to get the general meaning or gist.

**Sample answers**

a 6 After harvesting, treatment, process, is dried in special machines, This process consists of three stages. 7 Firstly, Secondly, they undergo a process where, are first crushed 8 The final and most important operation, This completes the process where
b 2 blooms, flowers, Each flower blooms
c 3 Commercially grown flax crops
d 2 Bees collect close to 15 kg of honey
e 1 200 varieties of flax plants
f 4 ancient/archaeological/as far back as/Neolithic times/ Bronze Age/early/Iron Age 5 5,000 years ago/3,000-4,000 BC/ancient

## Reading

**3** Elicit the process for doing questions 1–6. Look at the Tips for the next two sections. Follow the process for previous reading passages, but check students understand the information in the Tips and explain the structure of the flowchart.

**Answers**

| | | | |
|---|---|---|---|
| 1 | D | 7–9 | B, C, E in any order |
| 2 | E | 10 | parallel |
| 3 | C | 11 | (the) fiber/fibre |
| 4 | H | 12 | scraping |
| 5 | K | 13 | long fiber/fibre |
| 6 | J | | |

**Extension**
When students have finished answering the questions for the reading passage, ask them to describe the steps in the flowchart in their own words as far as possible. Then elicit a description from several students in the class.

## Intransitive/transitive verbs

**1/2** Get students to recall what transitive and intransitive verbs are and then read the instructions. After students do the activities, they can check answers as a whole class. If necessary, use the Grammar on page 152 to give students extra information.

**Answers**

**1**

Transitive:
1 spread into, turned
2 undergo, crushed
Intransitive:
1 make sure
3 blooms

**2**

Refer students to Unit 4, page 44.
Transitive verbs can be used in the passive. They are frequently used to describe manufacturing processes. Intransitive verbs cannot be used in the passive. They are often used for things which 'happen', (without the involvement of people in the process).
The present simple tense is used to describe a repeated process.

**3** Ask students to study the diagram in pairs. Explain any vocabulary as necessary. Some students may not be familiar with this way of presenting data and may need extra help here to show how to read the information.

**Answers**

*Grow/ripen* in the first stage can be active voice. The remaining stages need the passive voice as it is a manufacturing process.

**4** Elicit the meaning of any unknown words and ask students to do the matching in pairs. They can then check their answers with another pair before a whole-class discussion.

**Answers**

a 6   b 1   c 1   d 2   e 8   f 1

**5** Students can write the sentences individually and then check their answers in pairs before whole-class feedback.

**Answers**

1 The oranges are delivered.
2 The oranges are sorted.
3 The orange juice is shipped.
4 The orange juice is canned.
5 Water is added.
6 The orange juice is bottled.

**6** Give students an introduction to sequencers, writing the examples in the questions on the board. After they have practised, ask the students to ask you questions about the diagram. For extra practice, students can do the exercise on page 152.

**Answers**

Students' own answers.

## Process language: Nouns and verbs

**1** Remind students that they have been describing processes and ask them what kind of tenses and voice they've been using. Go over the nouns in the box and get them to fill in the spaces individually and then check their answers in pairs.

**Answers**

| | |
|---|---|
| 1 storage | 5 condensation |
| 2 irrigation | 6 transportation |
| 3 delivery | 7 packaging |
| 4 evaporation | 8 harvesting |

**2** Elicit the difference between *natural* and *man-made* and elicit the answers from the whole class.

**Answers**

4 and 5 are natural. The others are related to man-made processes.

**3** Ask students to write these words in their vocabulary books.

**Answers**

condense/condensed
deliver/delivered
evaporate/evaporated
store/stored
harvest/harvested
transport/transported
irrigate/irrigated
package/packaged
bottle/bottled

**4/5** Do the matching as a class activity, then students do the pairwork. Tell them you'll be looking for passive forms, sequencers and logical process. Sort out any problems with vocabulary before they start. Choose three students to demonstrate.

**4**

1 the making of apple juice
2 the production of tea
3 the production of a music DVD

**5**

**Sample answers**

1 Apples are grown in an orchard. When they are ripe they are harvested. They are then taken to a factory where they are sorted. After that they are squeezed to extract the juice. The squeezed juice is then canned or bottled and put into storage before it is delivered to shops.

2 The tea is grown in special plantations where it is picked by hand. After sorting and grading the tea, it is dried and blended. The tea is then tested and packaged before shipping. Then it is delivered to shops.

3 The music is written or composed and then it is recorded and filmed. After these two stages, the film is edited and prepared for production. The cover of the CD is designed and the CD is packaged and sent for storage in a warehouse. It is then delivered to shops and sold to the public.

# Writing 2 page 63

## IELTS Writing Task 1: Describing a process

### Aim
This section builds on the previous two sections, Language focus and Vocabulary 3, to help prepare students to describe a process.

### Suggestion
Some students may need more practice in describing processes. As a revision exercise, use the photocopiable material on processes on page115. You can also find images on the web of natural processes or manufacturing processes.

### Exam information
In Task 1, students might be asked to describe a process, using one or more diagrams. The process can be a natural process or a manufacturing process or a combination of both.

**1** After students have read the Exam information and the Tip, ask them questions about the contents. Refer back to previous activities, if necessary, to exemplify. Give students two to three minutes to study the diagram in pairs. Then elicit what the diagram shows and ask them to justify their answers. Clarify the meaning of any words students do not know.

2

**2** Write the stages on the board and then elicit the verbs made from the nouns.

**Sample answers**

Stages: 1 heating, 2 evaporation, 3 condensation, 4 blowing of wind, 5 catching, 6 forming droplets, 7 dropping, 8 storing/storage, 9 drinking/irrigation
Verbs: 1 heat, 2 evaporate, 3 condense, 4 blow, 5 catch, 6 form (droplets), 7 drop, 8 store, 9 drink/irrigate

**3** Students can do this exercise by themselves first, before checking their answers in pairs. Then elicit the answers from the whole class. If students ask you the meaning of words in the description, write them on the board with their meaning. Point out that they do not need to change the form of the verbs to complete the description.

**Answers**

| | | | |
|---|---|---|---|
| 1 | is used | 5 | is carried along |
| 2 | occurs | 6 | are caught |
| 3 | condenses | 7 | form |
| 4 | forms | 8 | is fed |

**4/5** After students have completed the exercises, ask them to explain the difference between adverbs and conjunctions, using the examples in the description. Elicit the difference in the use of punctuation.

**Answers**

**4**

It is clear that there is a number of stages involved <u>before</u> the water 1 ................. on farms and is drunk by people. The first stage of the process 2 ................. <u>when</u> the sea water is heated by the sun. <u>After that</u>, evaporation takes place <u>when</u> the heated moisture rises into the air. <u>Once</u> the air cools, the moisture in the air 3 ................. and a mist 4 ................. which is full of water droplets. The mist 5 ................. by the wind towards the land. At the next stage, the mist reaches the mountainside <u>where</u> it passes through a series of special nets. The droplets in the mist 6 ................. by the nets and 7 ................. larger drops. These <u>then</u> drip into the tank <u>where</u> the water is stored.
<u>Finally</u>, the water in the storage tank is used for drinking or it 8 ................. into the farm irrigation system <u>where</u> it is used to grow vegetables.

**5**

Conjunctions: before, when, where, once
Adverbs: then, finally, after that

**6** These words can be added to students' vocabulary books. For extra practice, ask students to work in pairs, cover the description in exercise **3** and then take turns to describe the diagram in exercise 1.

**Answers**

1 when, once
2 after that, then
3 when, once
4 then, after that

**7** Write the example on the board and ask students to identify what changes have been made and how the stages are linked. Students can do the exercise on their own, followed by checking in pairs. Then check answers as a whole class. Make sure students check the sentences for errors in verb/subject agreement and word order.

**Answers**

1 When the concentrate is made, it is put into refrigerated storage.
2 Before the peas are frozen, they are graded.
3 The next stage of the process is canning, where the food is canned.
4 As soon as the tea is picked, it is taken to a factory.
5 Once the olives are pressed, they are refined in/by special machines.
6 The apple juice is stored in refrigerators, and then it is bottled.
7 After the bread is baked, it is delivered to the shops.

**8** This can be done in class or for self-study.

**Answers**

1 The concentrate is made. Then it is put into refrigerated storage.
2 The peas are frozen after they are graded.
3 The next stage of process is canning, when the food is canned.
4 The tea is picked. After that, it is taken to a factory.
5 When the olives are pressed, they are refined in/by special machines.
6 The apple juice is stored in refrigerators. After that, it is bottled.
7 As soon as the bread is baked, it is delivered to the shops.

**9** Look at the diagram as a whole class and elicit the meaning of any unknown vocabulary, eg, *pruning* and *refining*. Elicit key words and the main ideas. Point out that in the IELTS examination, candidates need to write at least 150 words. Elicit an introduction and an overview and write them on the board, or give students the sentences from the model answer on page 163. They can count the words as part of the 100 words in the rubric. Give them 20 minutes to describe the process and check for errors.

**10** Students can peer-correct and then compare their answers with the model answer on page 163.

## Photocopiable activity    page 115

### Buying a book online

**1** Students can be given a copy of the bubbles to cut up and put in order before they label the text.

**2** Before they look at the text, students can describe the sequence in their own words. They can also dictate the order of the steps for you to attach them to the board.

**3** After students have completed exercise **3**, ask the questions to the whole class.

**Answers**

see page 123

## Study skills    page 65

### Writing: Making a revision card for process language

**1** Students can add the table to their vocabulary books and complete it for self-study. The answers can be checked at the start of the class. Getting students to create their own revision card makes them revise the unit. A class master card can be created electronically for the IWB, students' mobiles, etc.

**Sample answers**

Common transitive verbs in processes: sort, add, deliver, transport, produce, harvest, bottle, ship, package, pick, grade
Common intransitive verbs in processes: become, happen, occur, take place
Verbs – transitive and intransitive: grow, ripen

### Speaking Part 3: Cause and effect chains

**1/2** Look at the way the information flows in a cause and effect chain with the class. Show students how the verb in italics can be made into a sentence: *Learning to speak English makes people more confident.* By way of demonstration, get students to ask you the question and develop the answer using items 1–6 as prompts. Then ask students to do the same in pairs.

## Sample answers

**1**

1 make
2 make/generate
3 improve
4 become
5 produce
6 lead to

**2**

... make new friends in their social life, for example at parties. When people make friends like this, they are usually happier, which, in turn, gives them confidence. And if they have more confidence when speaking to people, they can improve their English.

## Content overview

### Theme

This unit is based on the topic of reading, books and comics, and activities related to the topic.

### Exam-related activities

#### Reading

Matching headings
Matching
Multiple choice

#### Writing

Task 1    Future projections
Task 2    Writing a paragraph for an essay

#### Listening

Section 2
Sentence completion
Matching

### Speaking

Part 2    Organizing your answer
          Describing something you enjoyed/didn't
          enjoy reading
Part 3    Beginning your answer
          Speaking fluently

### Language development

#### Language focus and Vocabulary

Collocations related to reading
The future
Collocations: Evaluating adjectives
First conditional

#### Study skills

Reading/Writing: Cause and effect
Speaking: Developing ideas – using *if* clauses

---

## Vocabulary 1    page 66

### Collocations related to reading

#### Aim

This section helps students focus on vocabulary that they can use throughout the unit.

#### Suggestion

As students go through the unit, point out, or ask them to look out for, words that relate directly or indirectly to reading. Ask them to create a vocabulary list starting with the words in this section.

**1** If necessary, review the meaning of the word *collocation*. After the discussion about the pictures, ask students what other kind of things they like to read. Elicit different kinds of reading material they might not have mentioned, eg, *textbooks, novels, factual books, websites, newspapers, science fiction, manga* and make a list on the board. Ask them which types of fiction/non-fiction from the list they like to read or have read.

#### Answer

Students' own answers.

**2** Students can do this exercise in pairs. Encourage them to give at least one reason and example for each question and ask additional questions. If there is time, ask them to change partners with another pair and repeat the process.

#### Answers

Students' own answers.

**3** Once students have done exercise **3** individually, check the answers as a class. Students can practise reading the questions from the point of view of stress and rhythm. Ask them to read the stressed words in each question, eg, *0 find books English easy read* and then to read the whole question. You might like also to point out the pronunciation of *read* in the past form. Monitor the activity and then select individual students to read each question. Ask students to add the collocations to their vocabulary books.

#### Answers

| | | |
|---|---|---|
| 1  reading | 4  read | 6  reader |
| 2  reader | 5  reading | 7  read |
| 3  read | | |

**4/5** After students have checked their answers for exercise **4** in pairs, give them time to think of their questions and answers for exercise **5**. Point out the importance of beginning the answers to questions well. When they take turns to ask and answer the questions, encourage them to begin their answers as in the book. For additional practice, students can choose another two or three questions and then develop the answers in their own way. Elicit alternative beginnings to answers, write them on the board and discuss why they are suitable.

Students can do the additional practice on page 159 in the class or for homework.

### Answers

| 0 e | 1 g | 2 c | 3 f | 4 b | 5 h | 6 d | 7 a |
|-----|-----|-----|-----|-----|-----|-----|-----|

### Extension

This is a good time to introduce students to guided readers if your school has them. You could take them to the resource centre, show them how the coding works (if they haven't already had an induction) and get them to choose a book to take out and read later. Point out how reading is a great way to expand their vocabulary and increase their confidence in the language. Students can report back to the class about books they have read. This can be done in groups once a week or fortnight.

## Speaking 1   page 67

### IELTS Speaking Part 2

**1** Give students one minute to make their notes. By now they should be able to make brief, efficient notes.

#### Sample answer

science fiction book (*Dune*), 12, secondary school, exciting, enjoyable, film, (read) more

**2** Before students start, read through the items in the box. Remind students of the meaning of *to appeal* and other adjectives from Unit 1 Word building on page 10. When they have finished, they can check their answers in pairs.

#### Answers

what it is: What I'm going to describe is/I'd like to describe
when you read it: when I was 12/I read it in secondary school.
where you read it: I read it in secondary school.
explain why you enjoyed or didn't enjoy reading it: Another reason why it appealed to me was because/and I loved it/didn't like it at all/It was very enjoyable because

**3** Before students begin, get them to read the Tip. When making notes, suggest they write the notes in the order they want to present them. Point out that it is probably easier to read them if they are written vertically. Remind them to expand on their notes as much as possible within the time limit, especially when they explain why at the end. Time them as they practise the speaking. When they finish, ask them to consider how they could have improved their answer.

#### Sample answer

What I'm going to describe is a science fiction book called *Dune* which I read when I was in secondary school. I was 12 at the time. It was a very enjoyable book. It was so thrilling that I couldn't put it down. I really enjoyed reading it because the story was very exciting. It was about different worlds and it meant you could really escape into it. Another reason why it appealed to me was because it was full of action and the story moved very fast. I read it very quickly even though it was quite long. It even made me want to read other science fiction books and now I am a really big fan of science fiction.

## Photocopiable activity   page 116

### I read them a lot because ...

**1** Alternatively, students can tear up or cut up all the boxes and assemble the information in the correct arrangement.

**2** For free practice, encourage them to talk about the types of material suggested here.

#### Answers

see page 123

## Listening   page 67

### IELTS Listening Section 2

#### Aim

This section aims to give students practice with the type of monologue they will encounter in Section 2 of the Listening module. The length of the recording is shorter than students will encounter in the IELTS exam. The content is also simpler, as are the questions, but the latter mimic the exam format.

## Pre-listening

**1** To introduce the Listening section, ask students what they think a book fair is. If you have access to one, show a picture of a book fair or point out the picture on page 68 and ask them what it shows. Get them to go through the list and decide what they would find at a book fair. Elicit the meaning of the word *stand* or *exhibits* using the picture on page 68. If someone has been to one, ask them to describe it to the class.

**Answers**

Students' own answers. All are possible.

## Listening

**2**  Look at both Tips and the picture again. Elicit whether students expect to hear a dialogue or a monologue. Ask them to read through the questions and describe what the speaker is going to say about the book fair, using the questions. Remind students of the word limit in questions 1–4 and to listen for the days of the week in questions 5–7. Play the recording once. When students have checked their answers in pairs, play it again and check the answers as a whole class.

**Answers**

| | | | |
|---|---|---|---|
| 1 | four/4 | 6 | C |
| 2 | UK | 7 | A |
| 3 | free | 8 | C |
| 4 | electronic devices | 9 | B |
| 5 | B | 10 | A |

**◉ 1.13**

Welcome to *The Book Corner*. My name is David Horne and as always we have some exciting reports for you today. We're going to look at whether literacy does matter and how we can encourage young people, especially boys, to read more in this digital age. And what better way to start the show than news about The International Book Fair here in London which runs for four days, including today.

There are 20 major publishers' stands from the UK and another 30 from around Europe and another 30 from around the world. With some publishers having more than one stand to exhibit their publications, there are 110 stands, including 30 stands in the digital zone, devoted to electronic media, including devices and software. The fair is open to all members of the public, and all ages over 16. To encourage young people to come to the fair, entrance, which normally costs £10, is free on day two of the fair for those under 25. This is the first year that the book fair has introduced such a scheme. So if you are under 25, get down

there with your student card and proof of age tomorrow for your free entrance.

At lunch time today, when we were at the fair, there were large crowds of visitors of all ages, including many young people. If more visitors turn up tomorrow, the book fair will be very busy this year. By far the most popular stands for young people were those devoted to electronic devices for reading books and surfing the net, etcetera. The stands are all very lively, modern and appealing. It will be the most successful fair ever, according to the organizers.

Over the four-day period of the fair there are many different events taking place ranging from seminars, talks and workshops to advice sessions for young and old amateur writers. Tomorrow, Tuesday, there are over 10 talks scheduled during the day, but I think the most popular one will be on writing children's books by the famous children's author Charles Shaker. This will be very stimulating. Then on Wednesday, if the talk is not full, I'm personally planning to go to a talk on encouraging boys to read by the well-known TV presenter, Edward Chaucer. This should be a very interesting talk. On Thursday, everyone on our show, *The Book Corner*, is planning to visit the fair and we will broadcast live from the fair. If you are there, we'll be happy to meet you and have a chat. So come and see us.

…

We've already had some messages on Twitter, emails and instant messages about the show. Angus Dean, the organizer of the fair, has written: *Show a huge success. Hoping to see you all there over the next couple of days.* And from Maria Lopez we have a message, … she says *If you go to the fair, you'll love it. I'm going to visit the fair again.* Let's see if we can find another message from someone else. Ah, yes, here we are. This is a message from Cheng Ming who visited the Book Fair this morning and he says: … *My visit was an invaluable experience. All young people should make use of the free day.*

## The future

**Aim**

This section introduces the future in preparation for Writing Task 1 in the next section, where students write about predictions relating to data.

Talking about the future can be challenging for some students. Some may have been taught only *will* as the future form, and some errors will ensue from this. Note also that some languages don't have tenses for the future. The first activity here will help clarify this, but you may need to do a mini-presentation using the Grammar on page 152. If students still need extra help, do the grammar practice on page 153.

**1** Students can do this exercise in pairs, followed by whole-class checking. Check they all understand the different forms and functions presented here. They may not know the use of the present continuous in this function but tell them how commonly it is used. Write a few supplementary sentences on the board and ask students to identify the tense. Then read the sentences to the students with their books closed and ask them to name the tense and explain why it is being used.

**Answers**

a 3    b 1    c 4    d 2

**2** This activity is a useful diagnostic test to check whether students have grasped the different forms and functions used to describe the future. They should do this individually and check their answers in pairs. Give extra examples if necessary.

**Answers**

| | | | |
|---|---|---|---|
| 1 | 'm going to read | 5 | Are (we) going to listen |
| 2 | Will (they) sell | 6 | won't be |
| 3 | 'm flying | 7 | 'm arranging |
| 4 | closes | | |

**3/4** Elicit possible question endings for each of these stems, before students ask and answer the questions in 4. Encourage students to change partners and ask the questions to at least one other student, developing their answers in their own way. When they have finished, allow them to ask you questions so you can monitor comprehension. As a further exercise, get students to ask you questions as before. Give answers which students have to decide if they are correct or not. If they think the answers are wrong, students should explain why and correct the answer.

**Sample answers**

2 How will you spend your summer holidays/weekend?
3 What will you do after the class/lunch today?
4 What are you planning to do this evening/after the class/this weekend/over the summer?
5 Why are you going to go back home/do the exam soon?

**5/6** Give students time to write their sentences and then share them with a partner.

For consolidation, put each of the forms across the top of the whiteboard and ask them to supply sentences. They then tell you under which heading you should write them. An alternative would be to write the different ways to talk about the future on the board. Then ask them in groups to give examples of contexts or situations in which they can be used. You then collate them on the board.

**Sample answers**

I'm going to study at university.
My parents are planning to take me on holiday this year.
I'm spending the weekend with friends in Paris.
I'm starting a new job next month.
I'll go back to my old job when I go home.

## IELTS Writing Task 1: Future projections

**1** Get students to look at the graph in pairs. Elicit the part of the graph that represents future projections. Ask them how this is indicated and also ask what the axes represent.

When they have matched the sentences, discuss how the same information is written in different ways. Draw their attention to passive/active forms and synonyms.

**Answers**

1 and 6; 4 and 5

**2** Look at the language presented. Write it on the board as stems. Elicit the rewritten sentence and write it up next to one of the stems. Ask students to copy it down and write the sentence again using two different stems.

**Answers**

It is forecast/predicted/estimated/expected/projected (that) expenditure on education will fall between 2011 and 2050.

**3** Elicit from students the difference between this sentence and the others: it is very general and provides a summary of the trend.

**Answer**

3

**4** Write the sentences on the board as students dictate them to you. Then using the sentences on the board, ask students to transform the sentences back to the original form. Give students further practice with this transformation: *1 Car sales rose dramatically./There was a dramatic rise in car sales. 2 Cinema attendance fell sharply./There was a sharp fall in cinema attendance. 3 There will be a significant increase in traffic next year./Traffic will increase significantly next year.* Point out the form changes from adverb to adjective and the preposition *in* is added after the noun. Students can practise saying the sentences to a partner, who then transforms them.

**Answers**

2 There was a peak in expenditure on education around 2005.
5 It is expected that there will be a fall in expenditure on education between 2011 and 2050.

**5** Students should work in pairs and look for the answers. After checking the answers, they should work with another partner and take turns to ask the questions. When they have finished, ask the questions around the class.

**Answers**

1 The graph shows the past and projected expenditure on education as a percentage of GDP in New Zealand between 1950 and 2050.

2 Despite the projected decline between 2011 and 2050, the trend in expenditure over the whole period is still upward.

3 It increased from about 2 per cent to approximately 6.5 per cent.

4 It peaked at about 5 per cent.

5 It plummeted/dropped to below 4 per cent.

6 sharp

7 It is predicted to fall/decrease/decline.

8 gradual

**6** Give students 20–25 minutes to write about the data. When they have finished they can check their answers (encourage them to spend 2 minutes doing this). Ask students to compare their answer with the model on page 163. Alternatively, if possible display the sample on the board and ask them to match the sentences to the graph.

**Extension**

At the end of the section, students can work in pairs and draw their own graphs about predictions. They can draw the two axes for a line graph, and write numbers 10–100 on the vertical axes, where 10=10,000 and 100=100,000. Along the bottom axis they can write *2018, 2020, 2025, 2030.* They then draw three lines on the graph for the sale of cars, vans and motorcycles. Students can change partners and dictate their graph to another partner, who then draws it.

## Vocabulary 2   page 71

### Collocations: Evaluating adjectives

**Aim**
This section aims to provide students with the type of adjectives that are useful in all parts of the IELTS exam.

**Suggestion**
Use such adjectives as part of your meta-language or teacher language so students become used to hearing them.

**1** You can use pictures to introduce the adjectives if necessary, eg, a car, a house, a field, something wooden, snow. Ask students to describe the pictures. Write two headings on the board: *descriptive* and *evaluating*. Ask students under which heading you should write adjectives like *big, small, green, wooden, cold, loud* and adjectives like *wonderful, delicious, kind, interesting, ugly.* Ask them: *Can we disagree with the adjectives in the first list? (No.) Can we disagree with those in the second list? (Yes. The second list of adjectives indicates opinion: something that is not fact, but a personal evaluation.)* Elicit from students why they think the adjectives they underlined are evaluative.

**Answers**

1 exciting

3 lively, modern, appealing

4 the most popular, stimulating

**2** Go through the adjectives in the box and ask the class: *Are they descriptive or evaluative?* Students can do the exercise in pairs. At this point, don't help them with meaning – see if they can work it out from the context. Tell them they can use dictionaries if they can't guess the meaning.

**Answers**

| | |
|---|---|
| 1 suitable | 4 convenient |
| 2 invaluable | 5 beneficial |
| 3 useless | 6 successful |

**3** Point out to students that they have to learn which adjectives and adverbs collocate. There is no set rule for this. Students can write the collocations in exercise **2** and the adverbs and adjectives in their vocabulary books.

**Answers**

*Very* cannot be used with *invaluable* and *useless.*
*Hugely* cannot be used with *suitable, invaluable* and *useless.*
*Extremely* cannot be used with *invaluable* and *useless.*

**4/5** Give students 5 minutes to write the sentences before putting them into groups to share.

**Sample answers**

The festival I went to last weekend was very stimulating.
I found a new leisure centre near here which is very convenient for going to the gym.
I went to study in Greece. It was an invaluable experience.

## Reading   page 71

**Aim**
The aim of the reading passage is to show that all forms of reading are valuable.

**Suggestion**
Get students to write down all the types of reading that they have done in the past 24 hours or since they got up. They can then compare their lists in groups and discuss. Collate all the various types on the board and include any type of sign or label students might have read. Include your own examples if possible.

### Pre-reading

**1** Ask students to predict the contents of the reading from the title and the picture. Elicit what the reading will be about.

**Answer**

reading comics

**2** Check students have got the type of word correct before they scan for the opposite words in the reading passage. Time them looking for the antonyms – allow between 3 and 5 minutes.

**Answers**

| | | |
|---|---|---|
| 1 | verb | blamed/condemned |
| 2 | adjective | found |
| 3 | adjective | positive |
| 4 | noun | fact |
| 5 | verb | support |
| 6 | adjective | extensive |
| 7 | adjective | useful |

**3** Do the questions together as a class. Then discuss the different purposes of a text, i.e., *Why is the writer writing this? (to persuade/to complain/to inform/to discuss/to give an answer, etc)* Students are now moving towards identifying the author's attitude from the language he/she is using.

**Answers**

1 positive
2 blamed/condemned
3 the negative words are mainly at the beginning
4 supporting. Look at the title. Also the negative comes at the beginning, followed by the positive, which is a common pattern in texts.

## Reading

**4** Review the procedure for reading as in previous units. To help students, you can focus on one set of questions at a time, giving them 7–8 minutes for each section and then checking the answers. Once you have established the text is positive about reading comics, you can use this to help discuss the headings with students. You can, for example, ask the students to look at the headings and then ask them questions: *i: Is this about a skill or skills? Is it related to children? ii: Is this about a method? Is it about all children? iii: Is this likely to be the introduction? Why not? Is this about all kinds of problems? v: Is this general or is it specific? Is this change likely to be from positive to negative or negative to positive? (Think of the title.)* If necessary, spend some time preparing students for the reading from now on by focusing on one set of questions for each reading passage. Get students to add a section in their vocabulary books for words and patterns that can occur frequently in paragraph and section headings. Tell students to look at the Tips and Glossary. When students have checked their answers, ask them whether they read comics; and whether they agree with the contents of the reading passage.

Ask students to select 7–10 items from the reading passage to add to their vocabulary books. You can collate the selection on the board with part of the context. At this halfway stage, it might be an idea to check to see if there is any particular question type they are having difficulty with as a class. If so, give them some extra practice from supplementary material before doing another sample reading test.

**Answers**

| | | | |
|---|---|---|---|
| 1 | Section A v | 8 | D |
| 2 | Section B iii | 9 | E |
| 3 | Section C i | 10 | A |
| 4 | Section D vii | 11 | A |
| 5 | Section E ii | 12 | C |
| 6 | B | 13 | D |
| 7 | C | 14 | C |

# Language focus 2 page 74

## First conditional

**1** Use the exercise as a diagnostic test, referring students to the Grammar on page 153 to complete it. If they are still having difficulties, give a mini-presentation, eliciting the form and function of the first conditional.

**Answers**

2 The simple present is used in the *if* clause and *will* is used in the main clause.
3 *If, provided* and *unless* are conjunctions, so you need a comma between the two clauses instead of a full stop.

**2** When students have finished, you can write the beginning of several conditional clauses on the board, eg, *If children read comics … ; Provided libraries in schools are pleasant … .* Ask students to complete them in pairs, collating the answers on the board. As an extra exercise, students can do the grammar practice on page 153.

**Answers**

3 Provided children are able to read and write well at a young <u>age, they</u> will develop fast.
4 If <u>you go</u> through your homework afterwards, then you will find some mistakes.
5 <u>If</u> young people don't study, their chances in life will not be good.
7 If children ~~don't~~ read for pleasure, they will develop their imagination.
8 Unless young <u>people are computer</u> literate, they will not find a good job nowadays.

**3/4** Encourage students to use all the options, not just *if*. You might like to drill for intonation and stress here, eg, *If I <u>pass my exams,</u> (fall) I'll go to <u>university.</u> (rise-fall).*

## Speaking 2  page 74

### IELTS Speaking Part 3

**1/2** Remind students how important it is to begin their answers well. When they have finished exercise **1**, discuss why the fourth option is unsuitable. In exercise **2**, explain that there are many different ways to begin the answers. Then ask them to practise asking and answering the questions in different ways, using just the beginning of the answers. Students can do this first with their books open and then closed. Monitor as they practise and encourage them to expand their answers and use all the alternatives.

#### Answers

1  A, B, C
2  A, B, D
3  B, C, D

**3** **(O)1.14** Tell students that native speakers run sounds together in connected speech. This helps fluency. There are certain sounds, as well as contractions, that allow this in speech. Write the sentence on the board, using linking curves under the words in the sample sentence. Ask them to read the sentence aloud. After they have listened, write several answers from exercise **1** on the board, eg, 1c, and ask them to think about which sounds they can run together. Ask them to practise answering the questions in exercise **1** again in pairs, focusing on the elision between words.

**(O)1.14**

Yes, it's vital to be able to read nowadays, because ...

**4** Students can do this exercise individually before checking in pairs. Write the sentences on the board, leaving space between lines for adding the curved links. Read the sentences aloud, then ask several students to do so.

#### Answers

No I/so at all/I think it's/the opposite/there is/so much/ want to have/and earn/a lot of/And if/have a good

**5/6** Write the cues given on the board and elicit the answers. When they have finished, ask them to take turns to ask and answer the question. Monitor students for linking between words when they practise in pairs.

#### Answer

Competition → good jobs → money → good lifestyle

**7** Point out what features the 'observer' will give feedback on and put them on the board. When students

## Writing 2  page 75

have finished, get several pairs to demonstrate to the class.

### IELTS Writing Task 2

**Aim**
This section helps students write a paragraph for a Task 2 essay, with guidance.

**Suggestion**
For extra practice, elicit another paragraph from students which you can write on the board.

**1** Look at the picture and discuss the situation as a whole class. Elicit the three best ways from students and write them on the board, with justifications and examples below the appropriate reason.

#### Answers

Students' own answers. All the reasons can be used.

**2/3** Go through the Tip with students and emphasize the importance of paraphrasing the essay title. When students have discussed their choices in pairs, go through the reasons as a whole class, eliciting explanations and giving reasons.

#### Answers

**2**

Students' own answers. All are possible answers.

**3**

2, 3, 4, 6

**4** Students can do this exercise in pairs. Check answers with the whole class. Elicit reasons for the answers. Get them to copy out the introduction into their notebooks along with the paragraph so they can see them together. Point out the linking devices used: *moreover, so, for example, then*. Ask them to add a section on Writing to their vocabulary books entitled *Linking devices*. Alternatively, ask them to keep a separate record for writing words and phrases.

#### Answers

1  b     2  d     3  c     4  a

**5** Remind students of Vocabulary 2 on page 71. Emphasize that writers don't always have to use phrases such as *I think*. They can use adjectives as well.

#### Answers

a  I think     b  certainly

**6** Point out that arrows are useful for showing cause–effect relationships when making notes. Ask students to explain why 1 is correct. Ask them to relate the three stages to the text in **4**.

**Answer**

1

**7/8** An alternative method for doing this is to get students into groups of four. They plan and write the paragraph together on a large sheet of paper, a computer or an overhead transparency. When they have finished, they can display the paragraph for peer-correction and feedback. Ask students to compare their answers with the model paragraph on page 163. Read through the comments with them. Ask them to match the specific parts of the comments to the model paragraph.

Point out that writing the summary is good academic skills practice. It should be encouraged as a checking tool after students write both Tasks 1 and 2.

## Study skills   page 77

### Reading/Writing: Cause and effect

**Aim**
This gives students further practice in an important feature of academic writing which they will encounter in all four skills.

**Suggestion**
Dictate four or five sentences to students, eg, *Flooding is caused by heavy rain. Investment in schools improves education. Airplanes are responsible for pollution. Qualifications can lead to a good job.* Then ask students to identify the cause and the effect in each sentence.

**1** Go through the Tip and encourage students to do this by adding a section in their vocabulary book or in a separate notebook for writing.

**Answers**

| | | | | | |
|---|---|---|---|---|---|
| 1 | cause | 4 | cause | 7 | effect |
| 2 | effect | 5 | effect | | |
| 3 | cause | 6 | cause | | |

**2** Students can do this exercise individually and then check in pairs. Alternatively, it can be done as a homework exercise.

**Sample answers**

1 Reading newspapers daily can lead to <u>an increase in general knowledge</u>.
2 He became much more educated as a result of <u>studying part-time in the evenings</u>.
3 Competition between different companies reduces <u>the price of goods</u>.
4 <u>People's lives can be</u> improved by spending on education.

5 <u>The flooding became worse</u> and the bridge then collapsed.
6 With the increase in pollution, the water <u>became too dirty to use</u>.
7 <u>People demonstrated</u> when the price of bread rose.

**3** Students can do this on their own first, followed by checking in pairs.

**Sample answers**

| | | | |
|---|---|---|---|
| 1 | detrimental | 4 | produce |
| 2 | beneficial | 5 | impact |
| 3 | harmful | 6 | effective |

## Speaking: Developing ideas – using *if* clauses

**1** This can be worked through step-by-step in class if students still require a lot of guidance. If they are more confident, they can do this activity on their own. Encourage them to think not only of the language, but the pronunciation, stress and elision when they are speaking.

**Sample answer**

If children enjoy reading comics, then they will want to read more and will buy comics or can be encouraged to visit a library. If they visit a library, they will come into contact with books and newspapers. If they come into contact with books, some will borrow books and want to read some. If they read more, some will want to learn more.

**2** Students can do this in pairs and then compare their answers with other students, if they are doing the exercise in class.

**Sample answer**

If children enjoy reading comics, then they will want to read more and will buy comics or can be encouraged to visit a library. *When they are there,* they will come into contact with books and newspapers *and* some will borrow books and want to read some. *Once* they start reading more, some will *not be able to stop learning.*

**3/4** In exercise 3, students can first take turns to read through the question and answer, and then answer the question in their own way. After preparing their *if-* chains in pairs, students can think about it first individually before practising with a partner or other students. Point out that they can make similar *if-* chains for writing paragraphs in IELTS Writing Task 2.

## Content overview

### Theme

The theme of this unit is the mind and psychology.

### Exam-related activities

#### Reading

Identifying writer's claims – Yes/No/Not Given
Sentence completion
Multiple choice

#### Writing

Task 2    Punctuation
Task 1    Describing tables

#### Listening

Section 3
Multiple choice
Table completion
Choosing items from a list

### Speaking

Part 1    Describing frequency/Talking about media
Part 2    Fluency and accuracy/Talking about TV programmes
Part 3    Talking about children and imagination

## Language development

### Language focus and Vocabulary

Collocations: Technology
Second conditional
Defining and non-defining clauses
Word building: Nouns and adjectives

### Study skills

Reading: Yes/No/Not Given

---

## Speaking 1    page 78

### IELTS Speaking Part 1

**Aim**
The aim of this section is to get students to talk about and develop brief answers about everyday activities.

**Suggestion**
Remind students that they do not need to speak at length in this part of the exam. Encourage them to say no more than a few sentences in answer to each question. At this stage, they can start collecting topics that might occur in IELTS Speaking Part 3 and write sample questions as part of self-study or as an extension exercise in class.

**1/2** To orient students to the theme of the unit, ask them to predict what they think the unit is about. Ask them whether they think technology helps people's minds or not.

Ask students to do exercise **1** in pairs. Write the words relating to the pictures on the board. After class feedback on exercise **1**, elicit the meaning of the words and phrases in the box in exercise **2**. Check

comprehension around the class. If there are some adverbs of frequency they don't understand, draw the line below on the board and ask them to tell you where to write the words. They can then copy it into their vocabulary books for reference.

| 0% | 50% | 100% |
|---|---|---|
| never | sometimes | always |

**3** Give students several minutes to look at the question and the table. Elicit possible questions and answers, eg, *I (often) read newspapers online.* Encourage students to move around the class, asking different students. When they finish the exercise, ask for feedback, eg, *How many people use games online? (I found two people who often use games online.)*

Additionally, ask students to draw another table and write the names of each student they asked in the relevant box. They then write sentences, eg, *Lee rarely uses apps.*

**4/5** Students should first work in pairs. When they have finished, ask students several of the questions. Monitor them to ensure they give reasons, gently prompting by saying *Give a reason/example*, but not interfering in the pairwork activity. Also, get them to ask you questions before the whole-class discussion.

## Listening    page 79

### IELTS Listening Section 3

**Aim**

This Listening Section 3 gives students practice in dealing with more academic topics.

**Suggestion**

If students find this type of listening practice challenging, play the recording in sections, ie, questions 1–3, questions 4–6 and 7–10. Then play the whole recording without stopping so students can listen to check how much they understand.

### Pre-listening

**1/2/3**  After students have discussed and compared their answers with other groups, elicit the main things the listening test covers and write them on the board. Students can work out quite a lot about the discussion from reading the questions. It is easy to forget that the questions are a summary of the recording. This is a skill needed for the exam – and life. Remind them to look at the Tip for questions 7 and 8. Play the recording, but ask students not to look at the questions. They should just listen to see if their predictions are correct. Then check the predictions on the board with the whole class.

**Answers**

It's a discussion about a presentation, with slides. The presentation is about technology and the effect of technology on the brain.

### Listening

**4**  Before students listen and answer the questions, give them a chance to underline key words in the questions. Give them 2 minutes to do this. After listening to the recording, students check their answers in pairs and then listen again. Get them to mark any changes to their answers in a different colour.
It might be an idea for students to start keeping a record of their scores in both listening and reading from classwork and self-study. They could have two columns, one with correct answers within the time limit, and one with correct answers in extra time. Using this, they will have a goal they can work towards in terms of decreasing the time it takes to be accurate.

**Answers**

| | | | |
|---|---|---|---|
| 1 | B | 5 | confidence |
| 2 | C | 6 | thinking strategies |
| 3 | A | 7/8 | B, E |
| 4 | background details | 9/10 | A, D |

### 2.1

(H = Henry; C = Caroline)

H: Hi, Caroline!

C: Oh hi, Henry!

H: Do you mind if I join you?

C: No, by all means. I'm just sitting here thinking about what to do for this presentation next week. I've been in the library all morning.

H: Ah … I know what you mean. What are you doing the presentation on?

C: Oh, it's mmm, something for my psychology module. My aim is … mmm … to show how modern technology has an impact on people's brains, such as memory, skills and so on.

H: Wow. Sounds interesting! But why did you choose that topic?

C: Oh, mmm … I'm just fascinated by the way the brain functions. I think if I had to choose my course again, I'd do psychology as my main course.

H: Really?

C: I can't believe how interesting it is. There're masses of data on the negative effects of technology, … like making people lazy, … because they don't have to remember everything like telephone numbers.

H: Even Samuel Johnson, the dictionary writer, who lived and worked in the 17th century, once said there are two types of knowledge: the one you know and the one you know where to find.

C: Oh, that sounds good. Can I use that in one of my slides?

H: Yeah, sure. I'll have to find where it came from. I can't remember …

C: I've got a plan here of my talk.

H: That looks very organized.

C: It's only a plan! The first five slides are about statistics relating to the use of technology and then slides six to eight are basically on background details regarding unreal or virtual worlds on the Internet. Just by chance I found an article on how being avatars in these virtual worlds works.

H: OK.

C: In virtual worlds or 'unreal worlds' on the Internet, people … mmm … people become virtual people with a different personality.

H: Ah, OK.

C: And they adopt this personality and way of life, etcetera, in this world. It's like a game.

H: That sounds weird, but very interesting. Can you send me a copy of the article?

C: Yeah. But there is an interesting effect and that is that even if people are avatars for only a short period of time, it increases their confidence in the real world.

H: Yes, that *is* interesting.

C: And then slides nine to twelve are on … the development of young people's manual skills. There's evidence to show that playing video games really helps motor skills.

H: OK.

C: And slides thirteen to twenty are on memory and thinking and how using technology alters people's <u>thinking strategies.</u>

H: It sounds very impressive.

C: Do you think so? <u>I spent a lot of time putting together the slides.</u> In fact, I've been working on them for the past week. I have to say, I didn't think it would take me quite so long.

H: Well, they do take quite a while to make.

C: And <u>the other thing which took me ages was dealing with the handouts</u> to go with the presentation.

H: Is that a copy there?

C: Yes.

H: Do you want some suggestions?

C: Yes, sure.

H: The presentation is 30 minutes, yes?

C: Yes.

H: Well ... mmm ... <u>I think you've got too many slides.</u> Ten to twelve would be more than enough.

C: Do you think so? Just ten to twelve?

H: Yes, well, ... mmm ... with 20 slides, that is one-and-a-half minutes per slide.

C: Oh, yes. That's not a lot.

H: And also if I were you, <u>I'd then make notes on paper copies of the slides to help you as you speak.</u>

C: Oh yes, that's a good idea.

## Vocabulary 1   page 80

## Collocations: Technology

### Aim
This section aims to build students' confidence in talking about technology, which is a topic that they might encounter in the IELTS exam.

### Suggestion
As well as making revision cards for collocations (see exercise **5**), ask students to keep a vocabulary list of the types of technology they encounter. They can write brief notes about reasons for using or liking/disliking the technologies and then use the list for revision purposes.

**1/2** Review and elicit the types of technology we use these days generally, and in schools specifically. Get students to complete exercise 1 and identify and then add the collocations, eg, *state-of-the art technology*, *a technological revolution* (cf *the industrial revolution*), to their vocabulary books. After discussing the statements in groups, take a vote on the statements, writing the results against the sentence numbers. Get one person from each group to feed back to the class, giving justifications for their answers.

### Answers

| | | | |
|---|---|---|---|
| 1 | Solar | 4 | state-of-the-art |
| 2 | skills | 5 | revolution |
| 3 | developed | | |

**3** Ask students to describe the picture and ask: *How is it linked with the topic?* They can then do the exercise in pairs. Go around the class and help with ideas if necessary. Collate the answers on the board.

### Sample answers

1 digital technology – camera
2 green technology – wind farms
3 low-carbon technology – electric cars
4 educational technology – interactive whiteboards
5 the most reliable technology you have – laptop
6 a technology you'd like to see adopted – hydrogen cars/ buses
7 state-of-the-art technology you want to have – iPad2

**4** Students can write the sentences individually and then check them in pairs. Elicit examples to write on the board.

### Sample answers

2 A (good) example of green technology is wind farms.
3 Electric cars can have a positive effect on the environment.
4 Interactive whiteboards are very common in modern classrooms.
5 The most reliable technology I have is my laptop, which I can take everywhere.
6 I'd like to see more hydrogen buses, especially in large cities.
7 The iPad2 is a good example of state-of-the-art technology.

**5** When students have completed the card, it can be transferred to their vocabulary books on a page titled *Technology*. Encourage them to leave space so they can add more words during the course. Students can also use the revision card to make notes about other words.

### Sample answer

| | | Notes/Examples |
|---|---|---|
| Adjectives | modern: | up-to-date |
| | type: | agricultural |
| | good: | effective |
| | environmental: | green/clean |
| Verbs | use | adopt |
| | start to use | introduce |

### Extension
As a consolidation activity, get students to prepare a short 2–3 minute talk in groups on a piece of technology they have or would like to have. They can describe it, say when/how they (would get) got it, how they (would) use it, and why they (would) like it. Get them to present their ideas to the class.

# Language focus 1    page 80

## Second conditional

**1** Review the first conditional by writing the words *buy/BlackBerry®/do many things* on the board. Then elicit a sentence in the first conditional, eg, *If I buy a BlackBerry®, I'll be able to do many things.* When students have completed the grammar pattern, elicit an explanation of the second conditional and refer them to the Grammar on page 153 for more information, if necessary. Point out the use of *were* rather than *was* for *I* in the second conditional, ie, *If I were you.*

**Answer**

If

**2/3** Students should do these exercises individually, checking their answers in pairs, before a whole-class check. After completing exercise **2**, students can cover the right-hand column and complete the sentences in their own words. Elicit examples from the class. In exercise **3**, ask students to give reasons for their answers.

**Answers**

**2**

1 d    2 b    3 e    4 c    5 a    6 g    7 f

**3**

1 did    2 do    3 not    4 unless    5 will be

**4/5** Help students prepare their questions, if necessary. You may have to explain the word *react*. When they have finished, ask students questions using the question stems in **4**.

# Speaking 2    page 81

## IELTS Speaking Part 2

**1/2** Time students as they make notes. After they have checked their notes in exercise **2**, elicit examples of the notes to write on the board for comparison.

**3/4/5** (O) **2.2** Students should check their answers with a partner. They can then listen to the recording and check their answers.

## Answers

**3**

why you chose the programme

**4/5**

Another reason why I liked the programme was that it was stunning <u>to</u> watch. It <u>used</u> the latest technology to show how the human brain <u>works</u>. The images were very effective. It was <u>more</u> exciting than an adventure film. If the documentary were shown in 3D, I<u>'d</u> love to see it again. And I can say that I<u>'d</u> definitely recommend it <u>to</u> my friends to watch.

**6** Get students to time each other and give constructive feedback about the points in the instructions. Ask one student to talk about the card as a class demonstration.

# Reading    page 82

## Aim

The section gives students practice of a more formal type of reading passage. The passage is shorter than students will encounter in the exam and some of the vocabulary has been simplified. The questions are in the exam format, but are simpler versions of the type of questions they will encounter in the exam.

## Suggestion

If necessary, ask students to answer the questions in stages. They could start to answer in the class and finish for homework, or you could divide the class into groups and allocate one set of questions to each group. Then, the questions can be discussed as a whole class.

After students have read the first Tip, check comprehension by asking them questions about the contents. Point out that guessing unknown words from the context is a necessary skill in reading. For some students this may be contrary to how they have been taught to read in English, so encouragement to practise this will help them.

## Pre-reading

**1/2** Allow students to check their answers in a dictionary. Then elicit the meaning of the words from the class.

This might be a good time to explain that while bilingual dictionaries are very useful when starting to learn a language, they can also be limiting as there are many shades of meaning to words that cannot always be directly translated.

## Answers

| | |
|---|---|
| 1 improving | 5 long-term |
| 2 shines | 6 to do with space |
| 3 results | 7 a short sleep |
| 4 bringing together | 8 people who sleep |

**3** Ask students to look at the title, the picture on page 83 and the sentences in italics. Discuss the second Tip.

## Answers

The writer is positive: he/she uses words like *better, well established, important tool, enhancing, new study, important process*

## Reading

**4** Discuss the questions, asking students to read the Strategy. Then with the whole class, work through the first two questions, explaining the answers. Point out that there is more practice with Yes/No/Not Given statements on page 89. Students discuss the answers in groups as usual. Finally, ask students whether they think sleep helps their memory and helps them to learn.

Elicit from students 5–7 phrases from the reading passage that they think are worth remembering and write them on the board. Discuss students' choices and make sure they are phrases that are useful. Get them to write them in their vocabulary books.

## Answers

| | |
|---|---|
| 1 No | 8 described dreaming |
| 2 Not Given | 9 scenarios |
| 3 Yes | 10 C |
| 4 Yes | 11 B |
| 5 Yes | 12 A |
| 6 No | 13 D |
| 7 improvement | |

## Language focus 2    page 85

### Defining and non-defining clauses

**Aim**
This Language focus aims to show students how they can add information to their writing using defining and non-defining clauses.

**Suggestion**
Encourage students to use such clauses in their writing, especially in Writing Task 2, and in speaking. Remind them of the type of language they can use each time they prepare for a writing task. They can prepare a checklist of grammar features with brief examples that they can read through before they write.

**1/2/3** Check the students' answers as a whole class, writing the examples on the board. Elicit what the difference between defining and non-defining clauses is. Emphasize the difference in the punctuation. If necessary, give students a mini-presentation using the Grammar on page 154. Then elicit the answers for exercise **3** from the whole class and suggest they transfer the definitions in exercise **3** to their notebooks.

## Answers

**1**
1 and 2 are defining, 3 is non-defining

**2**
1 b    2 d/e    3 d/e    4 c    5 a

**3**
1 a    2 b

**4** Point out that some spaces can be left blank. This exercise can be done individually and the answers checked in pairs, followed by a whole-class discussion.

## Answers

**4**
| | |
|---|---|
| 1 that/which/– | 4 that/which/– |
| 2 whose | 5 that/which/– |
| 3 that/who/– | 6 who |

**5/6** In exercise **5**, give an example for 1 and explain it. Elicit why there is no punctuation. When students have finished writing, ask them to read out their sentences. Point out the intonation in both defining and non-defining sentences. In the latter, there is a rising tone before the commas which indicates the punctuation.

*A journey, which I went on quite recently with my brother, taught me a lot about North Africa.*

When students have practised in pairs, ask individual students questions about the statements. Encourage them to develop their answers giving reasons and examples.

## Writing 1    page 86

### IELTS Writing Task 2

**1** This exercise develops what students learnt about defining and non-defining clauses, using a paragraph. Look at the picture and get students to discuss what they think it represents. After students have finished the exercise, ask them to justify their answers.

**Answer**
The world wide web, which we generally now call the Internet, was introduced at the end of the last century.

Since that time its use, which was initially quite limited, has spread rapidly. So every home in the developed world now has an Internet connection. The benefit of the Internet that appeals to most young people is the possibility of being able to connect to social websites like Facebook. Such sites, which have millions of users, link people all over the world. People who move to other countries can also keep contact using video links on the web.

**2/3** Give students 20 minutes to write the paragraph in pairs or groups. After they have finished, give them 2 minutes to check the punctuation. Ask them to exchange their paragraphs with other students for peer-correction.

### Answer

Refer students to the model writing on page 163.

## Vocabulary 2     page 86

### Word building: Nouns and adjectives

**Aim**
Vocabulary 2 aims to help students expand their vocabulary.

**Suggestion**
During each lesson, aim to include some work on word families, even if it is just to remind students of words they already know.

**1** Ask each group to nominate a student to give feedback to the whole class. This could lead to an interesting discussion and bring up some cultural attitudes regarding the creative arts. You might like to add an additional question: *How have these attitudes changed in the last 20 years?*

**2/3** After students have completed the table, they can transfer the nouns and adjectives to their vocabulary books. Check they understand the differences and similarities in meaning between any of the words.

#### Answers

**2**

| | | |
|---|---|---|
| 1 intelligent | 4 flexible |
| 2 able | 5 cleverness |
| 3 imaginative | 6 creative |

**3**

talent/gift, intelligence/cleverness

**4/5** Some students might find it easier to talk about someone else as in the examples in **4**, but encourage them to talk about themselves.

**Answers**

**4**

1 talented/gifted, flexible
2 imagination
3 able
4 gifted

#### Sample answer

**5**

I think that I am quite creative, because I like making things. I paint and draw and like making drawings and plans of buildings. Sometimes, I make drawings in the street or in parks. And I also think that I am flexible, as I can fit in anywhere. I don't get stressed when things have to change, for example at work or at my college.

## Speaking 3     page 87

### IELTS Speaking Part 3

**1/2/3** An alternative is to put students into groups of three and give each group a different question to work on. Stress the importance of each person in the group having a copy of the notes. Give each member of the group a letter, A, B or C, and regroup with all the As in one group, all the Bs in another and all the Cs in another. They can now take turns to answer the question they prepared with one student being the Examiner. The Examiner should ask supplementary questions .The third student in the group listens and gives feedback on the candidates' answers and their notes.

## Writing 2     page 87

### IELTS Writing Task 1

**Aim**
This section gives students practice of writing about more than one set of data in tabular form.

**Suggestion**
To increase students' awareness of interpreting data of different types, give them data from the Internet and ask them to describe it orally. There is a wide range of data at www.ons.gov.uk.

**1/2** Point out the first Tip. Remind students that they should do this every time they see a Task 1 question. Ask students to look at both tables and describe the contents in their own words. Point out the second Tip at this stage. After they have answered the questions in pairs, as in exercise **2**, check comprehension by asking the questions to the whole class. These are very useful sample questions for students to get into the habit of asking to extract the main points of a table.

### Answers

1 no
2 crime
3 yes
4 A street lighting, B the economy
5 yes
6 The trend is similar – males and females are more likely to describe safety at railway stations as 'good' rather than 'poor'. However, more women than men are likely to describe safety as 'poor'.
7 yes
8 Both tables contain figures for crime. Concern grew about the environment and the economy, as well as crime.

**3/4** Check the answers with the whole class.

### Answers

**3**
1
**4**
2

**5/6** Give students about 20/25 minutes to write the remainder of the answer individually or in pairs. At the end, give them 3 minutes to check for errors. They can ask other students to check their answers for mistakes. Ask students to compare their answer with the model on page 164 and to notice any differences.

This might be the time to introduce a simple error-correction sheet to explain the symbols you use when marking work and their meanings. When you return students' writing, encourage them to correct their errors and keep a record of the three most common errors they make, so they can focus on these next time they write.

## Photocopiable activity    page 117

### A healthy mind

Once students have completed the table, they can describe the contents of the table in pairs. Then ask the whole class questions about the data. You can ask them to write a description in class or for homework.

### Answers

see page 123

## Study skills    page 89

### Reading: Yes/No/Not Given

**1** Go through the Strategy, which is an important one in reading: students should give answers based on what is written in the text. Ask students questions about the information in the text. Elicit the topic and ask for evidence.

### Answer

Brain implants

**2** Give students 10 minutes maximum to do this, asking them for reasons for their answers when you check as a whole class.

### Answers

1 A Y     B NG     C N
2 A N     B NG     C Y
4 A N     B Y      C NG

**Extension**
As a follow-up, you might like to give them some synonyms for *claim*, like *allege, assert, contend, maintain*, etc. If they are still having problems with Y/N/NG exercises, give them some further controlled practice in class.

## Content overview

### Theme

This unit is based on the topic of water and focuses on canals, waterways and the marine environment.

### Exam-related activities

#### Reading

Identifying information – True/False/Not Given
Table completion
Matching

#### Writing

Task 1    Pie charts, proportions and the future

#### Listening

Section 4
Multiple choice
Completing notes
Matching

### Speaking

Part 1    Talking about the environment
Part 2    Talking about people and things you admire
Part 3    Building an answer

### Language development

#### Language focus and Vocabulary

Adjectives and nouns related to the environment
Modal verbs and adjectives
Collocations: Research

#### Study skills

Writing: Proportion
Speaking: Developing ideas

## Vocabulary 1    page 90

### Adjectives and nouns related to the environment

**Aim**
The Vocabulary section aims to provide students with vocabulary which will help them as they progress through the unit.

**Suggestion**
Apart from keeping vocabulary books, students can make vocabulary revision cards (paper or electronic), which they can organize around themes. You can turn this into a competition for the best organized 'cards' on particular topics.

Write the word *environment* on the board in a circle in the middle and elicit words about the topic. Write the words in circles around the word *environment*, eg, *trees, countryside, wild animals, rivers, sea, fields*. Alternatively, you can get students to do this in pairs, followed by collation on the board.

**1/2/3** Ask students to explain their choice of adjectives in exercise **1**. After they have matched the phrases in exercise **2**, in exercise **3** encourage them to use the adjectives from **1** as well and add any of their own words. To check comprehension, ask students to describe the pictures.

**Sample answers**

**1**
A  rural, natural
B  marine, natural
C  urban, residential, built-up
D  urban, industrial, commercial, built-up

**2**

| | |
|---|---|
| A  1, 4, 5, 8 | C  2, 3, 6 |
| B  1, 4, 7 | D  2, 3, 6 |

**4** Read through the example with the students, eliciting reasons for using the adjectives, eg, they are more precise, and summarize the information. Students should write any new vocabulary in their vocabulary books.

## Answers

1 New industrial parks are often located outside towns.
2 It's an organization that helps young people who live in urban/built-up areas.
3 The place where I was brought up used to be rural, but it is now very urban.
4 My neighbourhood is residential, with only one or two shops and no businesses. It's very quiet and peaceful.
5 To improve an urban/built-up environment, trees, plants and flowers can be used.
6 The commercial district is right in the centre of my home town.
7 The natural environment is being destroyed all over the world.
8 Public open spaces in cities and towns should be attractive and relaxing.

**5** This is an opportunity for students to activate the vocabulary they have learnt in this section. Monitor them to ensure they are using the new vocabulary.

A consolidation activity might be to ask them to make up their own sentences using five of the new words/phrases.

# Speaking 1    page 91

## IELTS Speaking Part 1

### Aim
This section aims to give students the opportunity to use the vocabulary they learnt in the previous section.

### Suggestion
Always try to give students an opportunity to activate vocabulary by speaking, writing or reading. Point out words that students have already come across so that they get into the habit of 'noticing what they know'.

**1/2** If necessary, give students an example of a verb as a phrase, eg, *get up, take up*. After checking the answers, ask them to look at the ideas in the box and check for meaning and pronunciation. When you have explained the example, demonstrate exercise **2** by asking students questions and getting them to ask you.

### Answers

**1**
1 protect – positive
2 harmed – negative
3 look after – positive
4 improve – positive
5 make (residential areas in cities) attractive – positive
6 damage – negative
7 destroy – negative
8 save (the marine environment) from harm – positive

**2**
Sample answers:
by reducing fishing – 8/3
by building playing fields – 5
by making it dirty – 6
by making it unattractive – 6/7
by making the air dirty – 2
by banning new houses – 1
by educating children – 3
by planting trees and plants – 4

# Listening    page 91

## IELTS Listening Section 4

### Aim
This listening section gives students practice in listening to a lecture and the type of questions such as note-taking that are associated with IELTS Listening Section 4. The speed of delivery is still below natural speed to help students process the information. The focus of the pre-listening is on synonyms for words used in the lecture.

### Suggestion
Repeat exercise 3 in the pre-listening before you do every listening test, if you have time. The same technique can be used for reading.

## Pre-listening

**1** After checking the answers as a whole class, read the Tip and get students to add words to their vocabulary books.

### Sample answers

| | | | |
|---|---|---|---|
| 1 | split | 5 | waterside |
| 2 | systems | 6 | function |
| 3 | extensive | 7 | gems |
| 4 | links | | |

**2/3** (O) **2.3** After checking the answers in exercise 2, elicit information about the talk. Ask students to describe the picture on page 92 and speculate where it might be.

## Listening

**4** (O) **2.3** Ask students questions about the Tip. Draw parallels with reading skills. You can introduce the concept of 'redundancy' in speech here. Give them 2–3 minutes to skim the questions and underline words that will help them 'scan' the talk for the answers. Play the recording only once as students have already listened to it. Encourage them to note the section they had most difficulty with so they can work on it in self-study. When students have checked their answers, elicit the students' reaction to the talk. Ask them whether they like rivers and canals and why; and what benefits rivers and canals have for communities and countries, eg, leisure facilities, transport and commerce.

**Answers**

| | | | |
|---|---|---|---|
| 1 | B | 6 | cycling visits |
| 2 | C | 7 | partnerships |
| 3 | A | 8 | E |
| 4 | leisure facilities | 9 | A |
| 5 | 159 bridges | 10 | D |

 **2.3**

Good afternoon everyone, my name is Dr Angela Christie from the Department of Engineering. My lecture today is titled 'Waterways of the world – Engineering wonders'. In my talk I shall be looking at both canals and rivers, particularly <u>those in built-up, city environments</u>. There are some canals which are vital trade links for shipping between major oceans, such as the Panama Canal and the Suez Canal, <u>but they need to be dealt with separately. The talk is split into two main sections.</u> First, we will look at the location of four waterway systems in the world and then at the engineering construction in each area. The first section will take about 15 minutes and the second section will last about 45 minutes.

If we look at this map of the United Kingdom, we can see that the country has an extensive system of waterways totalling 3,100 kilometres or 2,225 miles that covers many parts of the UK. Let's take London as an example, where the waterways are a source of employment and <u>leisure facilities</u>. Regarding the extent of the network in London, we can see from this slide with facts and figures that London has 161 kilometres of canals and rivers, along with <u>159 bridges</u> owned by British Waterways. It's also worth pointing out that London's canals have four links with the River Thames.

There are 128 people employed on the waterways and there are some interesting population facts here. We can see that there are nearly 6 million people living within 5 miles of London's waterways, which is a large number of people and nearly one-third, that is about 2 million people, live within 15 minutes' walk of these waterways.

If we move on next to the use of London's waterways, they are a centre of activity. We can see from this chart that a huge number of people visit London's waterways each year. In the year 2002/3 for example, there were 16 million people. Additionally, from this chart we can see that the number of <u>cycling visits</u> was 740,000 and the number of events was 200, with 67 waterside attractions.

There are already many organizations, including businesses and volunteer organizations, involved in keeping the system available to the public, but it is possible that in the future there will be more and more attractions on or around the waterways with local <u>partnerships</u>.

…

If we now move on to my next slide; here we can see that we are going to look at canals in three other areas of the world, namely China, Russia and Italy, where there are important canal systems. Each has a different function and character.

In China, we're going to explore the Grand Canal which links Hangzhou in Zhejiang in the north of China with Beijing. The canal stretches some 1,747 kilometres and as we will see it has a dual function, <u>one of which is to irrigate rice fields</u> and the other commercial, as it carries trade along its route. The next canal system we will look at is in St Petersburg in Russia. It has numerous canals and <u>hundreds of attractive bridges</u>, which is why it is often called the Venice of the north. St Petersburg is a city of great beauty, one of Russia's gems. We shall be looking at the importance of the canals in the city's history. <u>We then look at Venice in Italy, which has an intricate system of canals, most of which can only take small boats.</u>

## Speaking 2    page 93

### IELTS Speaking Part 2

**Aim**

The purpose of this section is to help students focus on the notes they write prior to speaking so they become more organized.

**1** Elicit names of some international organizations, eg, *UNICEF, UNESCO, WWF*. Then ask students to think of some more local ones. Elicit the meaning of the words *voluntary* and *charity*. Then ask students to look at the card and discuss the prompts.

**2**  **2.4** Students look at the picture and say what the people are doing. Ask them if people do this kind of thing in their countries and when. Give them a minute to look at the list of words. After they have listened to the candidate speaking, check their answers and pronunciation.

**Answers**

| | | | | | | | | | | | |
|---|---|---|---|---|---|---|---|---|---|---|---|
| 1 | c | 2 | b | 3 | a | 4 | c | 5 | a | 6 | c |

 **2.4**

I am going to describe a <u>volunteer organization</u>, called Water Direct, that helps to protect the river in my home town. I first came across the organization when I went <u>walking</u> along the river one day and saw people taking <u>rubbish</u> out of the river. There are many reasons why I admire the organization. First of all, it helps <u>improve</u> the city surroundings. If the river banks and the water are clean, it makes the place <u>pleasant and healthy</u>. It is now possible for people to enjoy the river by going <u>swimming and having picnics</u> on the river banks, as most of the rubbish has been removed. This is a big difference as in the past it was very dirty. I think that <u>similar organizations</u> could soon be set up all over the country. In fact, I think it is highly likely.

**3** In pairs, students talk about the Task Card using the words they circled in exercise **2** as their notes. They can use the other words and phrases from exercise **2**.

**4/5** Students follow the normal procedure for preparation. After talking about the Task Card they chose, students can talk about the second card. They can use their partner's notes to help them make their own notes. Each time, students should give feedback based on the criteria given. Give your own general feedback of the whole class using the same criteria.

**Review**

As a revision exercise, ask students to compare how they lay out their notes; how long the notes are, how clear they are for looking at quickly, whether they should spell the words correctly, whether they should use abbreviations.

# Language focus  page 94

## Modal verbs and adjectives

### Aim

This section encourages flexibility in the use of language and helps students focus on paraphrasing.

### Suggestion

Always elicit different ways of saying things in practice for all four skills, for all types of language – not just the use of the modals and adjectives as here.

**1** First elicit examples of modal verbs, then the difference between *possibility* and *probability*. Refer students to the Grammar on page 154 if necessary. Encourage them to read the Grammar as self-study after the class. The exercise can be done together as a whole class.

#### Answers

Possibility
It is now possible for …
… could soon be set up …
Probability
I think it is highly likely.

**2** Students can do the exercise in pairs. Check the answers as a whole class. To check comprehension, read some of the sentences aloud to the class. In some cases, use the wrong modal verbs and elicit whether the statements are correct.

For extra reference, you could get students to draw a line with *mustn't* at one end and *must* at the other. Draw their attention to the fact that *don't have to* is not the opposite of *have to*. The former implies choice, the latter no choice.

#### Answers

| | | | | | |
|---|---|---|---|---|---|
| 1 | may | 4 | should | 7 | can |
| 2 | cannot | 5 | might | 8 | must |
| 3 | can | 6 | could | | |

**3/4** After completion of both exercises, point out to students how using adjectives like *possible*, etc, as alternatives to modal verbs can add variety to their speaking and writing. It also helps with paraphrasing in other parts of the exam.

#### Answers

**3**

| | | | |
|---|---|---|---|
| 1 | possible | 5 | possible |
| 2 | impossible | 6 | possible |
| 3 | possible | 7 | possible |
| 4 | likely | 8 | necessary |

**4**

2 It is impossible for the trees to/that the trees will be chopped down as they are protected.

3 It is possible for people/that people will make their own lives better by measures such as recycling.

4 It is likely that the environment will improve dramatically in the near future.

5 It is possible that the new park will/for the new park to be completed on time. We're not sure.

6 It is possible that the fares will be/for fares to be subsidized on public transport. It's a good measure.

7 It is possible for city streets to be made attractive. Only flowers, plants, seats and fountains are needed.

8 It is necessary for coral reefs to be protected by law. It's essential.

**5/6** Students should write the sentences individually, before discussing in groups. Encourage them to disagree with each other where possible, giving reasons and examples. Monitor the discussion for accuracy.

As a final comprehension check, ask students to match modal verbs with appropriate adjectives.

#### Sample answers

It's possible that I'll sit my exams in December.
It's unlikely that I'll finish my essay this evening.
It's not necessary for me to work this week. I'm free.

# Speaking 3  page 94

## IELTS Speaking Part 3: Building an answer

**1** Before students start, point out that this section gives them further practice with modal verbs and corresponding adjectives from Language focus. Students can decide what extra details can be added to the candidate's answer before looking at the information in the box. Once they have added the extra information, get them to identify and underline phrases with adjectives and possibly rephrase them using modal verbs.

## Answer

I personally think it's definitely a good idea, <u>as this will have a number of important advantages</u>. For example, people are then more likely to keep the water environment clean by taking action themselves <u>such as preventing their children throwing rubbish into waterways.</u> It is also possible to involve groups like primary and secondary school children <u>by showing them how important the water environment is in school lessons</u>.

**2** Monitor students and write down good examples and any corrections for class feedback at the end of the exercise. Ask several students the questions to check comprehension. Note the difference in the types of questions. In question 1, students are asked to evaluate / reason; in 2, to speculate; and in 3 to describe, explain and classify.

# Vocabulary 2    page 95

## Collocations: Research

### Aim
This vocabulary section focuses on collocations that can occur in all modules of the IELTS exam.

### Suggestion
Encourage students to collect collocations related to specific topics or words, such as *research*. Students can give mini-presentations of their collections in groups. You can also collate master lists for the class and display them. Point out they will remember the collocations better if they have a context. When students finish the reading passage on pages 96–97, ask them to find the word *research* and words related to it.

**1** Start by discussing the kinds of research governments fund and for what reasons. Show students pictures of different types of research taking place, eg, in a laboratory, street questionnaires, archaeologists in the field. Go through the questions as a class and see what ideas they produce. You may need to have some prompts ready, eg, *What is research? What do you think happens when people do research? What kind of people do research?* After students have finished discussing, elicit a summary from students for each question.

**2** Students complete the exercise in pairs. Check the answers as a whole class. They can add the words to their vocabulary books, putting the word *research* in a circle in the middle of a page and adding the words form the exercise in bubbles around it.

## Answers

| | | | |
|---|---|---|---|
| 1 | funded/financed | 6 | Current/ongoing |
| 2 | published/reported on | 7 | conducted/carried out |
| 3 | focused/concentrated | 8 | Collaborative/joint |
| 4 | project/programme | 9 | extensive/detailed |
| 5 | performed/carried out | 10 | confirmed/support |

**3/4** Go through the questionnaire prompts and elicit the questions students will ask. Put the following question on the board as a prompt: *Should the government finance research <u>into the environment</u>?* After they have studied the questionnaire, ask them just put a tick or cross for each person they interview in the appropriate box. In the meantime, put the questionnaire on the board and get as many students as possible to give you the numbers for each box. After completing exercise **4**, students can discuss the results as a whole class.

### Answers

Students' own answers.

### Extension
As an optional activity, you could give students a guided writing activity using the questionnaire to write a report on the findings. How much control you exercise over this will depend on the level of your class.

# Reading    page 96

## Pre-reading

**1** If more help is needed, ask students to look at the picture on page 97 and the Glossary.

### Answer

The topic is connected with the sea and creatures that live in it.

**2** Students can do this individually before they check their answers in pairs. Elicit the facts and write them on the board.

### Sample answers

**Paragraph 1:** 1 Norman Myers created the concept of hotspots; 2 Around 25 hotspots have been identified for conservation. **Paragraph 3:** 3 A temperature of around 22 degrees means there can be more species of fish and more large fish in a hotspot; 4 hotspots are located in areas where there is lots of plankton.

**3/4** Discuss students' answers as a whole class.

## Answers

**3**

The places, (the Costa Rican Dome, the Galapagos islands, waters east and west of the Baja peninsula), are all in the Pacific Ocean. The places are all areas where different waters meet.

**5** As students have now looked at the questions, elicit as much information about the reading passage as you can and write it on the board. This will help build students' confidence and show them how they can predict content using different techniques.

Look at the Tip and get students to write the numbers 1–13 in a column on the left-hand side of a blank page to act as an answer sheet. Point out to students that they need to write their answers on the answer sheet as they read in the exam, as there is no time at the end as in the listening module.

## Reading

**6** Remind students to look at the Glossary. Time them and follow the usual procedure for test practice. When you check the answers, make sure spelling and word limits are correct.

### Answers

| | | | |
|---|---|---|---|
| 1 | False | 8 | Mexico |
| 2 | True | 9 | concentration |
| 3 | True | 10 | C |
| 4 | Not Given | 11 | A |
| 5 | sea surface | 12 | D |
| 6 | plankton | 13 | B |
| 7 | waters | | |

## Reading discussion

**7/8** Ask students to choose a spokesperson to report their answers to the whole class and ask them to make a list of ideas for each question, eg, *Question 1: the destruction affects everyone, it will affect the food chain/fish stocks, sea creatures, people's jobs/livelihood; question 2: education, TV advertisements, government policies.*

# Writing   page 98

## IELTS Writing Task 1: Pie charts, proportions and the future

### Aim
The aim of this section is to introduce students to language for describing pie charts and to talk about the future.

**1** Elicit what a pie chart is and what sort of information it is useful for representing. Students can do the exercise in pairs or groups. Check the answers as a whole class. When you check, point out the words and phrases like *proportion, devoted to, consist of, constitute, compared to, account for* and elicit the meanings using the pie chart. Give other examples if necessary.

### Answers

1 T

2 T

3 F A small proportion of the land (<u>15</u> per cent) consists of water.

4 F Woodland constitutes a smaller proportion of the Ocean Park compared to farmland, <u>15</u> per cent and <u>5</u> per cent respectively.

5 T

6 F Sixty percent of Ocean Park consists of <u>grass</u>./<u>Five</u> per cent of Ocean Park consists of farmland.

**2** Ask students to do the exercise in pairs, ensuring they use the language in exercise **1**. Collate the answers on the board once students have finished.

### Sample answers

Farmland accounts/accounted for 5 per cent of Ocean Park in 2011.
Fifteen per cent of the Park consists/consisted of woodland.
Buildings constitute/constituted only a small proportion of the park at 5 per cent.
The water reservation accounted for 15 per cent of the Park./Fifteen per cent of the Park is accounted for by the water reservation.

**3** Ask students to look at both pie charts for Ocean Park. Before they answer the questions in pairs, ask them what the time difference is between them and elicit the most striking differences. Students then answer the questions about the second pie chart.

### Answers

1 10 per cent

2 60 per cent

3 increase – 15% per cent

4 decrease – to 5 per cent

5 50 per cent drop – significant

6 larger proportion

**4** You might like to review some comparative language here so students can make comparisons between the two charts in their answers. Also elicit contrast linking devices such as *whereas, while,* etc.

**5** Ask students to read the Tip on page 99. Elicit why the information is important. Ask students to decide what kind of word is missing before they complete each space.

## Answers

**5**

| | | | |
|---|---|---|---|
| 1 | show | 4 | dramatic |
| 2 | expected | 5 | rise/increase |
| 3 | 2011 | 6 | proportion |

**6** After checking the answers for exercise **5**, students should continue to work in pairs and adapt the text. In exercise **6**, encourage them to write out the text rather than just add the phrases to the text in the Student Book. After checking the answers, ask students to read the completed texts in **5** and **6** aloud to the whole class, or in pairs.

### Sample answer

As regards farmland, <u>it is expected that</u> there will be a <u>huge</u> increase in land devoted to farming. <u>It is predicted that</u> farmland will increase from just 5 per cent in 2011 to 60 per cent <u>by 2025</u>. Conversely, the <u>proportion of</u> land devoted to grass is forecast to decrease significantly <u>(60 per cent to just 10 per cent)</u>. <u>Similarly, it is projected that</u> the proportion of land covered by the water reservation will fall <u>from 15 per cent to 10 per cent</u>, while the area of built-up land will increase (from 5 per cent to 15 per cent). Moreover, the proportion of land devoted to woodland is also expected to shrink <u>by two-thirds from 15 per cent to 5 per cent</u>.

Note here the difference between *by 15 per cent* and *to 15 per cent*. Illustrate on the board to show them how an error in preposition here can change the meaning of the information.

**7** Ask students to look at the Strategy and ask questions about the contents. Give students several minutes to study the Task 1 instructions, the charts and the plan. Remind them of the Strategy and point out the words *By contrast/While* that help students compare rather than list the data. Elicit other conjunctions like *whereas*. Ask students questions about the task and plan, using questions similar to those in exercise **3**. Remind them of useful verbs such as *account for* and ask them to write the answer in pairs or groups. At this level, do not worry too much about the length, but point out that in the exam they need to write a minimum of 150 words. Give them about 25/30 minutes to write and then check their answers.

Refer students to the model answer on page 164 when they have finished and ask them to read the comments. Then ask them to match the parts of the text to the relevant parts of the pie chart.

## Photocopiable activity    page 118

### The charts show ...

When students have finished the pairwork exercises, ask them questions about the trends and attendance patterns for the three venues, the overview and the conclusion.

#### Answers

see page 123

## Study skills    page 101

### Writing: Proportion

#### Aim

The Study skills section focuses on writing about proportions in pie charts.

#### Suggestion

When students make cards like this, ask them to study them before they have to write about proportions in future and think about the mistakes they normally make before and after they write. They can do this with other aspects of grammar and vocabulary.

**1/2/3** Go through the Tip with students. Go over the instructions and suggest students do the exercises for self-study. The exercises are very useful for self-analysis and for guiding students' self-study. Encourage them to share their ideas and work together outside the class in this way and make revision cards for other words such as *research*.

#### Sample answer

Revision card: Proportion
Synonyms: *part, section*
Verbs: *account for, constitute, consist of*
Examples of sentence structures
1 *Farmland accounts/accounted for 5 per cent of Ocean Park in 2011.*
2 *Fifteen per cent of the Park consists/consisted of woodland.*
3 *Buildings constitute/constituted only a small proportion of the park at 5 per cent.*
Mistakes I normally make
The farmland consists of 50 per cent. [Fifty per cent consists of farmland or Farmland accounts for 50 per cent.]

## Speaking: Developing ideas

**1** Look at the Tips with the class. Students work with a partner to decide which of the items 1–8 are most useful in giving spoken answers. They can share their ideas with another pair. This also can be done outside the class.

**Answers**

All are correct except for 6

**2** Students can do this exercise individually before checking their answers in pairs. Collate the answers on the board and encourage students to keep lists of examples of the words in context in their notebooks.

**Answers**

| | | | |
|---|---|---|---|
| 1 | because, since | 4 | while, if |
| 2 | for example/for instance | 5 | however, but |
| 3 | and so/as a result | | |

## Content overview

### Theme

The theme of this unit is finance.

### Exam-related activities

**Reading**

Completing a summary
Identifying claims – Yes/No/Not Given
Matching sentence endings

**Writing**

Task 2
Writing an introduction
Organization and structure
Writing a paragraph
Writing about how to solve poverty

**Listening**

Section 1
Completing a form

### Speaking

Part 1    Talking about your home country
Part 2    Talking about jobs
Part 3    Complex sentences

### Language development

**Language focus and Vocabulary**

Words and phrases related to *pay*
Complex sentences: Concession
Opinion

### Skills development

**Reading**

Skimming

**Study skills**

Vocabulary: Word association
Speaking and writing: Rewriting sentences

## Listening    page 102

### IELTS Listening Section 1

#### Pre-listening

**1/2** Introduce the theme of the unit and ask students if they have ever taken part in a survey, either conducting one or answering questions. Ask them: *What different ways are there of conducting surveys? What kinds of things do people want to find out from a survey?* Elicit the kinds of questions the person in the picture might ask. Then ask students to discuss both exercises **1** and **2**. In **2**, you can allocate the questions to the groups or allow them to choose their own statements. Encourage them to give examples and reasons.

**Sample answers**

**1**

currency, trips, travelling abroad, credit cards, spending

**3** Give students 1 minute to skim the listening questions. After eliciting the topic of the listening test, ask students to underline the words that will help them as they listen.

**Answers**

The questionnaire is about travel and money. Other possible answers: trips abroad/currencies bought/ currencies held

#### Listening

**4** (o) **2.5** Point out the word limit for each blank space. When students have checked their answers, play the recording again. Students can make any changes using a different colour.

**Answers**

| | | | |
|---|---|---|---|
| 1 | two | 6 | snacks |
| 2 | 100 | 7 | hotels, meals |
| 3 | 10/ten (times) | 8 | (really) wasteful |
| 4 | 500 | 9 | email/e-mail address |
| 5 | many | 10 | 03452 4334 91 |

(W = woman; M = man)

W: Excuse me. My name's Melanie Broughton.

M: Yes?

W: And I'm doing a questionnaire on behalf of <u>Finance</u> Survey. Do you mind answering some questions about travelling?

M: OK.

W: Thank you. Have you travelled abroad in the last three months?

M: Yes.

W: How many times?

M: <u>Twice.</u>

W: And were the trips to the same place or different places?

M: Different places in Europe: France and Germany, etcetera.

W: You said you have been abroad twice in the past three months?

M: Yes.

W: Did you buy currency each time you went abroad?

M: It depends, mostly yes.

W: And can I ask you, how many euros did you buy each time?

M: Let's see ... for the first trip I bought ... mm 300 euros, ... and the second time I didn't buy so many, because the first trip was only for three days and I didn't spend it all. So I had about 150 left. And I only bought <u>100</u> for the second trip.

W: Was this second trip longer?

M: Yes.

W: OK, and how often do you normally travel abroad each year? One to three times, four to ten times, eleven or more?

M: I went abroad five times so it's four to <u>ten</u> times.

W: And my next question: is that for work or leisure?

M: Mmm ... it's mostly for work, though I sometimes have a few days to myself when I go abroad.

W: The next few questions are about currency.

M: OK.

W: When you come back from abroad, do you change the currency back into pounds sterling or do you keep it?

M: I always keep it, because I travel a lot.

W: Fine. Right. We can skip the next two questions. So can I ask you how much you have in a range of currencies?

M: Yeah, sure.

W: What about euros? Which band are you in: 1 to 50, 50 to 200, 200 to 500, or more than 500?

M: Oh, it's 50 euros.

W: And American dollars?

M: More than <u>500.</u>

W: And any other currency?

M: I've got dinars from various countries, but <u>not many</u>, and some Indian rupees.

W: Which band are they in? Do you want me to repeat the bands?

M: No. They are both quite small, in the 1 to 50 band.

...

W: Do you use only cards or cash when you travel?

M: A mixture.

W: And the next question is: what do you use the cash for?

M: Well, I spend it on taxis, newspapers and <u>snacks.</u> Taxis to and from the airport can be quite expensive and I have to use them if I'm in a hurry.

W: And do you use credit cards abroad?

M: Oh yes.

W: For what exactly?

M: To pay for <u>hotels</u>, if they are not paid for in advance, and <u>meals.</u>

W: OK, ... mmm ... I need to ask you for a few contact details.

M: OK.

W: We don't ask for an address, just an email and a contact telephone number.

M: OK.

W: That's fine. The company may want to ...

M: No, I don't want to receive any promotional literature. It's really <u>wasteful</u>.

W: OK. The company may want to check that you have actually done the survey.

M: You mean to prove that you didn't complete it, yourself?

W: Yes, exactly.

M: Mmm ... I'm happy to give you my mobile, but I don't want to give out my <u>email</u>, if you don't mind.

W: That's fine. Can I take your mobile number?

M: Yes, it's <u>03452 4334 91</u>.

W: Thank you.

# Speaking 1     page 103

## IELTS Speaking Part 1

**1** Give students 5 minutes to write down the questions. Monitor students as they do so. Collate examples on the board. Check for pronunciation and accuracy of question forms.

### Sample answers

1 Do people in your home country like travelling overseas?
2 Which countries are popular among young people?
3 How often do people make trips abroad?
4 Do people pay more electronically now than in the past?
5 Is cash more popular than credit cards?

**2** **2.6** Give students a chance to look at the answer stems. They can predict where the errors might be, thinking of their own common errors. Ask students to compare their answers in pairs after listening. Then play the recording again and check the answers as a whole class. Elicit from students the types of mistakes they normally make when speaking and collate their answers on the board.

### Answers

1 It depend<u>s</u> on age.
2 I think they probably main<u>ly</u> go to Australia.
3 At least three time<u>s</u> a year.
4 I<u>'m</u> sure they do.
5 The latter are <u>more</u> popular among young than older people.

**2.6**

(E = Examiner; C = Candidate)

1
E: Do people in your home country like travelling overseas?
C: It depend on age.
2
E: Which countries are popular with young people?
C: I think they probably main go to Australia.
3
E: How often do people make trips abroad?
C: At least three time a year.
4
E: Do people pay more by card than in the past?
C: I sure they do.
5
E: Is cash more popular than credit cards?
C: The latter are popular among young than older people.

**3/4** Before students work with a different partner, give them a few minutes to think of additional questions, eg, *Why do you like travelling abroad? Why do you think they are popular?* Elicit examples of mistakes that were made and write them on the board. Ask students to explain the types of mistakes and why they were made.

## Vocabulary 1   page 103

### Words and phrases related to *pay*

**1** Look at the picture with the class and discuss where it is and what the man is doing. Do the matching activity as a whole class. Elicit from students traditional methods of payment and how this is changing in the modern world. Ask: *What are the advantages and disadvantages of the different types of paying for things?*

**Answers**

1 a   2 b

**2** Use this exercise to help students avoid confusion when using *pay* and *pay for*. They can then transfer the diagram to their vocabulary books.

**Answers**

1 payment
2 pay rise – before; receive
3 for/at/to/in/by
4 Sample answers: *The job pays well. He paid in cash for the item. He paid the bill electronically/online.*
5 pay for
6 pay bills
7 pay cash
8 in dollars/euros
9 too much

**3** Check students understand what the phrases in the box mean. Go through the example before students do the exercise in pairs and/or groups.

**Answers**

1 job that pays well
2 students pay university fees
3 pay for small items
4 safe generally to pay for goods online
5 cash payments will disappear; will pay for everything electronically
6 improve pay and conditions
7 pay too much for entertainment

**4** Give students a chance to discuss the questions in groups. Encourage students to give reasons and examples. Monitor the discussion ensuring they expand on their answers as much as possible, and give feedback regarding mistakes.

## Photocopiable activity   page 119

### I try to pay for everything electronically

**1** This exercise helps recycle the words relating to *pay*. You can cut up the items in circles or boxes and ask them to match them or they can link the two using lines.

**2** This exercise should help students expand their answers to prepare for speaking for a longer period of time in exercise **3**.

**3** You can use this process to help students expand on their answers and help them be more specific. Try it after other speaking activities.

**Answers**

see page 124

## Speaking 2   page 105

### IELTS Speaking Part 2

**1/2** Look at the jobs and the adjectives with the class. Elicit the similarity between *exciting* and *thrilling*. Give students the phrase: *It depends …* to help them expand their answers. After they have completed exercises **1** and **2**, elicit additional reasons from students, if possible.

## Answers

**1**

Students' own answers.

**2**

**Sample answer**

3 b/d (I think being a pilot is very exciting) because working for an airline gives you a chance to travel./ I'd like to be a pilot because I'd be able to travel a lot.

5 a I think working in the business world is very interesting, because being a businessman/woman would pay very well.

**3/4** Elicit the names of different types of jobs and the reasons why people like them, writing them on the board. After eliciting what *career* means, give students one minute to look at the card and make notes. Make sure they give each other feedback about their ideas and how they expanded on them.

**Sample answer**

The job I'd like to have is being a pilot with a large international airline. So I would be able to work anywhere in the world. I'd like to be based in my own home country, Brazil, but I'd like to visit many different countries. The job would need a lot of training in flying an aeroplane. It'd be very technical, but I'd enjoy that because I like working with machines. The main reason I'd like to be is pilot is not the travelling but being in charge of the flying of a big aircraft. That would be really thrilling for me. Another thing is that being a pilot involves working with people as part of a team and being in charge of a team, which is also exciting and interesting. I don't think I'd find anything about it boring.

## Language focus   page 105

### Complex sentences: Concession

**1/2** Explain to students that they need to be able to use complex structures in their speaking and writing. Elicit what is meant by *promotional literature*. Refer students to the Grammar on page 155 if necessary.

**Answers**

**1**

The answer to both questions is probably no.

**2**

The use of *but*

**3** You can elicit the answers and write them on the board with example sentences. In the answers, the words *although, while, whilst* and *but* are conjunctions and require commas between the clauses. The word *though* can be a conjunction or an adverb. If it is the latter it requires a full stop between the two sentences.

*Nevertheless* is an adverb. Adverbs link sentences, but there is a full stop between the sentence the adverb is in and the sentence before it.

**Answers**

but – nevertheless
although – while, whilst, though

**4** Students can do this exercise in pairs and check their answers with other students, before whole-class feedback. Point out that students need to use the other clause in the example in the exercise itself.

**Answers**

0 Although credit cards are becoming more common, <u>older people still use them less them young people.</u>

1 Even though the workforce in my country is better educated than in the past, <u>the economy is not performing well.</u>

2 While mathematics is taught at school, <u>it doesn't mean that people are good at managing their finances.</u>

3 Whereas energy costs are rising year by year, <u>pay rises are not increasing at the same pace.</u>

4 My home city is certainly richer than ever before, <u>but there is still poverty everywhere.</u>

5 Cash is still used by many people to make small and large payments, <u>though this is likely to change in the near future.</u>

6 More and more young people are now taking vocational qualifications. <u>Nevertheless, there is still a shortage of skilled workers.</u>

7 People in some countries are generally richer. <u>They are still not happier than previous generations.</u>

**5** Students can follow the same procedure as in exercise **4**.

**Answers**

0 Credit cards are becoming more common, but older people still use them less them young people.

1 The workforce in my country is better educated than in the past. Nevertheless, the economy is not performing well.

2 Mathematics is taught at school, but/still, it doesn't mean that people are good at managing their finances.

3 Energy costs are rising year by year. Nevertheless, pay rises are still not increasing at the same pace.

4 Although my home city is certainly richer than ever before, there is still poverty everywhere.

5 While cash is still used by many people to make small and large payments, this is likely to change in the near future.

6 Whereas more and more young people are now taking vocational qualifications, there is still a shortage of skilled workers.

7 People in some countries may be generally richer, but they are still not happier than previous generations.

**6** The questions can be written on the board or students can write them by themselves first. When they ask each other the questions, encourage them to use the second clause to begin their answers, as in the example.

### Sample answers

1  Is the workforce in your country better educated than in the past?
2  Is mathematics taught at school?
3  Are energy costs rising year by year?
4  Is your home city richer than ever before?
5  Is cash still used by many people to make small and large payments?
6  Are more and more young people now taking vocational qualifications?
7  Are people in some countries generally richer?

## Writing 1    page 106

### IELTS Writing Task 2

#### Aim

This writing task aims to give students the opportunity to write a paragraph expressing their opinion.

#### Suggestion

In order to encourage students to give their opinion about Writing Task 2 questions, ask them to write at least three statements that they believe to be true about the topic generally. Ask them to compare their statements in groups and then select which statements are relevant to the essay question. They can follow this procedure for all types of Writing Task 2 questions.

**1**  Tell students to look at the photo on page 107 and decide what kind of after-school activity this is. Answering the 5 questions provides useful analysis of the writing task. Stress the importance of this in ensuring they don't include irrelevancies or omit aspects that are asked for.

#### Answers

2, 4

**2**  This exercise can also be done in groups. Come to a class consensus through discussion and write the ideas for the two best ways, or solutions, on the board. You can point out that there is no right answer.

**3**  Students can do this individually and then check with a partner. Write the sample answer on the board for comparison and elicit how it is connected with the Task 2 question in 1.

### Sample answer

The modern world is increasingly complex for people generally from the financial point of view. Although teaching finance at school is obviously important, there are other equally important measures.

**4**  Students can do this exercise in pairs, labelling the parts of the paragraph. Go over the paragraph carefully with them to see the different parts. Check that they understand what a topic sentence is: *a sentence which shows the reader the content of the paragraph*.

After checking the answers, ask several students to explain the organization using the labels. Point out they can follow this organization in their own essay paragraphs.

#### Answers

Topic sentence: Teaching finance in schools is undeniably important
Reason: because people need to make more financial decisions
Example: For example, if children are taught how to manage money from an early age
Concession: While children may not have a lot of money
Example: They can, for instance, set up scenarios
Result: As a result, they will be better prepared for the real world.

**5**  Explain that only one alternative, a or b, is appropriate and they have to choose which one to use to complete the next paragraph. They should justify their choice. Students should do this individually first before comparing their answers with a partner. Take feedback from the whole class. Ask students to explain the organization.

#### Answers

1  a    2  b    3  b    4  a

**6**  Ask students to review the previous activities to get a picture of the first paragraphs of the essay. Students should now do the exercise individually, comparing their answer with the model on page 164. Allocate 20 minutes for this exercise.

## Speaking 3    page 108

### IELTS Speaking Part 3: Complex sentences

**1**  After checking the answers in **1**, ask students to explain the agreement in their own words as far as possible. Stress the technique of balancing arguments (agreeing and then adding new information) as a way to open up the answers to the questions.

agree: Yes, for some people it does.

new: …there are other things like happiness and job satisfaction which are equally important.

**2** After students have done this in pairs, collate possible answers on the board and discuss.

### Sample answers

Skills and education are important, but I think money is vital.

Money is important, but I think these days skills and education are vital.

**3** Monitor students and select several examples of concession to write on the board. Elicit answers for one or more of the questions, after the pairwork activity.

### Sample answers

1 Although money is considered to be evil by some people, I think it is also crucial in the modern world.

2 Teaching children to be literate is important, but learning about finance is also essential because …

3 Although street surveys provide important information, more people can be asked questions using online surveys.

## Vocabulary 2 page 109

### Opinion

**1** Do this exercise as a whole-class activity. Point out that the phrase *I think* emphasizes that it is the speaker's opinion, but it is possible to leave it out. Also point out that often people give their opinion without giving overt markers. Ask them the difference between fact and opinion.

### Answers

Yes, because it makes it obvious the speaker is expressing his/her own opinion.

**2/3/4** When students have finished exercises **2** and **3**, elicit explanations for the words underlined. Point out how the adjectives *invaluable, key* and *effective* indicate opinion. You can, time permitting, turn one of the questions in **2** into a debate, dividing the class into two groups. Give each group time to prepare ideas before a whole-class discussion. If you think they need extra practice, provide a sheet with sentences that have a mixture of fact and opinion for them to identify and justify.

**2**

3 and 7

**3**

1 Education is an <u>invaluable</u> tool in the fight against poverty.

2 <u>In my opinion,</u> basic literacy and numeracy play a <u>key</u> role in improving living standards.

4 Setting up a business <u>could be</u> a <u>very effective way</u> of learning about people and the world.

5 <u>Personally, I feel that</u> the wealth of the richest countries should be shared with the poorest.

6 <u>It seems to me that</u> giving aid is only a temporary solution to a problem.

## Writing 2 page 109

### IELTS Writing Task 2

**1** The exercises here require students to write more than they have up to now. Elicit a few ideas about the Task 2 question in exercise **1**. Identify the different parts of the question.

Check students understand all the steps in exercise **1**.

**2/3/4** Give students 20–25 minutes for these exercises. You can ask students if you can copy examples of their answers for future use. Emphasize how useful it is to discuss ideas with one or two other students and to give their essay to another student to read and give feedback. Refer them to the sample answer and comments on page 164 and discuss the comments.

## Reading page 110

### Pre-reading

**1** Students can do this exercise in pairs or groups. They may be surprised about the volume of numbers that are part of their everyday lives. Collate the list on the board after their discussion.

### Sample answers

home telephone, mobile number, bus/tram number, bank card number, PIN, platform number, password(s), house/flat number, room number, number of Facebook friends

**2** Give them five minutes to scan for the answers and underline where they found them in the passage.

## Answers

1 zero
2 the Sumerians
3 there are no hundreds in the number
4 the Ancient Greeks
5 empty; place
6 by the middle of the twelfth century

## Reading

**3** Tell students to look at the Glossary and give them at least 20 minutes to complete the reading questions. When students have finished, ask for their reaction to the text. Also ask whether they knew where 'zero' came from. Students can go over the answers in the usual way in groups.

### Answers

1 C (B is not correct: cattle, etc, are not personal enough to be belongings: you can't pack them in your bag and take them away)

| | | | | | |
|---|---|---|---|---|---|
| 2 | A | 6 | Yes | 10 | E |
| 3 | G | 7 | No | 11 | B |
| 4 | I | 8 | No | 12 | A |
| 5 | F | 9 | Not Given | 13 | G |

## Reading discussion

**4/5** Elicit students' ideas on the importance of numbers and collate them on the board.

## Study skills    page 113

## Vocabulary: Word association

**1** Students can do this exercise and compare their answers. The answers do not necessarily matter as long as students can explain an association. The exercise is not just a way of checking association, but also a way of creating ideas for writing. Students can explain why they chose the words and take ideas from their explanation. Go through the Tip with students, which reiterates what they have previously learnt about selecting new words to be recorded in their vocabulary books. Refer them back to page 104 where they looked at a similar diagram for the word *pay* and other words that collocate with it.

### Sample answers

1 money, shop, time, budget, save, bank, earn, savings
2 shop, spend, happiness, leisure, coins, notes, currency, travel, necessary, earn
3 companies, government, personal, group, support, employers

**2** Making summaries, where students collect together what they 'know' about a word, will increase their knowledge of 'word depth', their confidence and their fluency.

### Sample answers

common verbs you use before the word *money:* spend, earn, waste, give, save, borrow

two common adjectives: enough, sufficient, additional, extra, spare

two idioms: to be in the money, to spend money like water

two meanings of money, eg, *cash:* savings, small change, ie, coins

a noun you can put after the word *money:* worries, problems

a verb that you use after the word *money:* come from, pour in, flow in

## Speaking and writing : Rewriting sentences

**1** Attention has already been drawn to the links in terms of ideas between Part 3 Speaking and Task 2 Writing. This is a good practice activity and could be incorporated into self-study as an exercise to do with, say, three new sentences every day.

### Sample answers

Although money is an essential part of our lives nowadays, job satisfaction and happiness are also very important.

Money is an essential part of our lives nowadays, but job satisfaction and happiness are also very important. Though money is an essential part of our lives nowadays, job satisfaction and happiness are also very important. Money is an essential part of our lives nowadays. Though, job satisfaction and happiness are also very important. Money is an essential part of our lives nowadays. However, job satisfaction and happiness are also very important.

# Content overview

## Themes

This unit is based on the topic of nature and science. It focuses on scientific subjects that students can study and how science can help nature.

## Exam-related activities

### Reading

Matching headings
Identifying claims – Yes/No/Not Given
Choosing items from a list

### Writing

Task 1    Describing tables
Task 2    Discussing views and giving opinions

### Listening

Section 4
Multiple choice
Labelling a diagram
Matching

## Speaking

Part 2    Talking about places
Part 3    Talking about studying at university

## Language development

### Language focus and Vocabulary

Countable and uncountable nouns
Noun phrases: *Nature* and *natural*
Word and phrase building: *Advantage* and *disadvantage*

## Skills development

Skimming

## Study skills

Reading: Matching paragraph and section headings

---

# Speaking 1    page 114

## IELTS Speaking Part 2

### Aim

This section aims to reinforce the need for structure in talking about the Task Card in IELTS Speaking Part 2.

### Suggestion

Always elicit from students the order they should give the information on the card. They can make an introductory phrase for the various stages (*where, when, what* and *why*) for each card before they start speaking, to help build their confidence. Build a bank of phrases for students to begin their description, eg, *I'm going to talk about ...*

**1** After the pairwork, elicit from students what the pictures show. Ask them how similar the places are to those they have studied in and whether they themselves can study anywhere. Elicit other possible places, eg, *trains, home, friends' homes.* Elicit how effective such places are for studying in.

### Answers

A shows students studying outdoors.
B shows students studying in a café.
C shows students studying in a library.

**2/3** ⊙ **2.7** Before they listen, elicit details about the prompts on the Task Card and check students understand what they have to do to complete items 1–6. Students can check their answers in pairs before listening again. Ask students to work in pairs and describe what the speaker talks about using the notes in items 1–6. As extra practice, students can listen a third time and note down the phrases and words the speaker uses to connect ideas.

### Answers

1  café/overlooks park/near university
2  3/three months ago
3  quite busy/lots of students (plenty of room)
4  his accommodation: quite small
   space: plenty of space, even when crowded
   furniture: modern/comfortable
5  watch the birds/daydream
6  he spends a lot of time in laboratories, so it's nice to look at nature/he enjoys spending time there

**2.7**

The place I am going to describe is a <u>café, which overlooks a park near the university</u> where I'm studying. I found the café only about <u>three months ago</u> and since that time I've been going there on a regular basis. The café is <u>quite busy with lots of students</u> discussing their studies. I like the café a lot because my accommodation is <u>quite small</u>. And there is <u>plenty of space</u> in the café … <u>even when it gets crowded</u> I can usually find a space at one of the tables that overlook the park. The furniture is all very <u>modern and comfortable</u> – it's much more pleasant than the room in the flat I share. I can sit and <u>watch the birds and daydream</u> when I am studying. I also prefer the café to the library because <u>I spend a lot of time in science laboratories doing research and it's very pleasant to sit and look at nature for a change. I really enjoy spending time there.</u>

**4** Students work in pairs, with each student choosing a different Task Card. Time them in the practice. Get them to give each other constructive feedback and enter ideas into their notebooks. When they have finished they can swap cards and repeat the process. Ask two students to talk about the cards as a demonstration for the rest of the class.

**Sample answer**

A

Notes: wood child river swim trees water happy games memories sun

The place I'm going to describe is a wood near my home when I was a child. I first went there with my family for a picnic when I was only about seven or eight years old, but I still remember it well. There was a river running through the wood and at one point it wasn't very deep and it was possible to play and swim in the water. There were lots of trees to shade us from the sun, and the water was very clean. It became my favourite place, because I was very happy playing there as a child and always asked my parents to take me back. I played games there like football and hide and seek. I still have very fond memories of the place, and for me the sun always shine there.

## Language focus   page 115

### Countable and uncountable nouns

**Aim**
This Language focus aims to help students to think not just about the grammar, but how an awareness of countable and uncountable nouns can help them make their speaking and writing more specific.

**Suggestion**
Each time students come across an uncountable noun, ask them for an example of a countable noun, eg, *(U) furniture (C) chair(s)*. For countable nouns, ask them for other examples and to supply the countable noun which helps to categorize them. They can then write the group nouns in their vocabulary books under the uncountable nouns.

**1/2** If possible, introduce the concept of countable and uncountable nouns using pictures, eg, books, coins, money. Elicit from students why you cannot show them pictures of knowledge or advice (they are concepts and you cannot count them). Refer them to the Grammar on page 155, if necessary. Encourage them to use the Grammar for self-study purposes after the class. Elicit an explanation about the differences between countable and uncountable nouns after exercise **1**. Exercise **2** can be done individually and checked as a whole class.

**Answers**

**1**

1   time – uncountable
2   space – uncountable; space – countable; tables – countable
3   time – uncountable; laboratories – countable; research – uncountable

**2**

1   uncountable (*job* = countable)
2   uncountable
3   both
4   uncountable
5   both
6   uncountable
7   uncountable
8   both
9   uncountable
10   both
11   both
12   both

**3/4** After checking students' answers, students can do an extension exercise in pairs (Student A and Student B). Student A can read the uncountable nouns in the box aloud to a partner. Students B then gives examples of countable nouns without looking at the book. Student B then reads the uncountable words and Student A provides the countable nouns, without looking at the book. Then elicit the uncountable and countable nouns from the whole class in the same way. In exercise **4**, remind students about verb/subject agreement changes they may have to make. These classifying nouns can make useful headings for their vocabulary books and help them to distinguish between countable and uncountable nouns.

## Answers

**3**

| | | | |
|---|---|---|---|
| 1 | accommodation | 6 | knowledge |
| 2 | fruit | 7 | technology |
| 3 | nature | 8 | litter |
| 4 | furniture | 9 | money |
| 5 | luggage | 10 | music |

**4**

1 flats and houses need
2 nature is
3 Fruit is
4 Technology is
5 knowledge has
6 litter ... makes
7 Furniture makes

**5** Ask students to look at several sentences in exercise **4** with and without indefinite articles. Elicit the fact that indefinite articles are used for singular countable nouns and that for uncountable nouns they aren't. After students have completed the exercise, read a few sentences from this section. Add unnecessary indefinite articles and leave some out. Ask students to identify correct and incorrect sentences. Clear up any difficulties they may have at this stage.

### Answers

1 In the modern world, we are surrounded by (a) noise from machines and (a) technology that is unnatural. It is (a) major problem.
2 (A) research into different aspects of (a) medicine is useful for (a) humanity.
3 (A) space in any city is (a) valuable asset, so spaces for parking vehicles are expensive.
4 He bought (a) furniture for the garden.
5 What I am studying combines (a) scientific knowledge and (a) lot of facts.
6 I don't like seeing (a) litter on the streets or in (a) park.

**6** Tell students to think about the use of countable and uncountable nouns. Ask two or three students to talk for one minute about the topics for the whole class.

### Sample answer

There are different types of accommodation, such as flats, houses, caravans, palaces and tents. Some accommodation, such as tents and caravans, can be moved around. In cities accommodation can be very expensive, especially in capital cities, because there is a shortage of space and cities attract a lot of people. Student accommodation is usually very small as students often cannot afford large flats or houses. In the future, the problem will become worse as city populations grow.

## Photocopiable activity    page 120

### Countable and uncountable nouns

**1** After students have checked their answers for exercise 1, ask them to work in pairs and choose a topic for their partner to talk about without hesitating for two minutes and without preparation.

**2** As they talk, monitor students for the correct use of countable and uncountable nouns and give feedback. When they have finished, ask students to report back to the whole class about how they felt about speaking without preparation.

### Answers

see page 124

## Vocabulary 1    page 116

### Noun phrases: *Nature* and *natural*

**1** Elicit from students what a noun phrase is or wait until they have finished the exercise and then ask. Ask students to look at the picture and elicit where/what kind of place it is and how they know. Write phrases they suggest on the board, especially if they are noun phrases. Show the two forms: adjective + noun and noun + noun.

### Answers

| | | | | | |
|---|---|---|---|---|---|
| 1 | natural | 4 | nature | 7 | natural |
| 2 | natural | 5 | nature | 8 | natural |
| 3 | natural | 6 | natural | | |

**2/3** Exercise **2** can be completed individually and checked in pairs. Before students do exercise **3**, ask them to ask you or other students several questions. Monitor students as they ask and answer the questions and give feedback on the noun phrases used.

### Answers

| | | | |
|---|---|---|---|
| 1 | natural habitat | 4 | nature study |
| 2 | natural resources | 5 | natural ability |
| 3 | natural ingredients | 6 | nature reserve |

## IELTS Listening Section 4

### Aim

This section gives students practice with listening to a more formal lecture of an academic nature.

## Pre-listening

**1** Ask students first whether they expect a monologue or dialogue in Section 4 of the Listening module; and what type of monologue: a lecture, a talk, or a presentation. Start the discussion by eliciting some of the problems the natural world is facing today. Write some of the more well-known examples on the board. Ask students to think how modern science can help nature, pointing out the example given.

### Sample answers

farms to protect animals from disease, zoos to rear endangered species of animals, research about wild animals, tracking animals, conservation

**2** Ask students to look at the diagram and describe it before they start the activity. Use the statements 1–5 to ensure students understand and can navigate the diagram. Ask one or more students to explain the diagram to check comprehension.

### Answers

| | | | | |
|---|---|---|---|---|
| 1 | True | 3 True | 5 | True |
| 2 | False | 4 Not Given | | |

## Listening

**3**  Point out the Strategy for questions 4–7. In any diagram of this kind, stress that it is a good idea to find where the description starts as students listen. They should listen for the noun phrase in the heading for the diagram, *Diagonal farm*. Also, ask them what other piece of information they need to note (the facing south arrow). Give them 2–3 minutes to skim the questions and underline key words. Play the recording and ask students to check their answers in pairs before playing the recording again. At the end, ask them what new ideas they got from the recording to add to their ideas for exercise **1**.

### Answers

| | | | |
|---|---|---|---|
| 1 | B | 6 | fruit |
| 2 | A | 7 | alternative energy |
| 3 | C | 8 | B |
| 4 | shop | 9 | C |
| 5 | vegetables | 10 | A |

### 2.8

My presentation today is on the different ways that <u>the world of science can help nature and humanity</u>. We see a lot of stories in the news about the negative aspects of science, but not enough information is made available about how scientists can help nature and thus the human race.

You will see from my first slide that the title of my talk is *Nature – Science gives a helping hand*. I'm going to provide different examples of how science is having and will continue to have a beneficial impact on the natural world. Then, I'm going to show how that is of great benefit to the human race in general. The presentation will last for <u>30 minutes and at the end there will be 10 minutes to ask questions</u>. I've prepared a handout for everyone, so there is no need to take notes.

According to current predictions, by the year 2050, nearly 80 per cent of the earth's population will live in urban areas. <u>And an area of new land which is about 20 per cent bigger than the size of Brazil will be needed to grow enough food to feed the extra population</u>. That is if we continue to use traditional farming practices as practised today. So what can be done to deal with this situation?

The solution, which at first sight seems rather strange, is a 'diagonal' farm in cities, as we see here from this diagram, which shows a simplified layout of a diagonal farm. Such farms are a neat solution to the lack of space in urban and rural areas.

If we look at the diagram, we can see the front of the building, which faces south and slopes at a diagonal, so the various levels can catch the sun. On the bottom level, we have a <u>shop</u> where produce from the farm can be sold. And on this next level, we have a floor where <u>vegetables</u> can be grown and then on the level above that <u>fruit</u> can be grown. On the level above the fruit, we can have animals, which would have marvellous views of the city. And at the very top, there could be a centre for <u>alternative energy</u> with wind mills and solar panels to power the building.

My next slide is an artist's impression of the simplified version of the farm, which as you can see is rather amazing.

Another example of science helping nature <u>is GPS technology, which is currently used</u> in cars for navigation and also to track animals such as birds and wild cats over large areas of the world with great accuracy. At one time, birds and animals were tagged with rings around their necks or legs. As technology has become advanced, it is possible to insert information in chips on the rings, so researchers can carry out research on animals in their natural habitats without having to monitor them constantly. The research can be done thousands of miles away in a laboratory. <u>In the near future, by using unmanned aircraft</u>, it will be possible not just to track animals, but actually see them in their own habitat. This will have the advantage of not disturbing natural habitats and will allow researchers to watch animals more easily. Such visual tracking may not work in areas where there is thick jungle, but <u>in the distant future</u> scientists might be able to develop <u>floating cameras</u> that can manoeuvre through even thick jungle with ease.

**Extension**

When students have finished, discuss the contents of the lecture. Then ask them to choose 7–10 words and phrases from the audioscript that they think it would be useful to remember and explain why. Then play the recording again and see how much more they understand.

# Speaking 2    page 118

## IELTS Speaking Part 3

### Aim

The table in this section is a stimulus to give students something to talk about. This section also prepares students for describing tables in the next section.

### Suggestion

Students may not have much knowledge about different types of subjects at university. To help students who may not have general knowledge about topics you want to discuss, give them lists of ideas, data or short paragraphs to read before they read or speak about a topic. You could also brainstorm or pre-teach vocabulary. Students do not need to give specialist information in their answers in the speaking or in Writing Task 2 answers.

**1** Give students several minutes to answer the questions in pairs. This is the kind of information a student should look at when faced with data such as this. It helps establish the context and the parameters of the information.

**2/3** Go through the example questions. After questioning each other, students can discuss the questions in exercise 3. Students can now roleplay candidate and examiner, and examine each other using one set of questions each.

### Sample answers

**2**

How many undergraduate students studied science in total? In 2004/5, the total was 539, 200 and in 2005/6 it was 550, 4000.

Why do the numbers for each subject not add up to the total? Because there are other subjects which are not on the list. The table contains a selection of subjects.

**4** After students have shared their ideas with the class, elicit whether it helped to discuss the questions first before being examined about them.

# Writing 1    page 119

## IELTS Writing Task 1

**1** Ask students to study the table in Speaking 2 on page 118 again, circling the significant points on the table. Give them 25–30 minutes to write their answer, following the plan. When they have finished, give them a few minutes to check their answers for mistakes and then compare their answers with another pair. They can then compare what they have written with the model on page 165, and check the model against the plan. Give your feedback on strengths and weaknesses in their answers.

# Reading    page 119

### Aim

The aim of the pre-reading is to help students deal with unknown words in a text.

### Suggestion

Try to encourage students to talk about a subject even if some of the words are unknown to them. As they discuss, the meaning may become clearer. Then give them the meaning or elicit it from them.

## Pre-reading

**1** Ask students to look at the title and the sentences in italics on page 120 and predict what the passage is about. Ask them to read the Strategy and emphasize that guessing the meaning of unknown words is important as they will not have a dictionary in the test. Thinking about root words is part of this strategy. Don't answer any questions about the vocabulary at this point. Tell them not to use their dictionaries, but to see if they can guess the meanings from the context.

**2** Again, prohibit the use of dictionaries at this point. If students still have difficulties when checking, assist them with other synonyms or explanations.

### Answers

| a 7 | c 6 | e 10 | g 4 | i 5 |
|-----|-----|------|-----|-----|
| b 2 | d 9 | f 1  | h 3 | j 8 |

## Reading

**3** Get students to write numbers 1–13 down the left side of a page in their notebooks to write down the answers as they do the test. Give them 20 minutes to complete the test. Do a diagnostic check here to see if there is any particular question type that they are having difficulties with. If so, give them some extra input on this in a later lesson, but before they do another reading test.

**Answers**

| | | | |
|---|---|---|---|
| 1 | Section A vii | 6 | Section F vi |
| 2 | Section B viii | 7 | Yes |
| 3 | Section C iii | 8 | Yes |
| 4 | Section D v | 9 | Not Given |
| 5 | Section E ii | 10 | No |

11/12/13  A, B, D in any order

## Vocabulary 2    page 122

### Word and phrase building: *Advantage* and *disadvantage*

**Aim**

This section aims to prepare students for Writing Task 2 in the next section.

**Suggestion**

Encourage students to keep a record of words and phrases related to *advantage* and *disadvantage* in their vocabulary books and to update the lists regularly. Encourage them to record the words and phrases with a context, if possible.

**1** Ask students to fill in the table and check their answers for spelling mistakes. If necessary, drill the words for stress and get them to mark the stress on the words, noting how it shifts depending on the word form, eg, *benefit; beneficial.*

**Answers**

| | | | |
|---|---|---|---|
| 1 | advantageous | 11 | support |
| 2 | disadvantageous | 12 | supportive |
| 3 | disadvantageous/ | 13 | support |
| | a disadvantage | 14 | be a hindrance to |
| 4 | prevention | 15 | opposition |
| 5 | preventative | 16 | oppose |
| 6 | preventative | 17 | opposition |
| 7 | help | 18 | defensive |
| 8 | help | 19 | defend |
| 9 | assistance | 20 | defence |
| 10 | assist | | |

**2** Students can do this exercise in pairs. Ask them to first decide what part of speech is needed and then change the word accordingly, if necessary. Go over the answers as a whole class. Check they understand the meaning of all the sentences.

**Answers**

1 There is no doubt that science has brought a range of benefits to the world.
2 The government faced strong opposition to the decrease in spending on science.
3 Correct
4 The university was very supportive of the research into the impact of science on nature.
5 Correct
6 Preventative measures need to be taken to prevent science and technology inhibiting creativity, especially in young people.
7 Correct
8 If the majority of students study science-related subjects at university, it is hugely disadvantageous to society.

**3** Emphasize that the word in italics can change form but the other words in each list need to remain the same as they write their sentences. Collate the answers on the board

**Sample answers**

1 The builders opposed/stated their strong opposition to the plans for a new supermarket.
2 The volunteer groups helped protect nature from harm.
3 Preventative measures should be taken to stop people relying too much on machines.
4 Relaxing outside can benefit/benefits everyone.
5 The government wasn't supportive of/didn't support environmental groups.

**4** Monitor students as they discuss in groups. Encourage them to use the new vocabulary from exercise **1** as much as possible.

## Writing 2    page 122

### IELTS Writing Task 2

**Aim**

This Writing Task 2 aims to help students focus on the connection between sentences.

**1** Get students to compare and contrast the two pictures and give their opinion about them. Then ask them to read Writing Task 2 and ask them questions about the contents and the organization.

They can then do the exercise in pairs. When you check their answers, elicit reasons.

**Answers**

1 A    2 A    3 B

**2** Point out the Strategy and ask students to explain the contents. Students can do the exercise individually and check their answers in pairs. Elicit reasons for the answers and stress the importance of connections like this in their writing. Point out the importance of understanding such connections for reading, listening and speaking.

**Answers**

1  Some people
2  increasing numbers of the young generation are living in cities
3  (increasing numbers of the young generation are living in cities) they have little contact with nature, as they spend most of their time inside buildings in enclosed spaces, working and playing on machines.
4  hindering the development of young people
5  to help pupils and students spend some time outside at school and university

**3** Students can do this exercise individually and then compare their answers with a partner. Check students' answers as a whole class and discuss how the language flows better with the changes.

**Answers**

1  This
2  They
3  This development (This situation)
4  This situation (This development)
5  They
6  to do this

**4** This can be done individually and checked in pairs. Elicit reasons for students' answers.

**Answers**

| | | |
|---|---|---|
| 1 development | 4 | situation |
| 2 research | 5 | solution |
| 3 problem | | |

**5** Ask students to read the Writing Task 2 question and ask them questions about it. Elicit the number of words that are required in the exam. Ask students to write only about 100–150 words, if you think 250 words is too long. Ask students to read the Strategy and the checklist. Point out that the word lengths for the paragraphs are guidelines only. Get them to copy the latter into their notebooks for self-study. They should refer to this every time they write the answer to a Task 2 question.

They can write the beginning of the answer (the introduction and the first paragraph) in pairs and then finish it for homework. In the exam, the suggested writing time for Task 2 is 40 minutes. At this level, allow them as much time as you think they need. When students have finished, they can compare their answers with the model and comments on page 165.

## Reading: Matching paragraph and section headings

**Aim**

The purpose of this section is to increase students' awareness of nouns in working out the meaning of paragraphs (and sections), and paragraph (and section) headings.

## Word strategies

**1** This can be done as self-study or in the class. Encourage students to follow the instructions and try the suggested strategies out on other passages. Inform them that while there are no rules as to what order they should answer questions in in a reading test, the matching headings questions are a helpful navigation aid to find the way around a text. The headings give guidance for the more detailed questions that follow.

If you feel students need more guidance, go through each of the questions in class. Students can use different coloured pens to highlight the text for the different techniques, instead of underlining. These are all useful strategies in picking out key words to help find the main ideas of a paragraph.

Emphasize strategy 7. It is important for students to recognize these nouns as they are central to headings. They are the words around which headings quite often are built; cleft sentences or clauses being the other main feature: *how ... what ...* The same applies to matching information to paragraphs. Teachers can help students by encouraging awareness of these nouns and showing how they work in IELTS exercises in all four skills (eg, advantages and disadvantages in writing). Encourage students to keep a list of these nouns as they come across them in reading passages; the nouns are often found in headings with synonyms in the reading passage. Give them a hint of how to collect these by going back to page 120 and picking out some of the general nouns in this list of headings, eg, *benefits, solutions, view, effective techniques.* You can also refer them to the table about advantages and disadvantages on page 122.

**Answers**

1

It says that the most promising <u>solution</u> is offered by artificial <u>trees</u>, <u>devices</u> that collect $CO_2$ through their "<u>leaves</u>" and convert it to a <u>form</u> that can easily be collected and stored. Tim Fox, <u>head</u> of <u>environment</u> and <u>climate change</u> at the <u>institution</u>, said that the <u>devices</u> were thousands of <u>times</u> more effective at removing <u>carbon</u> from the <u>atmosphere</u> than real <u>trees</u>.

In the first <u>report</u> on such <u>geo-engineering</u> by practising <u>engineers</u>, the <u>institution</u> calculates that 100,000 artificial <u>trees</u> — which could fit into 600<u>ha</u> (1,500 <u>acres</u>) — would be enough to capture all <u>emissions</u> from <u>Britain's</u> <u>homes</u>, <u>transport</u> and light <u>industry</u>. It says that five <u>million</u> would do the same for the whole <u>world</u>.

**2**

### Sample answer
It says that the most promising |solution| is offered by artificial |trees|, |devices| that collect |CO₂| through their "leaves" and convert it to a form that can easily be collected and stored. Tim Fox, |head| of |environment| and |climate change| at the |institution| …

**3**

### Sample answer
The most effective <u>technique</u> for reducing <u>carbon</u> in the <u>atmosphere</u> (*carbon* and *atmosphere* are things that we can identify – the word *technique* is a general noun)

**4**

technique – solution
carbon – $CO_2$/carbon
atmosphere – atmosphere
Note the fact that *technique* has a synonym, which is another general noun. Carbon is carbon and does not have a synonym. It does have a chemical formula. Headings are often built around theses general nouns, eg, *technique of/to/ for …/a … solution to …/a … impact on …*

**5**

how to solve the problem of pollution → (a) solution(s) to the problem of pollution

**6**

It says that the most promising solution is offered by artificial trees, devices that collect $CO_2$ through their "leaves" and convert it to a form that can easily be collected and stored. (Note the topic sentence corresponds to the heading, as it should do in an academic text.)

**7**

Students' own answers.

## Post-test strategy

**2** Ask students to read the post-test strategies and then ask them questions, eliciting reasons and examples relating to section B. You can also do this with another passage from a previous unit.

### Answers
4 technique, carbon, atmosphere
5 Specific: carbon, atmosphere; General: technique
6 solution (general); not physical
7 effective – promising
8 No, because they don't have synonyms. They are very specific.

## Content overview

### Themes

This unit is based on the topic of culture and the arts and focuses on arts events, exhibitions and types of art.

### Exam-related activities

#### Reading

Identifying information – True/False/Not Given
Short-answer questions
Matching – classifying

#### Writing

Task 1   Describing pie charts
Task 2   Developing ideas
Checking for mistakes

#### Listening

Section 3
Multiple choice
Completing a flowchart
Completing a table

### Speaking

Part 1   Talking about arts events
Part 2   Describing a favourite item
Part 3   Giving reasons and examples

### Language development

#### Language focus and Vocabulary

Art
Definite and indefinite articles

### Skills development

Skimming

### Study skills

Writing and speaking: Collecting and developing ideas

## Vocabulary   page 126

### Art

**Aim**
To introduce students to the different types of venues where art-related activities take place and give them practice in the four main skills.

1 Elicit students' preferences and reasons. Also elicit vocabulary and general knowledge about different art forms and write them on the board, eg, *sculpture, drawing, painting, writing, dancing,* etc.

2 Elicit explanations for the use of the word *event* in the sentences in the example. This exercise can be done in pairs, followed by whole-class checking of the answers.

**Answers**

1  1 performance 2 performances 3 performance
   4 performance
2  1 exhibition 2 exhibition 3 exhibitions 4 exhibition
3  1 festival 2 festival 3 festival 4 festival

**3/4** After each exercise, students should check their answers with a partner, followed by whole-class checking. Elicit reasons for students' answers in both exercises. Point out that the words *event, festival,* etc, are useful in the speaking module.

**Answers**

3
| | |
|---|---|
| 1 <u>live</u> performance | 5 the <u>art exhibition</u> |
| 2 correct | 6 correct |
| 3 The <u>festival organizers</u> | 7 The <u>festival programme</u> |
| 4 <u>performance artist</u> | |

4
| | |
|---|---|
| 1 remember it | 3 it disappoint you |
| 2 it impress you | 4 stun you |

5 When students have finished, write the words *event, festival, performance* and *exhibition* on the board and elicit examples of each from the students. Point out how the four words help to classify the examples.

# Speaking 1  page 127

## IELTS Speaking Part 1

### Aim
The purpose of this section is to help students prepare for Writing Task 1 in the next section.

### Suggestion
Use data for Task 1 as a way to introduce ideas for speaking and Writing Task 2, to build up students' general knowledge.

**1** The chart serves as input, giving students some ideas to talk about. Ensure students know the meaning of the sites listed on the vertical axis and point out the Glossary. Monitor students as they ask each other questions. When they have finished, either ask the questions to the class using the stems or get them to ask you the questions.

**2** This can be done in pairs or as a whole class. The discussion can be linked either to the country they are studying in, or their home country.

**3/4/5**  Ask students to study the answers in pairs and predict possible questions before they listen. In exercise **4**, pause at the end of each question for 1 minute for students to take notes and compare them with a partner. When they have finished, ask them to turn the notes into questions. Then in exercise **5**, monitor students as they answer the questions. Give feedback about students' answers.

### Answers

**3**
a 3    b 1    c 4    d 2

### (O) 2.9

1 Do you think museums or old towns are old-fashioned and not exciting? Why/Why not?
2 What kinds of arts events are popular among young people in your home country?
3 What kinds of festivals are held where you were brought up?
4 Do people prefer live performances of music to CDs nowadays?

# Writing 1  page 128

## IELTS Writing Task 1

### Aim
This section gives students the opportunity to practise writing about two sets of data, a bar chart and a pie chart, and linking them together.

**1** Ask students to describe the pie chart and elicit the connection between the pie chart and the bar chart on page 127. Ask students to give reasons for their answer. Read the Strategy with students and point out that in the exam there is often more than one set of data, eg, a graph or bar chart and a pie chart. It is, therefore, essential that they learn to link the data.

### Answer
3

**2/3** Refer to the questions and answers for the bar chart on page 127 and tell students to use these as the basis for their answer. Elicit information about the two charts and collate them on the board. Elicit a plan, which can also be written on the board: *an introduction, an overview, information about the bar chart, the connecting sentence from exercise 1, information about the pie chart.* Ask students to work individually and give them 20–25 minutes to write their answer. After checking for mistakes, students can swap their answers with a partner to peer-correct. They can then compare their answer with the model and comments on page 166.

# Listening  page 128

## IELTS Listening Section 3

### Aim
This Listening section introduces students to the completion of a flowchart.

### Suggestion
Encourage students to listen to the recording for Section 3 and read the audioscript at the same time as part of their self-study. Then can then listen without the audioscript and answer the questions again. They can also focus on one section only when they do this, eg, questions 4–7.

## Pre-listening

**1** Give them 2 minutes to decide and find reasons. Write their reasons on the board.

### Sample answers
Students choosing artwork for an exhibition. There are clues in many of the questions: 1 choose materials, 2 have already chosen, 3 pieces of art work, 4–7 words like *exhibition/art work/exhibition hall*, 8–10 words in the table such as *category*, etc.

**2/3** Ask students to do these two exercises in pairs. Elicit the reasons for the answers.

## Answers

**2**

1 note form
2 4 – noun, 5 – noun/adjective and noun, 6 – noun, 7 – noun/adjective and noun
3 Student's own answers
4 7
5 make sure right; assessment by; theme, impact; public, like

**3**

Students' owns answers.

## Listening

**4**  Ask students to look at the photo and have them describe what it shows. Read through the Strategy with the class and elicit information about it and the flowchart. Play the recording all the way through as usual, check the answers and play again.

### Answers

| | |
|---|---|
| 1 C | 6 craftsmanship |
| 2 A | 7 fifth judge |
| 3 B | 8 Roman ruins |
| 4 standard | 9 street art |
| 5 judging panel | 10 impress the judges |

**2.10**

(T = Tutor; C = Carla; W = Wills)

T: Hi, Carla.

C: Oh, hi, Dr Irvin. Hi, Wills.

W: Hi, Carla.

T: Shall we just get started selecting pieces for the <u>yearly exhibition at the end of the course</u>?

C: Yeah. Let's get down to it.

W: Yeah, mmm ...

C: Can I just ask if Wills and I are the last to make our selection?

T: Oh no, <u>just under half of the students have chosen their pieces.</u>

W: Oh, that doesn't make me feel so bad, then.

C: Yes, that is a relief.

W: We can choose three pieces. That's right, isn't it?

T: <u>Up to three.</u>

...

C: That makes it a bit easier. Mmm, before we make the selection, can you briefly go through the assessment process from selection to the judging for us?

T: Yes. It's quite simple really. First you, the students, choose the pieces of art that you want to be included in the end-of-year exhibition for the judges to consider.

W: That's what we're doing now. OK.

T: The exhibition organizers check if they think that the pieces are of a high enough <u>standard</u>.

C: And what happens if they are not up to standard?

T: Then you're asked to submit another piece.

C: Ah, OK.

T: Then the pieces are put in the exhibition hall and when the hall is tidied up, the members of the <u>judging panel</u> go round and give each piece a score based on a set of criteria. So it's the <u>judging panel</u> that makes the assessment.

W: Mmm. What are the criteria?

T: Generally the criteria vary from year to year slightly. This and last year's are basically the same: originality, theme, impact and ... mmm ... oh, <u>craftsmanship</u>. So that is what we need to bear in mind as we make our selection. Oh, and I forgot to mention that this year there is a new step in the whole process and that is that we are having a public vote as well, which will account for 20 per cent of the marking.

W: So ... the public will be like the <u>fifth judge</u>.

T: Effectively, yes.

...

T: So shall we get down to the selections? Carla, have you chosen anything from the drawing category?

C: Yes, I've got this building design that everyone seems to like.

T: It's just the right dimensions and it's really very fine indeed. I think that will impress the judges.

W: Oh yes, it's really beautiful.

C: Thank you.

T: Wills, have you got anything for the drawing category?

W: No, but I've got something for the painting category. I've had this one in my portfolio for a year now, but I like it.

C: Oh, the watercolour of the <u>Roman ruins</u> in North Africa. That's stunning.

T: Have I seen that one? No, I haven't. Oh you're right, Carla. It's wonderful. It really stands out.

W: Oh, thank you.

T: The next of the four categories is ... mmm ... film art. What about the film category?

C: I have a short film on <u>street art</u>.

T: Yes, that one you're putting into the arts exhibition at the annual film festival at the end of the month as well.

W: It's stunning.

C: I hope the judges think so too.

T: I think they won't be disappointed. And Wills?

W: I've got this short film on the process of creating a painting. I've called it *Mess and creation*.

C: I like that. It's very funny.

T: Are you submitting any other pieces?

C: I'd like to put in a third one in the electronic media.

T: OK.

C: It's an electronic painting done on an iPad.

T: That's very different. It will certainly <u>impress the judges</u>.

C: I've played around with it a lot. It's not as easy as you think.

## Speaking 2 page 130

### IELTS Speaking Part 2

**1** After students have compared their answers, elicit examples to write on the board. You can also elicit reasons for their choices.

**2** Check students understand the phrases in the speech bubbles and elicit whether they are weak or strong items. Elicit an example to write on the board, eg, 'The film *An Education* had a huge impact on me.' Encourage them to give reasons.

**3** Give students large sheets of paper to make the Task Card. When they have finished, ask them to display their cards and compare them.

**4** Point out to students that they are going to give feedback on the reasons they use. Remind them only to make brief notes about the Task Card. Finish with a general discussion about areas they feel they have improved on and areas they still feel they need to work on.

## Reading   page 130

### Aim

This section helps to show students that they can answer questions about a slightly longer and more complex reading passage. This helps to build their confidence in reading.

### Suggestion

If necessary, give students words and phrases from each or several paragraph(s) and ask them to predict what the paragraph or text is about. Alternatively, after students have read the text, choose a paragraph and ask them to select 7–10 words or phrases that would give them the meaning or gist of the paragraph. Write the words on the board and ask students to talk about the paragraph using the words and phrases.

**1** This can be done as a whole-class exercise. Elicit where the picture is from and what it shows (a sign for the Paris Métro). Write predictions on the board, which can then be checked after exercise **2**. You can give students hints by asking: *Is the passage about science? Or is it about art?* Also ask them for reasons.

**2** Be strict about the time limit. After students have shared their ideas with their partner, discuss them as a class and tell students to check them against their predictions.

**3** As students do the exercise, tell them not to underline the words as they find them, so they don't over-focus on them. Encourage them to select four or five words to write in their vocabulary books.

### Answers

| | |
|---|---|
| 1 embraced | 5 icons |
| 2 harmony | 6 outlines/patterns |
| 3 conformed to | 7 prosperity |
| 4 commissioned | 8 typified |

### Reading

**4** Ask students to answer questions 1–13 as usual. Allow 20 minutes to answer the questions as per the IELTS

exam, but extend the time if necessary. Point out the Tip relating to questions 10–13.

### Answers

| | | | |
|---|---|---|---|
| 1 | False | 8 | (the) World's Fair |
| 2 | True | 9 | (the) subway system |
| 3 | Not Given | 10 | B |
| 4 | True | 11 | C |
| 5 | Not Given | 12 | A |
| 6 | many key developments | 13 | C |
| 7 | (emerging) young designers | | |

## Reading discussion

**5** As students discuss, write their ideas on the board. This exercise can also be done in groups of three or four students. Ask them to choose someone in the group to take notes for whole-class feedback.

## Language focus   page 133

### Definite and indefinite articles

**1/2** Remind students of the use of indefinite articles they looked at on page 115 when they learnt about countable and uncountable nouns. Elicit what they remember. Elicit any rules they know about articles.
Students can complete exercise **1** as whole class. If necessary, use the Grammar on page 155 to help you provide an explanation for students and also ask them to read the page for self-study. Exercise **2** can be done as a pairwork activity, followed by whole-class discussion. Point out the definite article before the superlative in sentence 3.

### Answers

**1**

1 It was developed by <u>a</u> brilliant and energetic generation of artists and designers …
2 no articles
3 Paris was <u>the</u> most important artistic centre in Europe at this time (definite article)

**2**

1 Paris; Europe
2 life
3 artists; designers
4 a brilliant and energetic generation

**3/4** Students should do both exercises on their own, before checking their answers in pairs.

### Answers

**3**

1 ~~the~~ moons

2 ~~the~~ many cultural events
3 ~~A~~ Paris
4 ~~The~~ computers can be used to create ~~a~~ digital art.
5 I don't really like ~~the~~ plays
6 ... about ~~a~~ famous poets from Iran.
7 ~~A~~ research
8 full of ~~the~~ interesting events.

**4**

| | | | | | |
|---|---|---|---|---|---|
| 1 | a | 5 | – | 9 | the |
| 2 | – | 6 | the | 10 | the |
| 3 | The | 7 | – | 11 | an |
| 4 | – | 8 | – | 12 | a/the |

**5** Drill students for intonation before they practise, if necessary. After practising, several students can describe the type of art to the class.

Articles can be problematic as many languages don't have them. If students are still experiencing difficulties after doing these activities, give them the extra practice on page 156 or point out the extra practice for self-study.

## Photocopiable activity   page 121

### Articles

**1** After students have identified and checked their answers, they can conduct the survey. Encourage them to ask as many fellow students as possible.

**2** If necessary, elicit more example questions before students start the survey.

**3** Use the class discussion as a comprehension check of students' use of the articles.

**Answers**

see page 124

## Speaking 3   page 134

### IELTS Speaking Part 3

**Aim**

This section helps students prepare for answering questions in IELTS Speaking Part 3 by focusing on beginning their answers to the examiner's questions.

**Suggestion**

Make sure students realise that there are different ways to begin their answers. They can keep lists of different ways to begin answering questions. This will show how flexible they need to be in the IELTS exam and when they speak generally.

**1/2** After students have done exercise **1** and checked their answers, elicit reasons for their answers. In exercise **1**, point out that answers can begin in different ways. For example, the answer to question 1a can begin: *Yes, I do. The preservation ...* You can also elicit other answers for 1–3 from students.

**Answers**

1  a/b    2  b/c    3  a/c

**3/4** Elicit from students what the monitors are going to listen for and give feedback on. Monitor the roleplay and ensure the monitors give feedback.

## Writing 2   page 134

### IELTS Writing Task 2

**1/2** Ask students to look at the photo and describe it. Check if anyone has visited anywhere similar. You might want to elicit words like *ruins, heritage, site*, etc. When students compare their ideas, encourage them to support their viewpoint and concede the opposite viewpoint where appropriate. Decide which viewpoint has the best supporting ideas. Collate the ideas for both sentences and write them on the board under Sentence 1 and Sentence 2.

**Sample answers**

Sentence 1: buildings are attractive; give variety to the environment; pleasant and beautiful to look at; preserve history;
Sentence 2: accommodation a basic right; people especially children need shelter; people more important than buildings

**3/4** Before students do exercise **3**, point out the Strategy. The table is very useful for clarifying ideas, and while students won't have time to do this in the test, it's a good basis for self-study and class practice. After students have completed the table in pairs, elicit reasons for students' choices. Ask several students to explain the contents of the table.

**Answers**

**3**
a 2   b 1   c 2   d 1   e 2
**4**
1 b   2 d   3 e   4 a   5 c

**5** After students have practised connecting the ideas in pairs, elicit several sentences from the class.

**6** Point out that the guidelines are useful for writing introductions. Select two or three introductions to write on the board as samples. Also write the Sample answer below on the board.

**Sample answer**

While some people believe it is crucial to protect old buildings like ruins or old castles at the same time as constructing new roads and new accommodation, others feel that the emphasis should be on modern architecture. As with all discussions there are arguments on both sides, but I personally feel that the answer is to put the emphasis on both equally.

**7/8/9** Check the answers for exercise **7** and elicit which argument in the table in exercise **4** it relates to and ask students to give reasons. Students can then write the paragraph in their notebooks after their introduction. In exercise **8**, students first discuss how they will develop the next two paragraphs, using the table in exercise **4** as a plan. Ask students to read the model answer and comments on page 166. This can be done in class or as self-study.

**Answers**

**7**

Keeping old buildings such 1 <u>as</u> castles and ruins helps preserve 2 <u>the</u> past, because such buildings show the present generation and future generations what the past 3 <u>was</u> like. For example, children at primary and secondary 4 <u>schools</u> can visit old castles, where they can learn about how people lived. As a result, the children will have 5 <u>a</u> view of history and this helps reinforce the traditions of 6 <u>the/their</u> country and makes them proud 7 <u>of</u> their culture.

## Study skills   page 137

### Writing and speaking: Collecting and developing ideas

**1/2** To introduce the study skills, ask students to read the first Tip and discuss the contents. Ask them to copy the table into their notebooks/vocabulary books. Point out that as they prepare for IELTS, they can add to the table. The more ideas and vocabulary they have to hand, the easier it will be to plan writing and speaking answers.

**Answers**

**1**

Yes

**2**

**Sample answers**

Idea: Finance (relates to all of the topics in the box in 1)
Notes about topics: Role of finance = cost of measures to encourage recycling, cost of preserving old buildings, cost of travelling around the world, cost of using the computer (eg, Internet costs, anti-virus protection)

**3** Encourage students to copy the diagram onto cards. They can then add ideas around the words in circles when they plan a paragraph. Ask them to compare this with the table in exercise **2** and the table on page 135.

**Sample answer**

first argument from table on page 135

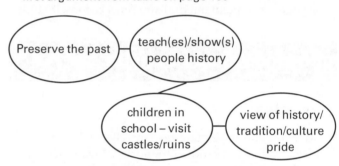

**4** Ask students to check their diagram with at least one other student.

**Sample answer**

Importance of teaching the arts

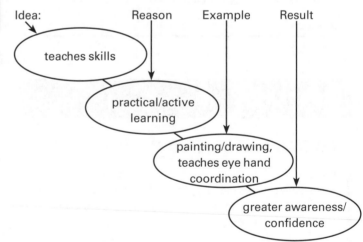

## Content overview

### Themes

This unit acts as a consolidation of the different parts of the IELTS exam and is thematically focused on communication and language.

### Exam-related activities

#### Reading

Matching information
Labelling a diagram
Matching sentence endings

#### Writing

Task 1    Describing data – two charts
Task 2    A range of essays

#### Listening

Section 3
Choosing items from a list
Multiple choice
Matching

### Speaking

Part 2    Choosing relevant ideas
          Practising giving answers
Part 3    Talking about the importance of learning
          languages

### Language development

#### Language focus and Vocabulary

Collocations: Communication
Ellipsis and substitution

#### Skills development

All skills
Fluency and flexibility

#### Study skills

Writing: Planning

## Vocabulary    page 138

### Collocations: Communication

**Aim**

This section aims to focus on building awareness of collocations related to communication.

**Suggestion**

Review the concept of collocations before or after the section. Encourage students to continue to build their collection of collocations in their vocabulary books. Remind them to record as much context as possible to help them remember the meaning of the collocations. Encourage them to use a collocation dictionary such as the Macmillan Collocations Dictionary.

**1** To introduce the unit, ask students what they think the unit is about and what types of communication there are, eg, *verbal, electronic, email, letters, body language, sign language*. Write the ideas on the board. After they have finished discussing the pictures in groups, ask them to add to the list on the board, by adding *videophone, Skype* and *videoconferencing*.

**2/3** Explain what *rank* means. After students have completed exercises **2** and **3** in pairs, elicit examples to match their reasons.

**4** To introduce the exercise, elicit the answer for the first question. Ask students to complete the exercise in pairs. After checking the answers, students can take turns asking and answering the questions. Ask them to add the words to their vocabulary book under the heading *Communication*.

**Answers**

1  electronic and non-verbal communication
2  mass communication
3  satellite communication
4  breakdown in communication
5  communication skills
6  instant communication
7  communication difficulties or problems
8  different methods of communication
9  cross-cultural communication
10  improve communication

**5/6** Students can do exercise **5** individually. Students check their answers first in pairs. Then take whole-class feedback. Students can then practise reading the dialogue in exercise **5** in pairs. When they answer the questions in exercise **6**, only the 'Examiners' should look at the book. Encourage 'Candidate' students to develop the answers in their own way.

### Sample answers

**5**
1 skills
2 methods; electronic; non-verbal
3 communication; difficulties
4 improved; Cross-cultural
5 mass

## Listening   page 139

### IELTS Listening Section 3

#### Aim
The Listening section aims to give students practice in listening to three people speaking in a conversation. Some students find this section in the IELTS exam challenging, so break up the recording into several parts if necessary.

#### Suggestion
To introduce the listening, ask students to describe the picture and suggest what the role of the tutor is.

### Pre-listening

**1** After students have done exercise **1** in pairs, discuss the questions as a whole class and give students time to underline key words in the questions.

#### Answers

a questions 5–7
b question 1 and 2
c questions 8–10
d questions 3 and 4

### Listening

**2**  Play the recording once only, as in the exam. Give students a few minutes to check their answers in pairs. Ask them to write the numbers 1–10 vertically in their notebooks and transfer their answers to their notebooks. Check the answers as a whole class. Then play the recording again so they can listen and check their comprehension.

#### Answers

| | | |
|---|---|---|
| 1 and 2 | B/D | 7  A |
| 3 and 4 | A/E | 8  B |
| 5 | B | 9  C |
| 6 | D | 10  A |

#### Extension
Before students listen to the recording for the final time, ask students to work in groups of three and to read the audioscript aloud.

**(O) 2.11**

(T = Tutor; F = Fatima; A = Alan)

T: So this is our last tutorial before you take your exams in communication skills and language. So, how can I help you both? Fatima? Alan?

A: Mmm ... on the course, mmm ... <u>I found the lectures really fascinating.</u> In fact, ... I don't think I missed any of them. But the best part ... <u>was going out into the schools.</u>

T: That's good to hear, Alan. Some people have found the final year quite tough.

F: And I changed over to the communication skills and language course at the beginning of the year as you know, <u>mainly because of the excellent name of the course among students and tutors</u> and among people outside the university <u>and also because of the practical work in the course.</u>

T: And are you glad you did so?

F: Oh yes. I loved the practical aspect of the course.

T: Well, you've both got to the end. So, ... what can I do for you both today?

A: Mmm ... we wanted some tips about getting ready for the final exams and some advice about the courses we're doing. I'm not sure I'm quite ready.

F: I'm sure you are more ready than you think you are.

T: I think that Fatima's right, ...

A: I <u>think that I could've spent more time on reading for some of the modules.</u>

F: I'm sure we all could have, but there's a limit to what we can do.

A: Yes, but I'm not very good under exam pressure. I panic more now, but when I was at school I didn't.

T: Maybe it's because you know more now.

A: Do you think so?

T: It's perhaps part of the problem. There's also the fact that it's your final exams.

A: I suppose so.

F: Is there anything you can advise us to do?

T: <u>I think the first thing is to make sure you are fresh and rested before the exam, so perhaps stop working about 24 hours before you sit each exam.</u>

A: Yes, perhaps we should try to.

F: I made an attempt to before the last set of exams, but I didn't manage to relax before all the exams.

A: Well, I didn't either.

T: You can only try. Another thing is make sure you don't go to parties around the exams and <u>read the advice sheet on exam preparation put together by the department. Here's another copy in case you haven't got it.</u>

F: Thanks.

A: Thanks.

...

T: So, have you decided where you'd like to go after you've graduated?

F: We've both been looking at the same places and have narrowed it down to three: Rockham College, Bart's Institute and St John's School of Languages.

T: All three are good places.

A: If I'm right, Rockham College has a very good postgraduate course in cross-cultural communication and linguistics.

F: Yes, but I think we should've applied for this one much earlier as we both got rejections.

T: That's a shame because it has a very dynamic department, the Centre of Media and Mass Communication. A couple of our students from last year went on to study at the centre.

A: I've got a place on an MA course in communication systems at Bart's Institute.

F: And I've also been offered a place on an MA course in language acquisition at the same place.

T: Both courses are very highly thought of and Bart's is undoubtedly a first-class institution. We've not had any students go on there from here, but it's very good. And St John's has a good track record for turning out film producers. There was just one student who attended St John's after leaving here. So well done.

## Language focus    page 140

### Ellipsis and substitution

**1** When you have elicited the answers, you may have to refer students to the Grammar on page 156 and give a mini-presentation.

**Answers**

1 left out of
2 another word

**2/3** Ask students to do these exercises in pairs. Elicit reasons for their answers.

**Answers**

**2**
1 changed over to the communication skills and language course
2 could have spent more time on reading
3 I didn't panic.

**3**
1 substitution
2 ellipsis
3 ellipsis

**4** This exercise can be done by students individually followed by checking in pairs. Elicit reasons for students' choices when you check the answers as a whole class.

**Answers**

1 I find it difficult to communicate by video, but my sister doesn't.
2 Although people used to write lots of letters in the past, they don't anymore.
3 Some people don't think that learning languages is valuable, while many do.
4 People often try to leave their mobile phones at home, but they find that they aren't able to.
5 People used to design products by hand rather than on computers, but nowadays they can't even if the computer breaks down.
6 The human race wants to communicate with beings on other planets, but if they do, will we be at risk?
7 Languages have disappeared from the school curriculum in some schools, but here they haven't.
8 The government hasn't spent as much money as other countries on making broadband available to everyone but they should have.

**5** Students can do this exercise in pairs. When students have checked their answers, read sentence 1 below and ask students to transform it as in exercise 4. Students can do the same in pairs.

**Answers**

1 I find it difficult to communicate by video, but my sister doesn't find it so.
2 Although people used to write lots of letters in the past, they don't do so anymore.
3 Some people don't think that learning languages is valuable, while many think so.
4 People often try to leave their mobile phones at home, but they find that they aren't able to do so.
5 People used to design products by hand rather than on computers, but nowadays they can't do so even if the computer breaks down.
6 The human race wants to communicate with beings on other planets, but if they do so, will we be at risk?
7 Languages have disappeared from the school curriculum in some schools, but here they haven't done so.
8 The government hasn't spent as much money as other countries on making broadband available to everyone, but they should have done so.

**6** Encourage students to use ellipsis and substitution in their answers. Monitor the pairwork and give feedback on good examples.

## Photocopiable activity    page 122

### I don't find it difficult to ...

**1** Students do not have to read each other all of the statements when they do pairwork exercise **2**. Point out that there is more than one answer.

**2** Encourage them to read the statements at random.

**3** Monitor students to check spontaneity.

#### Answers

see page 124

## Speaking 1    page 142

### IELTS Speaking Part 2

#### Aim
This section gives students an opportunity for greater independence and practice in IELTS Speaking Part 2.

#### Suggestion
Ask students to make a collection of all the types of Part 2 tasks, eg, under the headings of *describing people, places, events and processes*. They can also predict what types of topics might come up in the exam and keep topic lists.

**1/2/3** Students should choose the card they want to talk about, but try to ensure that they are not all doing the same one. Make sure they write their notes individually and choose the items in exercise **2** that are relevant to their chosen card. At this stage they should be completely independent when it comes to writing notes. Make sure they write brief notes. In exercise **3**, when students have finished, ask them to give their notes to their partner and discuss whether they followed them or not.

#### Sample answer

B
The method of communication I'd like to describe is my video phone. I bought the video phone six months ago and since then I have used it many times to speak to my friends and family back in my home country. I also use it to speak to my friends here in New York, as they all have video phones. I think I probably use it three times a week. I like using it because it is really practical and convenient. We can see each other very clearly, which is reassuring for all of us. It is also cheaper to use than I thought it would be, so I can call more frequently than I did in the past.

## Reading    page 142

#### Aim
As well as further practice in the question types that students have already encountered, this reading passage gives practice in completing a diagram.

### Pre-reading

**1** Elicit what the link is between the picture and the title of the passage. As students brainstorm ideas in pairs, limit them to three facts only. They can work with another pair to share ideas. When they have compared their answers in groups, collate all the ideas on the board. Allow students to add other ideas at this stage.

**2** Give students 5–8 minutes for this exercise. Then elicit their facts and write them on the board.

### Reading

**3** Follow the usual procedure for the reading passage, but before you start, make sure students understand the diagram in questions 7–9. Point out that they don't have to know the exact meaning of the words to complete the diagram. Give them 20–25 minutes to answer the questions.

Point out to students that when they answer the questions, they should put a mark next to the number of any questions they cannot answer. When they come back to it later on, they won't write the next answer in the wrong place.

Go over the answers with students as a whole class, showing them where to find the information in the text and ensuring they all understand the reasons for each answer. Get them to record their scores. Discuss with students which particular parts of the test they still find most challenging and advise them on further self-study.

#### Answers

| | | | | | |
|---|---|---|---|---|---|
| 1 | C | 6 | B | 11 | E |
| 2 | C | 7 | phonic lips | 12 | G |
| 3 | F | 8 | melon | 13 | A |
| 4 | A | 9 | echolocation | | |
| 5 | F | 10 | B | | |

### Reading discussion

**4** Follow the group discussion with a whole-class discussion.

# Writing 1  page 145

## IELTS Writing Task 1

### Aim
The aim of this section is to prepare students to write a full Task 1 answer on their own. The tasks in this section also give students practice in linking two sets of data.

**1** Ask students to work in pairs and discuss the Task 1 question and the two graphs. Elicit specific information about the graphs or get them to ask you questions. Elicit the differences and similarities in information that each diagram represents. Point out the last sentence of the rubric and emphasize the words *summarize, selecting main features* and *comparisons*. Ask them why these words are important.

**2** When students have done this in pairs, write the corrected text on the board as students dictate it. Ask them to identify which mistakes they commonly make.

### Sample answer
The graphs show the proportion of people in different age groups involved in teleworking in the United Kingdom between 1997 and 2005 along with the rates of teleworking in various industries in 1997 and 2005.

**3** Students can do this in pairs. Then elicit the sentence and write it on the board.

### Sample answer
Despite the slight decline in the proportion of those aged 25–34 towards the end of the period, the rates of involvement in teleworking for all ages are upwards.

**4** Students can do this orally in pairs before writing version B in their notebooks. You can then elicit version B from the students without writing it on the board. Elicit which version is better (version B) and ask them to give reasons and examples.

### Sample answer
Take those aged 50+, who had the highest proportion of teleworking. There was a rise in the rate of teleworkers from about 5 per cent in 1997 to approximately 12 per cent in 2005. The 35–49 age group saw a similar pattern, with the rate climbing to 10 per cent in 2005. Similarly, there was an increase in the rates for the 16–24 and the 25–34 age groups, who had the lowest proportions of teleworkers, from just above 0 per cent to about 2 per cent; and 3 per cent to about 6 per cent respectively. The bar chart clearly reflects the rising trend in teleworking in the selected range of professions. Construction, energy and agriculture and fishing almost all quadrupled the proportion of teleworkers.

**5** Students should do this exercise individually as a timed writing task in class. Set a 20-minute time limit, but allow students more time if necessary. When they have finished, they can compare their answers with a partner and check for mistakes. Then ask them to look at the model answer and the comments on page 166. Allow them to make any changes to their answer at this stage. Ask them to rewrite their answer with any corrections if they make too many mistakes.

### Extension
If you can display the model answer and the comments on an OHT or on the interactive whiteboard, ask students to match the comments to the text and explain why it is a good answer.

# Speaking 2  page 147

## IELTS Speaking Part 3

**1/2** Check that students understand the exercise. Monitor and give feedback on pairwork. To check comprehension, elicit the answers from the class.

### Answers
1 Less popular now than technology or science
2 I'd say that they are less so now ...
3 passport to further study
4 I think it's very popular/common, especially as ...
5 both, although not everyone is suited to languages or science
6 They are both equally important/essential, but ...

**3/4** Ensure students work with a partner they don't usually work with. Remind them to expand their answers as indicated. If students need some time to think of some ideas for expansion, allow them a minute per question.

# Writing 2  page 147

## IELTS Writing Task 2

### Aim
This section gives students an opportunity to write a full Task 2 essay after detailed preparation.

**1** After students have finished, analyse each essay question in turn, eliciting reasons from the students for their choice of ideas.

**2/3** Students can do these exercises in pairs. Collate the ideas on the board when they have finished and compare them with the sample answers below. Elicit students' opinions by taking a vote.

**Sample answers**

**2**

A Commercial benefit
  * better for business – talk in French/English to trading partners
  * communication – quicker by phone or email in a common language
  * easier overseas travel on business – can read signs, etc in, say, Japan/Russia/China
  * improved diplomatic relations – understanding of culture through language learning

B Languages for their own sake
  * personal enjoyment – satisfaction of learning a new skill
  * stimulating – keeps the brain active, like chess
  * travelling – can travel around more easily and meet people
  * studying – can use skills/language in other subjects, eg, business
  * learn about language(s) in general – helps when studying a third language

**4** This exercise can be done in pairs. Elicit students' reasons for their answers.

**Answers**

1 Learning a foreign language has great economic value.
2 As a result, trade relations can be improved enormously, showing the economic value of learning other languages. The paragraph supports the commercial benefit of learning a language.

**5** Students should write the paragraphs individually, followed by peer-checking. Read out some of the paragraphs to the class as examples, and ask them to choose which one is the best.

## IELTS Writing Task 2 Test

**6** This exercise can be done as a timed activity in class. Set a 40-minute time limit, including checking the answer. When they have finished, ask them to summarize their essay for a partner orally and then peer-correct. Discuss the model answer and the comments on page 167.

**Extension**
As a revision task, you can get students to write their own Task 2 essay questions, using the different types of questions they have encountered in the course. They can keep a list and use them for revision purposes. You can make your own list to use as supplementary materials in future courses.

## Study skills  page 149

## Writing Task 2: Planning

**1/2** These consolidation activities collect together the language of Task 2 questions and instructions. These can then be looked at in conjunction with the model answers to see the differences in what is being asked.

**3** After students have finished their plans, ask several of them to explain their answers. Point out that they can use this plan as a guide when they write. Ask students to read the Tip, and stress that the number of words is a guideline only: paragraphs do not have specific lengths.

**4** Students can make the plan on large sheets of paper. Display them so students can see each other's work and for peer-evaluation.

**5** Suggest to students that they should do this for self-study individually or in groups.

# Grammar key

## Unit 1

### Talking about the present

1  PS I do exercises in the gym every weekend.
   PC I'm doing exercises in the gym so I can't really talk now.
2  PS The airport doesn't close as it is open 24 hours a day.
   PC The airport isn't opening today at all.
3  PC She isn't working today as she's ill.
   PS She doesn't work today as it's her day off.
4  PC The river is flowing very fast today.
   PS The river has a lot of islands in the middle.
5  PS I spend the summer here every year.
   PC I am only spending the summer here this year.
6  PC Passenger numbers on trains are increasing this year.
   PS Passenger numbers on trains increase when petrol prices rise.

### Past simple

1  Did you <u>spend</u> a lot of time studying for the exam last week?
2  When he went to Canada he didn't <u>fly</u> because he was afraid of flying.
3  I <u>studied</u> science when I was at secondary school.
4  I <u>watched</u> the documentary on different cultures by myself.
5  I made a chair in a carpentry class. (correct)
6  The students asked a lot of questions about life in Melbourne. (correct)
7  I answered about 20 emails to friends on a social networking site this morning. (correct)
8  I began to learn English and Russian when I was 14. (correct)
9  How long <u>did</u> you stay in stay in the library yesterday?

## Unit 2

### Present perfect

| 2 b | 4 e | 6 g | 8 h | 10 i/a |
|-----|-----|-----|-----|--------|
| 3 a/i | 5 d | 7 j | 9 f | |

## Unit 3

### Likes/dislikes and preferences

1  I like to walk around cities because it helps me learn where everything is.
2  I love wandering around the countryside with no roads or buildings.
3  I dislike playing football and rugby as I don't like team sports.
4  As I am studying engineering, I enjoy watching documentaries on architecture.
5  My friends hate to travel by car. They generally prefer travelling by train as it's more relaxing.
6  Do people prefer living in houses or flats in your home town?
7  Some people can't bear living in the countryside as there are not enough amenities or entertainment.

### Comparative and superlative

1  larger
2  more common
3  the most exciting
4  more popular
5  better
6  most difficult

## Unit 4

### The passive

1  The old building was renovated and converted into a cinema.
2  The new houses were pulled down and the tower blocks were constructed.
3  A railway line was built and the town and the city were connected.
4  The town became larger as more people moved from the countryside.
5  The village changed dramatically over the period as the area was transformed.
6  As the population grew, many old houses were knocked down.
7  The market was demolished and replaced with a supermarket.

## Locations on maps

1 railway station
2 tower block
3 school
4 car park
5 artificial lake
6 cinema
7 supermarket

# Unit 5

## Intransitive/transitive verbs

**Sample answer**

First the mangos grow. When they ripen, the mangos are harvested. After they are crushed, the mango juice is bottled.

# Unit 6

## The future

2 The Book Show opens at 5 pm, but I won't get there until 6 pm.
3 The term ends in three weeks, but I think I'm going to stay here a little longer.
4 I'm doing a workshop at the conference on encouraging reading, which starts tomorrow.
5 E-books will change education dramatically in the future, but people are still going to use books as well.

## First conditional

1 value, will be
2 are developed, will also improve
3 are made, will appeal to
4 is given, will grow
5 are only sold, will disadvantage

# Unit 7

## Second conditional

1 *Were* children to exercise their minds more by doing problem-solving exercises, they would learn faster.
2 *The education system* would certainly be affected if subjects like psychology were not studied at university.

3 University students *need to focus on* learning for pleasure in order to be happier.
4 *As I* have a good memory, I don't have to work harder.
5 *I need to* practise speaking Russian regularly to learn to speak it fluently.
6 *Provided* people were generally more active physically and mentally, they'd have fewer health problems.

## Defining and non-defining clauses

1 The book on thinking skills that you leant me was very good.
2 Freud, who was a famous psychoanalyst, lived in London.
3 The speaker whose lecture on the human mind we went to is doing another one this week.
4 I'd like to describe a teacher who taught us how to think rather than just learn.
5 Philosophy, which many people think is difficult, is very enjoyable to study.
6 I'd like to talk about computer games, which I don't normally play as I generally don't like them.
7 Tasks which train children to use their brains should be the part of every course from primary school.
8 The subject that I found the most challenging at school was music.

# Unit 8

## Modal verbs and adjectives

1 humans won't be able to
2 it could
3 we might also
4 it's necessary for humans to
5 it's possible
6 it's possible that it will be
7 it's also likely to

# Unit 9

## Complex sentences: Concession

1 the lack of infrastructure prevents them from becoming very wealthy.
2 numeracy skills are becoming more of a problem.
3 While the standard of living is increasing in rich countries,
4 Nevertheless, I think it's inevitable.
5 many diseases are still dangerous.
6 Whilst expenditure on alternative energy is desirable,

# Unit 10

## Countable and uncountable nouns

countable: coin, apartment, orange, note, paper, bag, table, bottle, data, flat, apple, fact, detail, suitcase, chair, house
uncountable: furniture, money, music, blues, accommodation, knowledge, jazz, luggage, litter
both: space, technology, fruit, noise, plastic, business, medicine

# Unit 11

## Definite and indefinite articles

1  the, –, the, –
2  the, the
3  –, –
4  –, the, –
5  a, an, the
6  the, –, –, –

# Unit 12

## Ellipsis and substitution

1  doesn't
2  aren't/should do so
3  aren't
4  don't
5  thinks so/does
6  they should have
7  can
8  should

# Vocabulary key

## Unit 1

### Places to visit

**1**

1 countryside
2 beach
3 mountains
4 city

**2**

Students' own answers.

### Word building: Adjectives for describing places

1 Adventure holidays are exciting for people of all ages.
2 Visiting the countryside bores some people as they think there is nothing to do there, but I always find it interesting.
3 Do you think sightseeing in cities is appealing to people generally?
4 I find beaches very peaceful. Being at the seaside relaxes me.
5 Which do you think fascinates people more, exploring the countryside or visiting historical places?
6 The mountains in Peru really impressed me. I'll never forget them. The whole experience was really thrilling.

## Unit 2

### Collocations with *time*

1 Sometimes I kill time by playing games on my mobile.
2 Learning something new like a language takes time.
3 Time drags when life is boring.
4 Waiting for buses in cities can waste time. It's better to walk!
5 I never have time to surf on the Internet. I'm always too busy.
6 For me time flies when I'm in class. I love it.
7 Using computers saves time so people have more time for other activities.

### Synonyms

Technology has changed the entertainment and leisure world enormously. First of all, technology such as the latest mobiles and tablets, which the public find **fascinating,** are **important** means of entertainment, especially among young people. New tablets are **efficient** devices for storing and delivering not just music and films, but also games and books. This makes them very **practical.**

Some people argue that technology can be **harmful** to people's health, but devices like tablets are **helpful**, as there is no need to carry lots of heavy materials like CDs and books around. People find them very **enjoyable** to hold just like books. This helps explain why they are so appealing.

## Unit 3

### Collocations: Words related to organizing

**1**

**Sample answers**

1 plan a trip abroad, an exciting party, a long journey, an important meeting, an essay, events like conferences
2 sort out my room, letters and papers
3 tidy up my room, letters and papers
4 organize a trip abroad, an exciting party, an important meeting, events like conferences
5 prepare letters and papers, an essay

**2**

Students' own answers.

### Collocations: General nouns

1 Investment in transport can bring economic benefit to rural areas of a country.
2 Railways establish a strong link between remote towns.
3 Reducing the number of weapons is a key factor in contributing to world peace.
4 People's surroundings have a major effect on their mood.

# Unit 4

## Nouns and verbs

**1**

| | | | |
|---|---|---|---|
| 1 | replace | 5 | convert |
| 2 | expansion | 6 | extension |
| 3 | growth | 7 | develop |
| 4 | transform | 8 | construction |

**2**

1 An extension was added to the leisure centre.
2 My neighbourhood was completely transformed.
3 The economy has grown rapidly in the last decade.
4 The large house underwent conversion into a hotel.
5 The motorway was constructed very quickly.
6 The town experienced slow development over the years./There was slow development in the town .../ Slow development occurred in the town ...
7 There was no change in the street over the period./No change(s) took place/occurred in the street ...

# Unit 5

## Word building: Adjectives and nouns

**1**

| | | | |
|---|---|---|---|
| 1 | disappointed | 4 | relaxed |
| 2 | amazed | 5 | satisfied |
| 3 | fascinated | | |

**2**

| | | | |
|---|---|---|---|
| 1 | disappointment | 4 | relaxation |
| 2 | amazement | 5 | satisfaction |
| 3 | fascination | | |

## Cause and effect

1 The increase in private vehicles is harming city life.
2 Knowing foreign languages makes travelling easier.
3 TV plays a smaller role in our lives than in the past.
4 Education can improve people's career prospects.
5 Electronic communication has a huge impact on businesses.

## Process language: Nouns and verbs

**1**

fruit, eg, oranges, pineapples, apples, coconuts or anything that can be made into a liquid, eg, carrots, beetroot

**2**

**Sample answer**

At the first stage the carrots are harvested. The next stage is transportation where they are taken to a factory. At the sorting stage, the carrots are sorted or graded. Then the carrots are processed to make juice. The juice is then bottled and stored. At the next stage, the bottled juice is delivered to shops and supermarkets to be sold.

# Unit 6

## Collocations related to reading

1 are easier to read
2 become keen readers of
3 read much nowadays compared to the past
4 young people have to read widely
5 some may become fast readers

## Collocations: Evaluating adjectives

1 b   2 d(c)   3 f   4 a   5 c(d)   6 e

# Unit 7

## Collocations: Technology

In recent years, a **technological** revolution has been taking place around the world. **Advanced** technology **such as state-of-the-art computers** now plays an important role in our lives. It has changed the way people work, so that most people applying for jobs need **a wide variety of** skills. For example, workers need to understand the latest **innovations in** technology in the workplace like new software and **be able to use** new devices. As technology **develops and** becomes more widespread, people's lives will be improved enormously.

## Word building: Nouns and adjectives

| | | | |
|---|---|---|---|
| 1 | imagination | 5 | intelligence |
| 2 | flexible | 6 | able |
| 3 | creativity | 7 | talent |
| 4 | gifted | | |

# Unit 8

## Adjectives and nouns related to the environment

**1**

1 industrial
2 commercial
3 built-up
4 residential
5 urban
6 rural

**2**

Students' own answers.

## Collocations: Research

1 moneyed
2 carried
3 scheme
4 big
5 nowadays
6 Joining
7 fix

# Unit 9

## Words and phrases related to *pay*

1 I believe we pay **too** much for using the Internet, but soon it may be free. (missing word)
2 **Pay** and conditions should be good for all workers. (wrong word form)
3 I'd like a job that pays **well** when I finish studying at university. (wrong word)
4 Although credits cards are common, I like to pay by cash **for** small and large items. (missing preposition)
5 I don't think it's safe to pay for goods **electronically** or online. (wrong word form)
6 Cash **payments** will be around for a long time to come. (wrong word form)
7 Students should not pay for their education. They definitely shouldn't **pay university fees**. (additional preposition)

## Opinion

Sample answers

1 Personally, I feel life was cheaper in the past, because ...
2 Yes, definitely. In my opinion, people focus too much on money nowadays.
3 Yes, as far as I'm concerned, countries should help each other.

4 Yes, from my point of view it helps enormously.
5 No. I think that subjects like languages are just as important as economic courses.

# Unit 10

## Noun phrases: *Nature* and *natural*

**Sample answers**

1 A nature reserve is a place such a bird sanctuary or safari park where animals are protected.
2 Natural resources are items such as oil and gas which come from nature and which can be used by humans.
3 Natural ingredients are natural, raw products like oranges or potatoes that have not been processed.
4 A natural habitat is a place where a creature lives, for example a bird in a tree in the countryside or in the roof of a house.
5 A nature study is a study of plants or animals such as flowers or insects which children can do at school.
6 A natural state is a state where nothing such as artificial ingredients have been added.
7 A natural ability is something which cannot be learnt. It is something people possess naturally.

## Word and phrase building: *Advantage* and *disadvantage*

1 supportive, e
2 help, f
3 benefits, c/d
4 preventative, a
5 disadvantageous, c/d

# Unit 11

## Art

**1**

performance: live, dance, artist, stage

**2**

festival: annual, organizers, arts, programme
exhibition: of (art), hall, house (v), space
event: important, happy, organizers, management

## Collocations: Communication

A Electronic **communication is** here to stay. Each year different methods of **communication** become available. However, there are often so many different varieties to choose from that selecting one is difficult.

B The disadvantage of relying on electronic and non-verbal **communication** such as email and text messaging is that they can be easily misunderstood. Sometimes, breakdowns in **communication** also occur, when electronic devices like mobiles or laptops do not work. Developments in video technology, however, can now help overcome such **communication** difficulties or problems.

C In the modern world, the fact that we can have instant **communication** with anywhere in the world thanks to satellite **communication** is a benefit to the public, but especially to business. However, mass **communication** does not mean that everyone will communicate properly, so training in **communication** skills is relevant for everyone.

# 1 Finding out about the world

## Spot the differences

### Student A
Look at your graph and describe it to Student B. Make notes about what Student B tells you and try to find differences between the information. You should not look at each other's data.

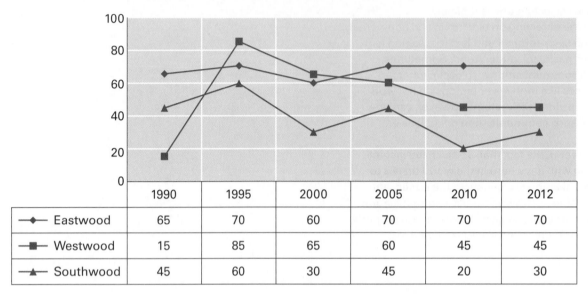

| | 1990 | 1995 | 2000 | 2005 | 2010 | 2012 |
|---|---|---|---|---|---|---|
| Eastwood | 65 | 70 | 60 | 70 | 70 | 70 |
| Westwood | 15 | 85 | 65 | 60 | 45 | 45 |
| Southwood | 45 | 60 | 30 | 45 | 20 | 30 |

### Student B
Look at your chart and describe it to Student A. Make notes about what Student A tells you and try to find differences between the information. You should not look at each other's data.

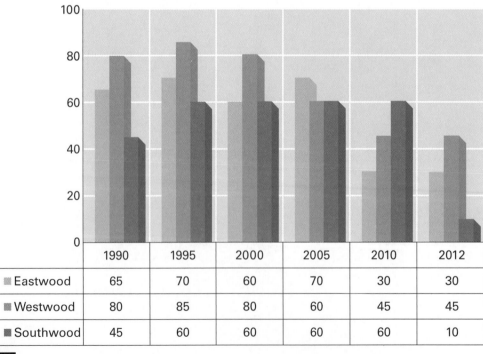

| | 1990 | 1995 | 2000 | 2005 | 2010 | 2012 |
|---|---|---|---|---|---|---|
| Eastwood | 65 | 70 | 60 | 70 | 30 | 30 |
| Westwood | 80 | 85 | 80 | 60 | 45 | 45 |
| Southwood | 45 | 60 | 60 | 60 | 60 | 10 |

## 2  In search of time

### How did you …?

**1** Choose one of the items in the table and write at least five questions using these phrases.
Has it …?
When was it? When did it happen?
What happened?
Why was it …? What made it …? What did you …?
Why did it …?
Why did you …?
How did you …?
Where was it? Who was it?

| | | |
|---|---|---|
| 1  a weekend where you have killed time | 2  something useful you have bought in the past month | 3  a fascinating place you have visited |
| 4  a period when time has dragged | 5  an interesting experience you have had | 6  a period when time has flown |
| 7  an important event that has taken place recently | 8  an enjoyable event that has happened recently | 9  something that has taken a long time |
| 10  something exciting that has happened to you in the last month | 11  someone you have found very helpful | 12  a place where you have spent a lot of time |

**2** Work in pairs. Give your questions to your partner and take turns to ask each other the questions. When you answer, give reasons and examples.
Useful expressions
It was so interesting because …
I found it …, as it was …
It was an invaluable experience because …
What made it interesting/useful/exciting/enjoyable was …

**3** Choose another item from the table. Ask your partner questions about it without preparation. Then swap roles.

# 3 Giving structure to our world

## Completing a text

### Student A

**1** Think of questions you can ask to complete the text below.

> There are 1 ..................... factors involved in choosing where to go
> on holiday nowadays. The 2 ..................... factor for many people
> is the type of holiday that they want to have. Some people want
> to relax by sitting on the beach 3 ..................... . Others want an
> adventure holiday 4 ..................... . Another 5 ..................... factor
> is the cost. Parents 6 ..................... nowadays need to think of the
> expense of paying 7 ..................... a long way from home.

**2** Ask Student B your questions and complete the text.

**3** Listen to Student B read the paragraph and check your answers.
Discuss how the text has been improved.

-----------------------------------------------------------✂

### Student B

**1** Complete the text with these words.

> for journeys and holidays    crucial    in a hot location such
> as the Seychelles    main    many    where they are climbing
> mountains and exploring jungles    with children

> There are 1 ..................... factors involved in choosing where to go
> on holiday nowadays. The 2 ..................... factor for many people
> is the type of holiday that they want to have. Some people want
> to relax by sitting on the beach 3 ..................... . Others want an
> adventure holiday 4 ..................... . Another 5 ..................... factor
> is the cost. Parents 6 ..................... nowadays need to think of the
> expense of paying 7 ..................... a long way from home.

**2** Answer Student A's questions about the text.

**3** Read the paragraph to Student A. Discuss how the text has been improved.

**112**

# 4 The land

## My town

### Student A

1 Cut out the images of places below and put them on the map.
  Give your town a name and a date.

2 Work with a partner. Describe the location of the places on your map.

3 Compare your map with Student B's map.
  Discuss any differences.

4 Swap roles and repeat the process.

- - - - - - - - - - - - - - - - - - - - - - - - - - - - - - - - - - - - - - - - - - - - - - - - - - - - - - -

### Student B

1 Cut out the images of places.

2 Listen to Student A describe his/her map.
  Put the places in the locations he/she describes.

3 Compare your map with Student A's map.
  Discuss any differences.

4 Swap roles and repeat the process.

- - - - - - - - - - - - - - - - - - - - - - - - - - - - - - - - - - - - - - - - - - - - - - - - - - - - - - -

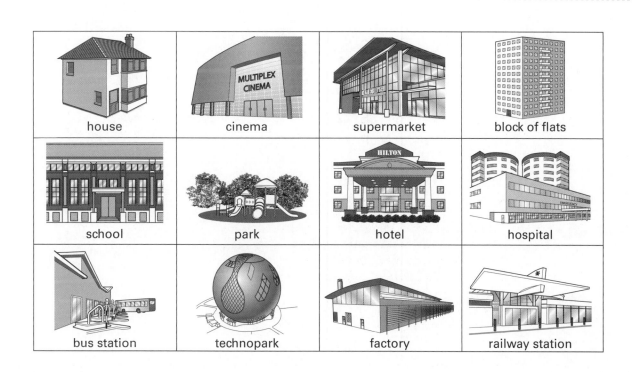

**113**

PHOTOCOPIABLE

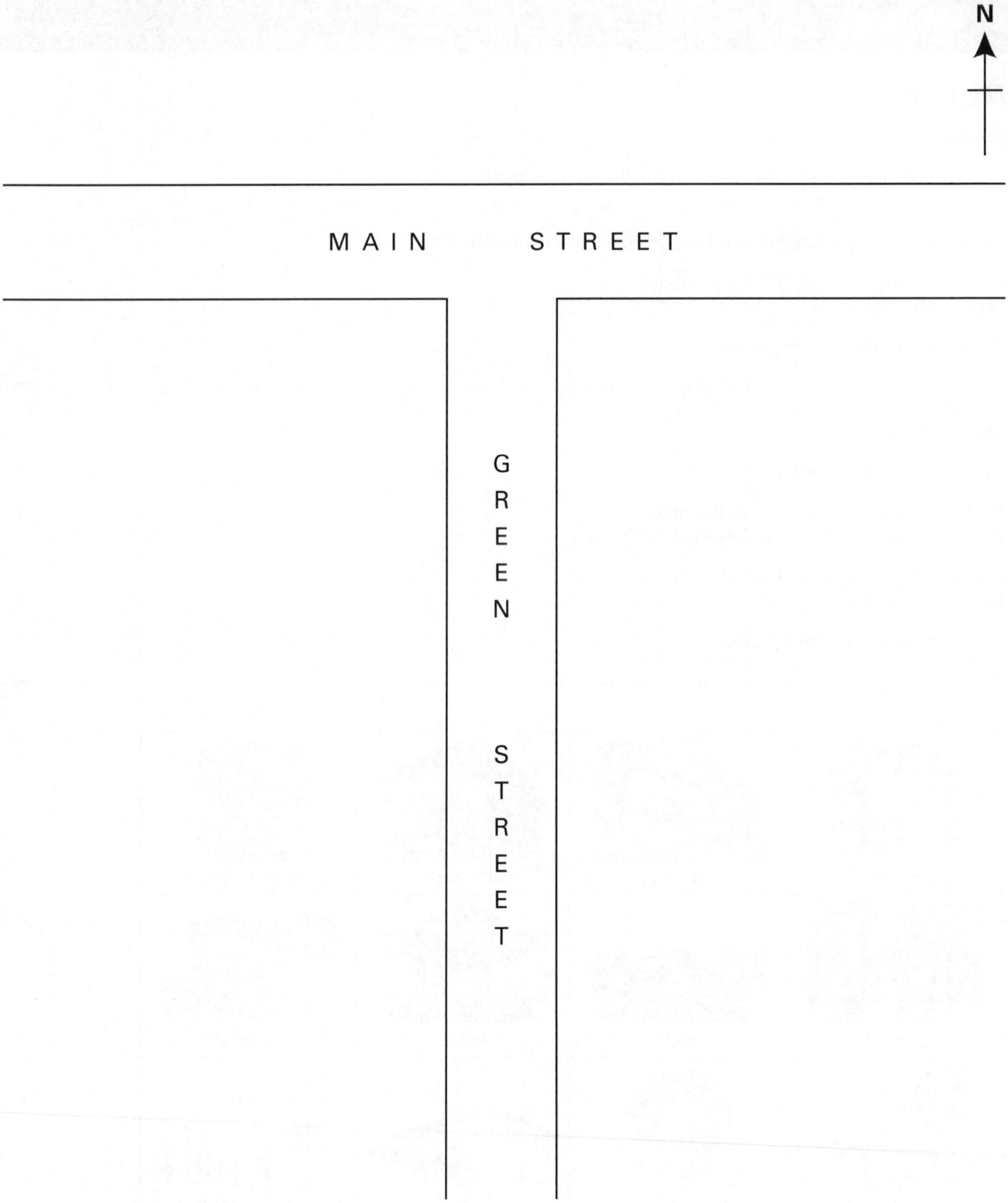

N

MAIN     STREET

G
R
E
E
N

S
T
R
E
E
T

Map of _____ Year_____

PHOTOCOPIABLE

# 5 The processes of life

## Buying a book online

**1** Work in pairs. Number the steps in the process of purchasing a book online.

B  the taking of the package to the post office

G  the reading of the book

C  paying for the book by credit card

D  accessing the website of an online bookshop

H  the recycling of the book/donation to a charity shop for resale

E  the opening of the parcel

A  the packaging of the book in the warehouse

K  the selection of a book

I  the arrival of the package to the buyer

F  the recycling of the packaging

J  the sorting of the package

M  keeping the book

L  the return of the book, if not satisfied

**2** Write the letter for each stage next to the line in which it occurs. Then compare your answers with your partner.

The diagram shows the stages involved in purchasing a book from an online bookshop for personal use.
It is clear that there are a number of stages involved in the process.
The first stage is accessing the website of an online bookshop.  1 __
Once a book is selected, it is purchased online and is paid for by  2 __ 3 __
credit card. The book is then packaged in the warehouse and  4 __
taken to the post office. When the package is sorted at the  5 __ 6 __
post office, it is then put into a van for delivery to the customer.  7 __
Then, the package is opened. If the customer is not satisfied the book  8 __
can be returned. If the customer keeps the book, the packaging is  9 __ 10 __
recycled and the book is read. The final stage is where the book  11 __ 12 __
is recycled or donated to a charity shop where it is resold.  13 __

**3** Work in pairs and ask each other questions about the process.
*What happens at the first/next/final stage? What happens first/next/after that?*

# 6 Read what you want

## I read them a lot because …

**1** Work in pairs. Add reasons A–D to the most appropriate boxes 1–4. Give reasons for your answer.

A They are often full of information that is very light and not very serious. They're often full of gossip.

B They really fire the imagination, even though they are really old stories like *Pride and Prejudice* by Jane Austen.

C But perhaps the main reason I like them is that books like history or geography books help me to understand the world.

D I read one every day because they are very stimulating and keep me up-to-date with world affairs.

| Types of reading material | Reason 1 | Reason 2 | Reason 3 |
|---|---|---|---|
| newspapers | 1 | They are also educational as they help me improve my reading skills. | If reading newspapers is encouraged in class, we can get a lot of ideas from them. |
| magazines | I don't read these as often as the topics don't interest me. | 2 | I can't afford to buy them, so I only read them if I find one on the train. |
| novels | I read them a lot because I find them really satisfying. | 3 | I also find novels enjoyable because reading them is a very good way to pass the time. |
| factual books | The kind of factual books that I like are history books because they are so interesting. | They are also invaluable for expanding your general knowledge. | 4 |

**2** Choose one of the types of reading material and with your partner take turns to give reasons why you like (or dislike) reading such material. You could also talk about reading comics, science fiction, romance, websites or blogs.

# 7 The mind

## A healthy mind

### Student A

**1** Study your table, which shows the results in percentages of a survey on the attitudes of various age groups to a range of factors for maintaining a healthy mind. Ask Student B questions to complete your table.

**Factors for maintaining a healthy mind (percentage of respondents)**

| Factors | Age 15–25 | Age 26–40 | Age 41–60 |
|---|---|---|---|
| Reading | 50 | | 70 |
| Watching TV | | | 30 |
| Socializing | 44 | 30 | |
| Puzzles (crossword puzzles and Sudoku) | | 78 | |
| Physical exercise | | 60 | 85 |
| Food | | | 80 |
| Computer games | 70 | | 20 |
| Other | 20 | 35 | 20 |

### Student B

**1** Study your table, which shows the results in percentages of a survey on the attitudes of various age groups to a range of factors for maintaining a healthy mind. Ask Student A questions to complete your table.

**Factors for maintaining a healthy mind (percentage of respondents)**

| Factors | Age 15–25 | Age 26–40 | Age 41–60 |
|---|---|---|---|
| Reading | | 65 | |
| Watching TV | 40 | 25 | |
| Socializing | | | 60 |
| Puzzles (crossword puzzles and Sudoku) | 70 | | 80 |
| Physical exercise | 15 | | |
| Food | 23 | 37 | |
| Computer games | | 35 | |
| Other | | | |

# 8 A world with water

## The charts show ...

**Student A**

1  Ask Student B questions to complete the text below.
2  Compare your text with Student B's charts. Discuss any differences.
3  Listen to Student B describing the charts. If necessary, refer to the text below and offer him/her help and suggestions.

> The charts show the numbers of visit in thousands on a yearly basis to three venues at the seaside between 2005 and 2010 along with the satisfaction rating in 2010.
>
> It is clear that the three venues have very different patterns of attendance with the ship museum proving to be the most popular at the end of the period. The trend for the ship museum was upward throughout the period, rising from approximately **1** ..................... visitors in 2005 to about **2** ..................... in 2010. By contrast, the reverse pattern can be seen for the marine park, where there was a fall in attendance during the six-year period from around **3** ..................... to just around **4** ..................... , a drop of approximately **5** ..................... per cent. While the ship museum and the marine park had very distinct patterns of attendance, the number of visitors to the aquarium fluctuated considerably between about **6** ..................... and **7** ..................... visitors. However, the attendance ended the period at about 55,000 visitors.
>
> It is clear that visitors to the three venues were happy with their experience with **8** ............ per cent overall being either very satisfied or satisfied.

--------------------------------------------------------------------------------✂

**Student B**

1  Study the two charts below. Answer Student A's questions.
2  Compare your charts with Student A's text. Discuss any differences.
3  Describe the charts, without looking at Student A's text.

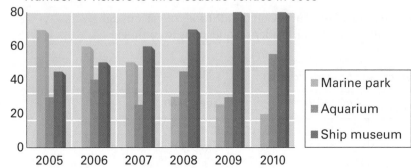

Number of visitors to three seaside venues in 000s

Chart 1

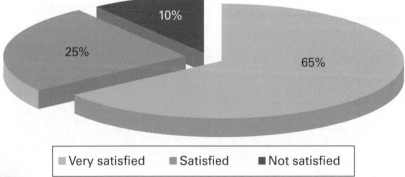

Satisfaction rating for the three seaside venues, 2010

Chart 2

# 9 Finance

## I try to pay for everything electronically

**1** Work in groups of three. Match 1–7 to A–G.

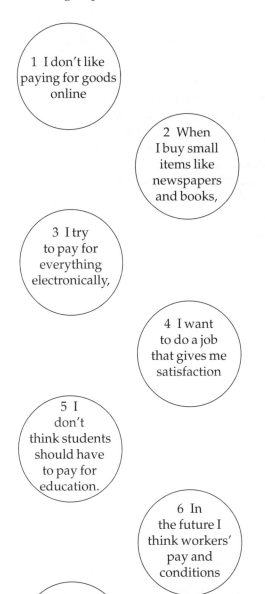

1 I don't like paying for goods online

2 When I buy small items like newspapers and books,

3 I try to pay for everything electronically,

4 I want to do a job that gives me satisfaction

5 I don't think students should have to pay for education.

6 In the future I think workers' pay and conditions

7 I don't mind paying for entertainment

A as I don't think it's safe.

B It should be free.

C as it helps me relax.

D will improve dramatically.

E I usually pay cash.

F so I don't have to carry lots of coins.

G rather than one that pays well.

**2** Student A: Select one of the items 1–7 at random and speak about it for one minute. Students B and C: Ask Student A questions about what he/she says, eg, *You said that … Can you explain a bit more about it?*

**3** Swap roles and repeat exercise 2.

## 10 Nature and science

### Countable and uncountable nouns

**1** Work in pairs. Use the hints 1–14 to decide what the missing word is in each case. Do not write the words down. Then take turns to read the text to each other, supplying the missing words.

> Listening to 1 _____ (uncountable noun) brings a number of 2 _____ (countable noun). For example, 3 _____ (pronoun) can help people to relax, which is enormously 4 _____ (positive adjective connected with *benefit*) in the modern world. If people have stressful 5 _____ (countable noun), playing a musical 6 _____ (countable noun) such as the violin, the guitar or the piano as a hobby can 7 _____ (verb) people stop thinking about their work. As a result, they are healthier. 8 _____ (an uncountable noun), however, can have various 9 _____ (countable noun). If people are living in 10 _____ (uncountable noun) such as flats, they can annoy their 11 _____ (countable noun) if they play 12 _____ (uncountable noun) too loud. 13 _____ (demonstrative pronoun) can damage people's 14 _____ (uncountable noun).

**2** Choose a topic for your partner to talk about for two minutes. Then swap roles.

**Beat the clock**

| | | |
|---|---|---|
| the advantage of doing research | the problem of crime | the importance of knowledge |
| the benefits of research | the danger of electronic waste | the problem of rubbish in the street |
| the benefit of travelling | the disadvantages of technology | the importance of nature |
| the benefits of science | the importance of water | the advantages of speaking another language |

## 11 Culture and the arts

### Articles

**1** Work in pairs. Decide whether the statements 1–13 contain a mistake relating to the use of the article: *a/an/the* or –. Correct the mistakes.

| | Agree | Disagree |
|---|---|---|
| 1 Government should invest more money in arts. | | |
| 2 I like the paintings and sculpture generally, but I don't like the works of modern artists. | | |
| 3 The art should be compulsory at primary and secondary school. | | |
| 4 Cultural events such as the festivals should be encouraged. | | |
| 5 The arts are as important as science in school curriculum. | | |
| 6 Performing arts such as the drama and dance are not serious subjects to study. | | |
| 7 Entrance to all museums should be free. | | |
| 8 Children should be encouraged to read book per week. | | |
| 9 Watching a good film is enjoyable and relaxing. | | |
| 10 I enjoy watching plays more than films. | | |
| 11 Theatres should be subsidized by a taxpayer. | | |
| 12 An education in the arts is useful. | | |
| 13 The arts will become less important in the future. | | |

**2** Conduct a class survey asking as many fellow students as you can whether they agree with the statements.

*Do you agree that the government should invest more money in the arts?*

**3** Discuss the findings of your survey.

## 12 Communication and language

### I don't find it difficult to …

**1** Study the statements below and decide how to respond using the following:

(But) I do/don't/wouldn't

I can't/could/couldn't/have/haven't/am/am not/will

But my sister/brother/(not) many people do/does/can/could/have/did/are/aren't

But … are

Mine is/isn't

**2** Work in pairs, Student A and Student B.

Student A: read the sentences one after the other.

Student B: respond without looking at the page.

Swap roles and repeat the process.

**3** Continue repeating the process until you can respond automatically.

---

**Statements**

1 I don't find it difficult to use the computer.

2 I'd love to learn Chinese or Japanese.

3 Some people can speak two or three languages.

4 Some children couldn't sit and watch TV for a long time when I was child.

5 I could create a computer game easily.

6 I have visited many tourist places in this country.

7 I think all adults whatever the age should learn to use computers.

8 Computers aren't changing as fast as they used to.

9 I'm not studying to go to university.

10 I won't return to the course next term.

11 People generally like travelling and seeing new places.

12 When I speak on the phone, I am usually quite shy.

13 My video phone is very modern.

14 I'm planning to stay in London during the holidays.

15 Some people don't write letters anymore.

---

# Answer key to photocopiable activities

## Unit 1

Differences: Eastwood 2010, 2012; Westwood 1990, 2000; Southwood 2000, 2005, 2010, 2012

## Unit 2

**1** (Sample answer) A weekend where you have killed time: *When was it? When did it happen? What did you do? How did you kill time? Why did you kill time?*

## Unit 3

### Student A

#### 1/2

1 How many factors?
2 What kind of factor?
3 Where is the beach?
4 What do you mean by adventure holiday?
5 What kind of factor?
6 With whom?
7 Paying for what?

### Student B

#### 1

1 many
2 main
3 in a hot location such as the Seychelles
4 where they are climbing mountains and exploring jungles
5 crucial
6 with children
7 for journeys and holidays

## Unit 4

Students' own answers.

## Unit 5

### 1/2

| | | | | |
|---|---|---|---|---|
| 1 D | 4 A | 6 J | 8 E | 10 M | 12 G |
| 2 K | 5 B | 7 I | 9 L | 11 F | 13 H |
| 3 C | | | | | |

## Unit 6

### 1

1 D    2 A    3 B    4 C

## Unit 7

| Factors | Age 15–25 | Age 26–40 | Age 41–60 |
|---|---|---|---|
| Reading | 50 | 65 | 70 |
| Watching TV | 40 | 25 | 30 |
| Socializing | 44 | 30 | 60 |
| Puzzles (crossword puzzles and Sudoku) | 70 | 78 | 80 |
| Physical exercise | 15 | 60 | 85 |
| Food | 23 | 37 | 80 |
| Computer games | 70 | 35 | 20 |
| Other | 20 | 35 | 20 |

## Unit 8

| | | |
|---|---|---|
| 1 45,000 | 4 20,000 | 7 55,000 |
| 2 80,000 | 5 66 | 8 90 |
| 3 70,000 | 6 30,000 | |

## Unit 9

### 1

1 A    2 E    3 F    4 G    5 B    6 D    7 C

## Unit 10

### 1

| | |
|---|---|
| 1 music | 8 Music |
| 2 advantages | 9 disadvantages |
| 3 it | 10 accommodation |
| 4 beneficial | 11 neighbours |
| 5 jobs | 12 music |
| 6 instrument | 13 This |
| 7 help | 14 health/relationships |

## Unit 11

### 1

1 **The** government should invest more money in **the** arts.
2 I like **the** paintings and sculpture generally, but I don't like the works of modern artists.
3 ~~The~~ Art should be compulsory at primary and secondary school.
4 Cultural events such as **the** festivals should be encouraged.
5 The arts are as important as science in **the** school curriculum.
6 Performing arts such as **the** drama and dance are not serious subjects to study.
7 Entrance to all museums should be free. (correct)
8 Children should be encouraged to read **a** book per week.
9 Watching a good film is enjoyable and relaxing. (correct)
10 I enjoy watching plays more than films. (correct)
11 Theatres should be subsidized by **the** taxpayer.
12 An education in the arts is useful. (correct)
13 The arts will become less important in the future. (correct)

## Unit 12

1 (But) I do/But most of us do/But my brother does.
2 I wouldn't/So would I.
3 (But) I can't/and I'd like to.
4 But I could.
5 I couldn't (but I'd like to).
6 I haven't.
7 I don't (think so).
8 But mobiles are.
9 I am.
10 I will/may.
11 (But) I don't.
12 I'm not.
13 Mine isn't.
14 I'm not.
15 I do.

# Macmillan Exams Portal

- Detailed overview of all English language exams
- Exams news
- Author videos
- Student and teacher course material recommendations and more...

# Apps for IELTS

This new range of Apps offers an innovative approach to preparing students for the IELTS exams. With a wealth of interactive content written by Sam McCarter, author of bestselling *Ready for IELTS* and the new lower-level *IELTS Introduction*, the apps focus on the skills needed for success at IELTS as well as providing a complete range of exam-type practice exercises.

### Key Features

- Covers areas such as reading speed, ability to respond effectively to the examiner and self-correcting in the writing paper
- Students can measure their progress by interacting with 'can do' statements linked to key skills areas

**For more information, visit www.macmillaneducationapps.com**

Apps for
**IELTS**

Courtesy of Apple Inc

## www.macmillanexams.com

# IELTS ESSENTIALS FROM

## IELTS Introduction

Sam McCarter

### Taking your first IELTS steps

▸ 12 units packed with exercises aimed at developing listening, speaking, reading and writing skills

▸ Essential IELTS task tips

▸ Collocation exercises

▸ Model answers for writing tasks

## IELTS Foundation
### Second Edition

Andrew Preshous / Rachael Roberts
Joanna Preshous / Joanne Gakonga

▸ For students aiming for IELTS band 4-5.5

▸ This course provides a comprehensive package, including extra self-study material that means students will achieve success with confidence and ease

▸ The scaffolding of the grammar allows clear strategies to be developed as students move from lower to higher bands

▸ Supported by a Teacher's Book with sample answers, photocopiables, full answer keys and recording scripts

▸ Includes Class Audio CDs

## IELTS Graduation

Mark Allen / Debra Powell / Dickie Dolby

▸ This focused, topic-based book will train the students in the skills required to achieve a high IELTS score

▸ Language Focus, Writing and Pronunciation sections build up the students' confidence and competence in these skills

▸ Strategy and tip boxes offer hints on how to tackle the various IELTS tasks

▸ The Student's Book is supported by the Teacher's Book with full information on all parts of the exam

# MACMILLAN EXAMS

## Ready for IELTS

Sam McCarter

This IELTS preparation course combines the successful elements of the 'Ready for...' series and an experienced author team to ensure students aiming for IELTS bands 5–6.5 are ready for success.

### Key Features

- Two-page review section at the end of each unit with exam-style tasks
- 'Ready for...' sections focus on each IELTS exam paper, giving extra support and tips
- Special emphasis on word building, collocations and phrasal verbs, paraphrasing, synonyms and polysemy
- Topic-based wordlists
- Model answers, graded by an examiner, provide excellent support for writing

## Tips for IELTS

Sam McCarter

This slim, definitive little book is packed full of all the information you need to know about the four skills tested in IELTS: hints on how to tackle specific types of questions; strategies on how to avoid common mistakes, and increase speed and accuracy; and useful language to be aware of and to use. This is the sort of book that can be used for quick reference, for revising and for checking progress.

## IELTS Language Practice

Michael Vince // Amanda French

An in-depth, detailed approach to English grammar and vocabulary.

A thorough and comprehensive series that ensures students' confidence with language through the progressive levels.

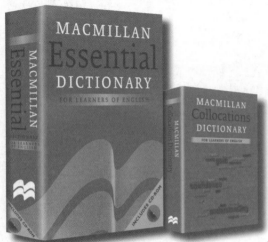

# Flavors of Tuscany

# Flavors of Italy

Sara Vignozzi
Gabriella Ganugi

# Tuscany

MᶜRAE BOOKS

Revised edition © 2008

Copyright © McRae Books Srl 1999

ISBN 978-88-89272-00-8

This book was conceived, edited and designed by
McRae Books Srl, Via del Salviatino 1 - 50016 Fiesole, Florence, Italy
info@mcraebooks.com

Text: Sara Vignozzi
Photography: Marco Lanza
Home Economist: Rosalba Gioffrè
Design: Marco Nardi
Layouts: Ornella Fassio, Adriano Nardi, Adina Stefania Dragomir, Sara Mathews
Translation from the Italian: Sara Harris
Editing: Alison Leach, Anne McRae, Mollie Thomson, Helen Farrell

2 4 6 8 10 9 7 5 3

Color separations: Fotolito Toscana, Florence, Italy
Printed and bound in Italy

# Contents

# Introduction

The origins of Tuscan cooking date back almost 3,000 years to when the region was settled by the Etruscans, a mysterious people who are thought to have migrated to central Italy from Asia Minor. Their tombs contain beautiful frescoes showing, among other things, *pappardelle* (noodles), pasta wheels for cutting pasta, colanders, cheese graters, grilled steaks, and even *Schiacciata con l'Uva* (Black Grape Sweet Bread—see recipe, page 104). Other frescoes show Etruscan diners reclining elegantly, plates and wine goblets in hand being served by graceful young men and women while musicians play nearby.

Etruscan civilization was eclipsed by the growth of Rome to the south and by the 3rd century BC the ancient region of Etruria had been absorbed into the Roman Republic. Something of Roman cookery has come down to us in the form of a cookbook containing five hundred recipes written or collected by Marcus Gavius Apicio in about 30 BC. None of the dishes described have survived, mainly because they relied heavily on spices and flavorings (at least ten in each recipe) and made generous use of a strong fish sauce, known as *garum*, which was smothered over everything in much the same way as some people use ketchup today.

The Roman world was destroyed by Germanic invaders in the 5th century. Florence and the other villages and towns of Tuscany endured their share of invasion and sacking; population declined and people moved away from the cities, back to the country. Many of Tuscany's most typical dishes date to this time. Starving peasants filled up on bread which was made without salt, a precious import that only the wealthy could afford. Tuscan bread is *sciarpo* (saltless) to this day. Servants in the great halls of the feudal lords learned to make nourishing soups and toasts with the scraps of meat- and oil-flavored bread their

The founding of the city of Florence is traditionally dated to 59 BC, when the Romans established a colony on the northern bank of the Arno, at a place where the river could be forded easily. The Romans in Tuscany, like their counter-parts elsewhere, are notorious for their banquets when rare and costly delicacies were served more with the aim of impressing guests than flattering their tastebuds. Menus included absurd dishes, such as the tongues of parrots and flamingoes, and peacocks' brains. Everyday food was more sober, based on cereals, fish, vegetables, and cheese.

In central Tuscany the wealth of Siena was based on trading cloth, locally produced saffron, wine, wax, and spices of all kinds. Like Florence, Siena was a republic, governed by powerful guilds rather than feudal lords. One of the best-known late-medieval frescoes was painted in Siena by Ambrogio Lorenzetti in 1337–39. Called *The Effects of Good and Bad Government*, it gives a complete and lively picture of life in the town and country. The detail above shows *Good Government in the Country* with peasants busily plowing, harvesting, fishing, and hunting.

lords left them. *Ribollita* (see recipe, page 31) and *Crostini toscani* (see recipe, page 15), are thought to be modern versions of these early medieval dishes.

These difficult centuries passed and by the 12th century the population had grown again, cities were flourishing, and trade and exchange of every sort reached far and wide. The larger cities of Tuscany became independent city-states, fighting among themselves for supremacy and control of valuable trade routes. As people grew richer, larger kitchens were installed in houses and cooking generally became more refined. The use of the fork was introduced in Florence during the 14th century, well before many other parts of Italy and Europe. A recipe book from the 14th century by an anonymous Tuscan cook lists fifty-seven recipes, many of which are quite familiar to modern cooks. Dishes include *ravioli*, *tortelli*, *maccheroni*, herbal pies, and marzipan.

During the 15th century the Medici family came to the fore in Florence, gradually taking over the government of the city and then the rest of Tuscany. Lorenzo the Magnificent ruled over a splendid court where fine food and drink were considered part of the new Renaissance way of life (see pages 76–77). Although the last of the Medici rulers in the 17th-18th centuries were mainly dreary religious bigots, the cities of Tuscany continued to celebrate traditional non-religious feast days, such as the *Palio* (a horse race through the city streets, still held twice each summer in Siena), flag twirling and throwing contests, archery, jousting, and football. Religious festivals included Christmas, *Carnevale*, Easter, the Virgin Mary's birth date, the date of the Annunciation, and many others. Most of these traditional festivals are still celebrated today. Now, as then, each occasion is marked by its own special array of dishes, and culinary lore and traditions (see pages 90–91).

When the last member of the Medici family died in 1737, Tuscany passed under the control of the Austrian Grand Dukes of Lorraine and, between 1799 and 1814, under the French when Napoleon defeated the Austrians. Local cooking was eclipsed under Napoleon and it was at this time that many French food words entered Italian, such as "menu," "restaurant," "café," "soirée," "dessert," and others.

Foreign rule of Tuscany ended in 1859 and the region became a part of the newly united Kingdom of Italy in 1860. Florence was capital of Italy from 1861 to 1875. The city was greatly damaged by the remodelling it was given for its new, prestigious role. The Old Market in the city center was destroyed, and many of the traditional trattorias and simple eating houses and their centuries-long tradition simply disappeared. Cooking at this time tended towards the pretentious and over-refined, having lost the dignity of its native heritage.

Tuscany lived its period of greatest glory during the Renaissance, which was practically invented in the region. This detail of a fresco, by Sodoma, comes from the abbey of Monte Oliveto Maggiore, in the province of Siena.

Fresh food and produce markets, as well as seasonal festivals, are held daily throughout Tuscany.

EMILIA ROMAGNA

TUSCANY

Carrara
Massa

Pistoia
Prato

MARCHES

Lucca

FLORENCE

Pisa

Livorno

Gorgona

Arezzo

Siena

TYRRHENIAN SEA

UMBRIA

Capraia

Grosseto

ELBA

Pianosa

LATIUM

Montecristo
Giglio
Giannutri

Since then Tuscan cooking has returned to its rural, peasant roots. It relies on the use of the finest and freshest of local ingredients prepared with care, but ideally brought to table as close as possible to the way Nature herself made them. Uncomplicated dishes are cooked simply and given extra taste by the use of local herbs, such as basil, rosemary, thyme, parsley, and sage. Meat and fish are typically broiled (grilled) or roasted with plenty of oil and herbs, or gently simmered in oil or a vegetable-based sauce until the meat is tender and flavorful. Meat, fish, and vegetables are also deep-fried in the region's excellent olive oil.

Pasta dishes are less common than in other regions. Tuscan first courses are often bread-based preparations, such as *Pappa al pomodoro* (see recipe, page 32), *Panzanella* (see recipe, page 29) and *Ribollita* (see recipe, page 31), or broth with beans or fava beans (broad beans) and a little pasta (*Pasta e ceci*—see recipe page 34).

*Bistecca alla fiorentina* (see recipe, page 78) is probably the most well-known Tuscan main course. For lovers of red meat it is the ultimate treat. Beef, veal, pork, and lamb are the most common meats, but there are also many dishes based on duck, rabbit, and other game. Fresh fish is plentiful along the coast and local traditions make the best of this. *Spaghetti allo scoglio* and *Cacciucco* (see recipes, page 57 and page 65, respectively) are two dishes typical of the coastal provinces. Further inland, freshwater trout are plentiful.

Along with tomatoes, potatoes, squash, and corn, beans were introduced by European explorers returning from America. Tuscan cooks have adopted them all but have reserved a special place in their hearts for beans. *Cannellini*, *Toscanelli*, and many others are a constant feature on Tuscan menus.

In simple trattorias dessert is often just the choice of a piece of the new season's fruit; other desserts are also simple, usually based on honey, nuts, spices, and other locally grown products and often served with *Vin Santo* (Holy wine).

Traditional cheeses are made of ewe's milk and are produced in small factories and on farms. Pecorino is the most common cheese, but ricotta is also popular.

The quality of Tuscan olive oil makes it an excellent choice for fried dishes. When frying food, don't go to the expense of using extra-virgin oil, plain olive oil is just as good.

Tuscan woodlands produce excellent porcini mushrooms as well as black and white truffles.

Chestnuts are another typical woodland fruit. As Christmas approaches the streetcorners of Florence are claimed by sellers of *caldarroste* (roast chestnuts).

Nowadays the restaurants and trattorias in the regional capital of **Florence** offer a broad range of Tuscan cuisine. The city's most typical dishes include *Trippa alla Fiorentina* (see recipe, page 71), *Fegato alla salvia* (see recipe, page 75), *Fagioli all'uccelletto* (often served with Italian sausages—see recipe, page 68), *Cenci* (see recipe, page 112), *Zuccotto* (see recipe, page 101), among others. The city's two main markets—San Lorenzo, in the center near the Duomo, and Sant'Ambrogio, near Santa Croce—offer an excellent range of fresh fish, meat, cheese, fruit, and vegetables on a daily basis.

**Massa Carrara**, the northernmost province of Tuscany, is known for excellent fish along the coast, while classic inland dishes include *tortelli*, *testaroli* (whole-wheat flat bread served with pesto or a mixture of oil, pecorino and parsley), and delicious minestrone.

The province of **Lucca** produces some of the best Tuscan olive oil; cooking with animal fats is practically unheard of in Lucca. The area is also known for its bread (the medieval town of Altopascio is particularly famous) and there are many *zuppe* based on cooked bread and vegetables, served with uncooked olive oil. The coastal resort of Viareggio is famous for its fish stew, a spicier version of the one made at Livorno. Inland, the wooded valleys produce black and white truffles and the streams are full of succulent trout.

Southward, along the coast, **Livorno** maintains a genuine tradition of fish cooking, based on the fresh catch caught daily off the coast. Its most famous dish, *Cacciucco* (see recipe page 65), has been the center of heated debate recently after a multinational firm announced plans to market a packaged, frozen version. The question is yet to be resolved and the directors of the international company have all been invited to

Livorno, courtesy of the mayor, to taste the difference. The tiny island of Elba, off the coast, makes its own version of *Cacciucco*, known as *sburrita*, together with a host of other fresh fish dishes, based on lobster, octopus, and bream, among others.

Nearby **Pisa** has a broad mixture of both fish and inland dishes. Local specialties include *Zuppa di ranocchi* (Frog soup) and *Stoccafisso in agrodolce* (Sweet and sour stockfish). The province is also known for its excellent game, including wild boar, duck, pheasant, and venison.

Moving inland in the direction of Florence, the provinces of **Pistoia** and **Prato** produce local sweets, including *Necci*, *Brigidini* (fennel-flavored wafers), and *Castagnaccio* (see recipe, page 107). Prato also produces salami and mortadella and a range of fruit for the Florentine markets.

Southeast of Florence the province of **Arezzo** has a distinctive cuisine. Specialties include *Pappardelle sulle lepre* (see recipe, page 40), *Scottiglia* (see recipe page 62), *Crostini all'aretina* (see recipe, page 23) and *Agnello arrosto* (roast lamb).

**Siena** is known for its cured meats, pecorino cheese, and olive oil. Many Siennese dishes make extensive use of local herbs, such as mint, tarragon, and calamint. A special local pasta, called *Pici* (see recipe, page 45), is worth trying. Siennese prosciutto is particularly tasty.

The southernmost province of **Grosseto** is famous for fish along the coast and game farther inland. Wild boar are plentiful in the Maremma. Local specialties include *Acqua cotta* (see recipe, page 48), *Polenta alla maremmana*, and *Risotto di carciofi*. The pecorino and ricotta cheeses produced in the province are exceptionally good.

The hilltop town of Montalcino in central Tuscany is famous for its local wines, the best of which—Brunello—is judged as one of Italy's top reds.

Fishing is an important industry along the entire coast of Tuscany. In summer tiny fish restaurants sprout up along the beach fronts and serve the day's catch fresh from the nets.

# Antipasti

Traditionalists will tell you that, with the exception of Chicken liver toasts and sliced cured meats, there are no antipasti in Tuscan cooking. This was true until a generation ago, but with the move to lighter meals in modern Tuscany, antipasti are often served instead of a pasta dish or second course. And on special occasions several antipasti will appear on the table, before the pasta dish!

# Crostini toscani

### Chicken liver toasts

Skin the calf's milt and cut into small pieces. ▪ Trim any connective tissue and discolored parts from the chicken livers and chop into small pieces. ▪ Finely chop the anchovy fillets and capers together. ▪ Melt two-thirds of the butter in a nonstick skillet over a moderate heat. Add the onion and sauté until tender. ▪ Add the chicken livers and calf's milt, if using, and sauté for 5 minutes. ▪ Season with salt and pepper, add the wine, and cook for 15 minutes, stirring frequently. If the mixture dries out, moisten with a little stock. ▪ Remove the skillet from the heat and set aside to cool a little. ▪ Place the liver mixture on a chopping board and chop finely. ▪ Heat the oil in the skillet over a moderate heat and add the liver mixture, anchovies, and capers. Stir well, add the remaining butter, and cook for 3–4 more minutes. ▪ Spread this deliciously rich, savory mixture on the toasts and keep warm in the oven until just before serving.

Serves: 6–8
Preparation: 35 minutes
Cooking: 30 minutes
Recipe grading: fairly easy

- scant 1 cup/200 g calf's milt (optional, see below)
- 1 cup/250 g chicken livers
- 4 anchovy fillets
- 1 tablespoon capers
- 3 tablespoons butter
- 1 onion, finely chopped
- salt and freshly ground black pepper
- ½ cup/125 ml dry white wine
- ½ cup/125 ml beef stock (homemade or bouillon cube)
- 4 tablespoons extra-virgin olive oil
- 1 long loaf firm-textured white bread, (about 3 in/7.5 cm in diameter) cut in ½ in/1 cm thick slices and toasted in the oven

Suggested wine: a young, fruity red (Chianti Montalbano)

*The traditional recipe calls for milt (calf's spleen). If preferred, omit and double the quantity of chicken livers.*

Serves: 4
Preparation: 10 minutes
Cooking: 5 minutes
Recipe grading: very easy

- 8 slices firm-textured white bread,
  ½ in/1 cm thick
- 2 large whole cloves garlic
- salt and freshly ground black pepper
- 3½ tablespoons best quality extra-virgin
  olive oil

Suggested wine: a young, sparkling red
(Vino Novello)

# Fettunta

## Toasted bread with garlic and oil

In Tuscany, the new season's oil, just pressed, is used for this simple but delicious snack. Ideally, the bread should be toasted over the glowing embers of a wood fire. Otherwise, toast it in a preheated oven at 400°F/200°C/gas 6 until crisp. It is important that the bread dries out while toasting, which it won't if browned in a toaster. ▪ Rub each slice all over with the garlic. ▪ Arrange the toasted bread on a serving platter. Season with salt and pepper and drizzle with the oil.

To make bruschetta, top each slice with about 2 tablespoons of diced and seeded ripe tomatoes and sprinkle with torn fresh basil leaves. ▪ Other Tuscan toppings include lightly boiled shredded dark cabbage leaves and home-cooked cannellini beans.

*Try to buy traditionally baked white bread, with a dense, ivory colored crumb, such as a Tuscan loaf or French pain de campagne, a day or two in advance. Mass produced steam baked bread is not suitable.*

# Insalata di campo

## Peasant-style mixed salad

Serves: 6
Preparation: 25 minutes
Cooking: none
Recipe grading: easy

Wash all the salad vegetables very thoroughly in cold running water, drain well and then gently squeeze them dry in a clean cloth. ▪ Place the leaves, whole or coarsely torn, in a large salad bowl. Sprinkle with salt and pepper and drizzle with the vinegar and, lastly, the oil. ▪ Toss vigorously and serve with plenty of fresh crusty bread.

- 2½ lb/1.2 kg (untrimmed weight) mixed endive/chicory and radicchio varieties (red, pale yellow and white, green and white)
- 7 oz/200 g young, tender, dark green cabbage leaves (optional)
- salt and freshly ground black pepper
- red wine vinegar
- extra-virgin olive oil

*The original Tuscan recipe calls for wild chicory, which is gathered by pulling the plant, root and all, from the ground; the slightly bitter roots are considered the best part, with only the outermost layer of skin scraped away with a small, sharp knife. If possible, use several types of radicchio and endive/chicory, chosen from red varieties such as Treviso, Chioggia, Castelfranco; white or white and green Belgian endive/chicory and escarole/curly endive.*

# Affettati misti

## Mixed platter of cured meats

Arrange the various meats on a serving platter or dish. ▪ Place the bread in a bread basket and serve with the meats, olives, and pickles.

Given the popularity of Tuscan cooking, all the cured meats listed here can usually be bought from Italian delicatessens or specialist sections of large supermarkets or city food stores. However, if you can't find the exact ones, replace with other, similar types of Italian cured meat.

Serves: 4
Preparation: 5 minutes
Cooking: none
Recipe grading: very easy

- 5 oz/150 g Tuscan prosciutto, freshly sliced off the ham
- 4 oz/125 g Tuscan salami
- 4 oz/125 g finocchiona, sliced fairly thickly
- 6 small wild boar sausages
- 1 lb/500 g sliced firm-textured white bread
- best quality green or black olives
- homemade pickles (optional)

Suggested wine: a dry red (Chianti Classico)

*Finocchiona is a large soft salami flavored with fennel seeds. The very best, freshest variety is called Sbriciolona (from the Italian sbriciolare, "to crumble"), because it falls apart as you slice it.*

# Fresh and cured meats

All the various provinces of Tuscany produce a variety of cured meats and sausages. Generally speaking, although their names vary from one place to another, they are usually made in the same way. Siena's *buristo* becomes *mallegato* in Lucca and *biroldo* in Pistoia, but the specialty is basically the same. *Buristo* consists of a mixture of pork offcuts, skin, blood, and spices encased in a skin. In Lucca, a handful of tiny sweet raisins and pine nuts are mixed into the blend before it is wrapped and cured.

*Finocchiona* is one of the most distinctive of Tuscan salami; it consists of a mixture of lean and fatty pig meat with fennel seeds (fennel is called *finocchiona* in Italian, hence the name). The Florentine version—called *Sbriciolona*—is very fresh, soft, and crumbly. It is difficult to slice thinly, so is usually served in rather thick slices. It is commonly served as an appetizer with globe artichokes preserved in oil.

Selection of cured meats and sausages in a butcher's shop in Florence. The salamini piccanti (spicy little salamis) in the foreground are made by adding hot chile peppers to the meat mixture before curing.

Tuscan cured raw hams (or prosciutto crudo), especially those from Siena, are treated with plenty of salt and pepper, and also often with garlic and juniper berries. This makes them much tastier than hams from Parma or San Daniele. Tuscan ham is often carved into fairly thick slices by hand rather than thinly sliced on a machine. Served on the saltless Tuscan bread and with a glass of good red Chianti, few Tuscans would exchange it for the more famous, sweeter hams from further north.

In keeping with the peasant tradition that produced so many Tuscan classics, when an animal was butchered every part was used and nothing wasted. *Soppressata* or *soprassata* (the name comes from the Spanish and means "sal presar", or to sprinkle with salt) is made from various cuts of pig meat, including the animal's skin and jowl. The chopped offcuts are highly seasoned with a mixture of chile pepper, cloves, coriander seeds, and cinnamon. This mixture is then tightly wrapped and sewn up in a linen cloth and simmered for several hours until ready.

The Maremma, a wild area of reclaimed marshlands along the coast of southern Tuscany, is home to many wild animals, including wild boar and deer. Many mouthwatering cured meats and sausages are made from wild boar meat, such as cured raw hams and small, lean sausages which can be sliced like little salami.

Undoubtedly Tuscany's most famous meat dish, *Bistecca alla fiorentina* (Florentine beef steak — see recipe page 78) is cut from Chianina beef (right), a breed native to the Val di Chiana, near Arezzo. The steak is cut from the animal's loin and includes the fillet and T-bone. For purists, there is no such thing as a well-done Florentine beef steak; it must always be *al sangue* (very rare). It is traditionally accompanied by a side dish of boiled white cannellini beans.

Arista (roast loin of pork) is another Tuscan specialty. Its name comes from the Greek *aristos*, meaning "the best." The loin of pork, with all the chops attached to the backbone, is spiked with garlic and rosemary and slowly roasted in the oven.

Serves: 4
Preparation: 20 minutes
Cooking: 25 minutes
Recipe grading: easy

- 1¼ lb/600 g fresh porcini mushrooms
- 1–1½ tablespoons butter
- 4 tablespoons extra-virgin olive oil
- ½ white or Bermuda/mild red onion, finely chopped
- 2 cloves garlic, finely chopped
- 1 tablespoon fresh calamint (or parsley or thyme), finely chopped
- salt and freshly ground black pepper
- ½ cup/125 ml vegetable stock (homemade or bouillon cube)
- 1 long loaf firm-textured white bread, (about 3 in/7.5 cm in diameter) cut in ½ in/1 cm thick slices and toasted in the oven

Suggested wine: a dry white
(Capezzana Bianco)

*Fresh porcini are the most prized wild mushrooms in Tuscany. However, they are often expensive or unobtainable. If you can't get them, experiment with other wild mushrooms, such as shiitake, chanterelles, morels, or oyster mushrooms (or combinations of these).*

# Crostini con i funghi

## Mushroom toasts

Remove any grit or dirt from the mushrooms, rinse quickly under cold running water, and pat dry with paper towels. ▪ Separate the stalks from the caps and dice only the firm, unblemished stalks. Chop the caps coarsely. ▪ Heat the butter and oil in a nonstick skillet over a moderate heat and sauté the onion, garlic, and calamint for 3 minutes. ▪ Add the mushrooms and season with salt and pepper. Cook for 5 minutes, stirring continuously. ▪ Gradually stir in enough stock to keep the mixture moist but not sloppy and continue cooking for another 8–10 minutes. ▪ Spread each toast with a generous helping of the mushroom mixture and serve.

Variation: Spread the mushroom mixture on squares of firm, cold polenta and bake in a preheated oven at 400°F/200°C/gas 6 for 10 minutes before serving.

# Crostini all'aretina

## Sausage toasts

Squeeze the sausage meat out of the sausage skins into a mixing bowl. ▪ Add the cheese and pepper and mix very thoroughly with a fork. ▪ Spread each toast with a generous helping of the sausage and cheese mixture and transfer to a large, shallow ovenproof dish. ▪ Bake in a preheated oven at 400°F/200°C/gas 6 for 5 minutes, or until the cheese has melted and the topping is bubbling. ▪ Serve piping hot straight from the oven.

Serves: 6
Preparation: 10 minutes
Cooking: 5 minutes
Recipe grading: easy

- scant 1 cup/225 g small, highly flavored fresh Italian sausages
- 7 oz/225 g fresh stracchino (crescenza) cheese or a coarsely grated semi-hard stracchino cheese
- freshly ground black pepper
- 1 long loaf firm-textured white bread, (about 3 in/7.5 cm in diameter) cut in ½ in/1 cm thick slices and toasted in the oven

Suggested wine: a young, dry red (Chianti Colli Aretini)

# Pinzimonio

## Platter of raw vegetables in olive oil dip

Only the freshest, most tender artichokes are suitable. Have one or two large, juicy lemon wedges ready to rub over all the cut surfaces as you work to prevent discoloration. Cut off the upper section of the remaining leaves, leaving the fleshy, edible base of each leaf attached to the stem. Doing this will expose a central "cone" of leaves: slice about 1 in/2½ cm off the top of this and part the leaves to gain access to the 'choke', the spiny filaments which must be carefully trimmed away, leaving the fleshy, dish-shaped heart intact. Use a small, sharp knife to scrape away the skin from the stalk. As each artichoke is finished, drop it into a bowl of cold water acidulated with the juice of a lemon. Set aside for 15 minutes. ▪ If the carrots are very young and tender, scrub well and leave whole with a little stalk attached. If larger, peel and cut lengthwise into quarters. ▪ Discard the outermost layer of the fennel, cut the bulbs from top to bottom, dividing them into quarters, and rinse well. ▪ Cut the celery heart lengthwise in half or quarters, wash and drain. ▪ Trim and wash the radishes, leaving any fresh, unwilted leaves attached. ▪ Trim the scallions, leaving only a short length of green leaf attached. Unless they are very fresh and firm, remove the outermost layer of the bulb. ▪ Drain the artichokes thoroughly and pat dry with paper towels. ▪ Arrange all the vegetables on a large serving platter. ▪ Place the platter in the middle of the table and give each person a plate and a small bowl. Place containers of oil, vinegar, freshly squeezed lemon juice, salt, and pepper on the table and let each diner prepare their own bowl of dressing for dipping the vegetables. ▪ Serve with plenty of fresh bread.

Serves: 6
Preparation: 20 minutes + 15 minutes' standing
Cooking: none
Recipe grading: easy

- 4–6 very young, fresh globe artichokes
- lemon wedges
- 12 very fresh small carrots, preferably with their leaves
- 2 small, tender fennel bulbs
- 1 celery heart
- 12 radishes
- 6 scallions/spring onions
- scant ½ cup/100 ml extra-virgin olive oil
- good quality wine vinegar
- scant ½ cup/100 ml lemon juice
- salt and freshly ground black pepper

Suggested wine: a dry, sparkling white (Spumante di Vernaccia di San Gimignano)

Serves: 4–6
Preparation: 5 minutes
Cooking: none
Recipe grading: very easy

- 14 oz/400 g fresh green or black figs
- 10 oz/300 g Tuscan salami, thinly sliced
- 6 fresh fig leaves (optional)

Suggested wine: a dry rosé (Bolgheri)

# Salame e fichi freschi

## Tuscan salami with fresh figs

Wash the figs thoroughly under cold running water, then pat dry with paper towels. ▪ Remove the rind from the salami. ▪ If you have them, place the fig leaves on a large serving dish and arrange the salami and figs on top.

*Figs begin to appear in the markets in Florence in June. In August, when the local trees are producing these delicious fruit, this dish becomes a staple in many homes and restaurants. The combination of the salty salami and the sweet flesh of the fruit is a perfect and refreshing way to begin a meal at the end of long, hot summer's day.*

# Cecina

## Garbanzo bean flat bread

Serves: 6
Preparation: 5 minutes
Cooking: 10 minutes
Recipe grading: easy

Place the garbanzo bean flour in a large mixing bowl and using a wooden spoon or a balloon whisk, gradually stir in enough water to form a thick pouring batter with no lumps. ▪ Beat in the oil and a generous pinch of salt. ▪ When the batter is smooth, pour it into a nonstick roasting pan or similar ovenproof dish, filling to a depth of less than ¼ in/5 mm. ▪ Bake in a preheated oven at 400°F/200°C/gas 6 for 10 minutes. A thin crust should form on the surface. ▪ Transfer the cooked cecina to a heated serving dish, sprinkle with freshly ground pepper and serve at once.

- 4½ cups/625 g garbanzo bean/chickpea flour
- 2 quarts/2 liters water
- ¾ cup/180 ml extra-virgin olive oil
- salt and freshly ground black pepper

Suggested wine: a dry rosé (Carmignano)

*This is just one of the many regional breads made in Italy. Simple and easy-to-make, it is delicious served hot with a platter of sliced cured meats.*

# Primi piatti

Tuscan first courses are strongly linked to the peasant tradition that created them. Bread was relatively cheap and formed the basis of many meals. Bread-based *primi piatti* are among the most typical Tuscan dishes even today. Soups were common fare, along with homemade pasta, often served with sauces from game typical of the region. Dried, store-bought pasta, such as spaghetti and penne, were not as common in Tuscany as they were further south, although they are now widely served.

# Panzanella

## Tuscan bread salad

Slice the bread fairly thickly and soak in water for 3–10 minutes, depending on how firm it is, until it softens but does not disintegrate. ▪ Drain in a colander and squeeze each slice well to remove excess moisture. The bread should resemble large, damp bread crumbs. ▪ Wash the lettuce leaves, dry thoroughly, and cut into thin strips. ▪ Transfer the bread to a large salad bowl, add the tomatoes, cucumber, onions, lettuce, and basil and mix gently but thoroughly. ▪ Drizzle with the oil and vinegar and season with salt and pepper. ▪ Chill in the refrigerator for at least 2 hours before serving. ▪ Serve cold.

Serves: 4–6
Preparation: 15–20 minutes + 2 hours' chilling
Recipe grading: easy

- 1¼ lb/600 g firm-textured white bread, about 2 days old
- 8 crisp Romaine/cos lettuce leaves
- 6 medium ripe tomatoes, skinned and cut in quarters or eighths
- 1 large cucumber, peeled and diced
- 2 Bermuda/mild red onions, very thinly sliced
- 10 leaves fresh basil, torn
- 6 tablespoons extra-virgin olive oil
- Italian red wine vinegar
- salt
- freshly ground black pepper

Suggested wine: a young, dry red (Chianti)

*The ingredients used to make Panzanella vary according to which part of Tuscany it is made. The addition of cucumber, for example, is shunned in the area around Siena, while it is always included in Florence. The salad can be enriched by adding diced carrots, fennel, celery, hard-cooked eggs, capers, or pecorino cheese.*

# Ribollita

## Vegetable and bread soup

Place the tomatoes in a large, heavy-bottomed saucepan with the beans, garlic, and sage. Cover with cold water. If using fresh beans, add salt to taste at this point. ▪ Bring slowly to a boil, cover and simmer for about 25 minutes for fresh beans or about 1 hour for dried beans. If using dried beans, add salt when they are almost cooked. ▪ Discard the garlic and sage and purée half the beans in a food processor or food mill. ▪ Put the parsley, thyme, onion, leek, carrots, Swiss chard, cabbage, tomatoes, and other vegetables in a large, heavy-bottomed saucepan with 4 tablespoons of oil over a moderate heat and sauté for a few minutes, stirring continuously. ▪ Add the puréed beans and the whole beans, followed by about two-thirds of the stock. Taste for salt. Cover and simmer gently for about 1½ hours, adding more stock if the soup becomes too thick. ▪ Heat a heavy-bottomed saucepan and add a ladle or two of the soup and a slice of bread. Keep adding more soup and bread until finished. Drizzle with 3 tablespoons of oil and sprinkle with pepper. Cover and leave to stand for 2–3 hours. ▪ Return to the heat and bring slowly to a boil. Simmer very gently for 20 minutes without stirring. Alternatively, reheat the soup in the oven at 425°F/220°C/gas 7 for about 10 minutes. ▪ This soup is equally good served hot, warm, or even cold, depending on the season. Traditionally it is served in small, round terracotta bowls with little handles on either side. Drizzle a little olive oil into the bottom of each, then ladle in the soup.

Serves: 6–8
Preparation: 45 minutes + 2–3 hours standing + 12 hours soaking if using dried beans
Cooking: 2–3 hours
Recipe grading: fairly easy

- 3 cherry tomatoes (pricked with a fork)
- 1 lb/500 g fresh white cannellini beans or 1¼ cups/275 g dried cannellini beans
- 2 cloves garlic
- 6 leaves fresh sage
- salt and freshly ground black pepper
- 1½ tablespoons finely chopped parsley
- small sprig of fresh thyme
- 1 onion, thinly sliced
- 1 leek, thinly sliced
- 2 medium carrots, diced
- 8 oz/250 g Swiss chard, shredded
- ½ small Savoy cabbage, shredded
- 1 cup/250 g chopped tomatoes
- a wide variety of seasonal vegetables can also be used, including new potatoes, French beans, zucchini/courgettes, peas or whatever you have on hand)
- 7 tablespoons extra-virgin olive oil for cooking + extra for serving
- 1 quart/1 liter beef stock
- 10 oz/300 g firm textured white or brown bread, sliced about ½ in/1 cm thick

Suggested wine: a young, dry red (Chianti dei Colli Fiorentini)

Serves: 4
Preparation: 15 minutes
Cooking: 25 minutes
Recipe grading: easy

- 1¼ lb/600 g firm-ripe tomatoes
- 5 tablespoons extra-virgin olive oil
  + extra for serving
- 3 whole cloves garlic, bruised
- 8–10 leaves fresh basil, torn
- 8 oz/250 g firm textured white or brown
  bread, 2 days old, cut in 1 in/2.5 cm
  thick slices and then diced
- salt and freshly ground black pepper
- about 1¼ cups/300 ml water or stock
  (homemade or bouillon cube)

Suggested wine: a young, dry red
(Chianti dei Colli Senesi)

# Pappa al pomodoro

## Tomato and bread soup

Place the tomatoes in a heatproof bowl. Add sufficient boiling water to cover and leave for 1 minute. Drain, rinse quickly in cold water, and then skin. Cut in half, remove the seeds and any tough parts, and chop into small pieces. ▪ Heat the oil in a heavy-bottomed saucepan over a low heat, add the garlic and basil, and sauté for 2 minutes before adding the bread. ▪ Increase the heat to moderate and cook, stirring continuously, for 2 minutes. Season with salt and pepper. ▪ Cook for 2 minutes more, then add the tomatoes and a little water or stock. ▪ Continue cooking, uncovered, for 15 minutes, stirring frequently. Add more salt and pepper, if needed, and more liquid if the soup begins sticking to the bottom of the pan, although remember that it is supposed to be very thick. ▪ Serve hot in individual soup bowls. Place extra oil and pepper on the table so that each person can season to their own taste.

*A classic peasant dish from the hills around Siena, Pappa al pomodoro is excellent when made in advance and reheated. Try adding a few finely chopped fresh rosemary leaves with the tomatoes for extra taste.*

Serves: 4
Preparation: 20 minutes + 12 hours' soaking
Cooking: 1¼ hours
Recipe grading: fairly easy

- 1½ cups/300 g dried garbanzo beans/
  chickpeas
- 1 teaspoon baking soda/
  bicarbonate of soda
- 4 cloves garlic, bruised
- 2 sprigs rosemary
- 6 tablespoons extra-virgin olive oil
- 2 tablespoons tomato concentrate/
  purée
- salt and freshly ground black pepper
- 1–2 cups/250–500 ml stock (homemade
  or bouillon cube)
- 7 oz/200 g tagliatelle, broken into short
  lengths

Suggested wine: a dry red (Pomino)

# Pasta e ceci

## Pasta and garbanzo bean soup

Put the garbanzo beans in a large bowl of cold water with the soda. Leave to stand overnight or for at least 12 hours. ▪ Drain, transfer to a colander, and rinse thoroughly under cold running water. ▪ Place in a saucepan and cover with cold water. Add 2 garlic cloves and a sprig of rosemary. Cover, leaving a space for steam to escape, and simmer for about 1 hour, or until the beans are very tender, adding a pinch of salt after about 50 minutes. ▪ Drain, reserving the cooking water. ▪ Purée three-quarters of the garbanzo beans in a food processor or food mill, keeping the remainder whole. ▪ Heat half the oil in a large heavy-bottomed saucepan and sauté the remaining garlic and rosemary sprig for 3 minutes. ▪ Add the tomato purée and continue cooking over a moderate heat for 2 minutes. ▪ Add the puréed and whole garbanzo beans and the reserved cooking liquid and bring to a boil. If the soup is very thick, dilute with a little hot stock. ▪ Add the tagliatelle and cook for about 10 minutes until the pasta is ready. Season with salt and pepper. ▪ Serve the soup in individual soup bowls. Place extra oil and pepper on the table so that each person can season to taste.

*In Tuscany this dish is cooked in a deep, flameproof earthenware dish.*

# Gnocchi di polenta

## Polenta gnocchi

Prepare the meat sauce. ▪ Bring the water to a boil with the salt in a large, heavy-bottomed saucepan. Sprinkle in the cornmeal while stirring continuously with a long-handled wooden spoon to prevent lumps forming. Continue stirring while cooking for 40 minutes. ▪ Just before removing from the heat, stir the butter into the polenta, which should be very thick, smooth, and soft in texture. ▪ Using a tablespoon, make oval dumplings, dipping the spoon in cold water to prevent the polenta sticking. Don't worry if the dumplings look rather untidy. ▪ Place a layer of dumplings in a fairly deep, heated ovenproof dish, spoon some meat sauce over the top, and cover with another layer of polenta dumplings. Continue in this way, finishing with a layer of meat sauce. ▪ Sprinkle with the cheese and bake in a preheated oven at 400°F/200°C/gas 6 for 5–8 minutes, or until the topping is golden brown. ▪ Serve immediately.

Serves: 4
Preparation: 5 minutes + 15 minutes for the meat sauce
Cooking: 40 minutes + 1–2 hours for the meat sauce
Recipe grading: fairly easy

- 2 quarts/2 liters water
- 1 heaped tablespoon coarse sea salt
- 3⅓ cups/500 g coarse-grained cornmeal
- 4 tablespoons butter
- 1 quantity meat sauce (see recipes on pages 45, 50, or 53)
- 1¼ cups/150 g freshly grated parmesan cheese

Suggested wine: a dry red (Chianti Classico)

*This hearty dish is perfect for cold winter evenings. Prepare in advance and bake just before serving. If pushed for time, use one of the precooked polenta flours which are now widely available.*

# Olive oil: Tuscany's liquid gold

The Tuscan landscape has been dotted with olive trees from Etruscan times, over 2,000 years ago. The fruity, aromatic oil they produce is among the finest in the world. Tuscan farmers harvest and press the slightly immature fruit according to centuries-old tradition. Hand-plucked or shaken from the trees into nets, the olives are pressed within a day of being harvested. The olives are washed, then crushed between large stone wheels into a paste. The oil is extracted from the paste using a centrifuge and then filtered to remove impurities. This *prima spremitura* (first pressing) produces extra-virgin oil, the highest quality available. The oil in the remaining paste is extracted chemically and is of inferior quality. Extra-virgin Tuscan oil is labor-intensive to produce and expensive to buy (even in Italy), but attempts to save by skimping on quality will ruin every dish. Buy small quantities of new oil and store it in a cool place (not in the refrigerator). Fresh, spicy Tuscan oil is perfect on salads and soups.

The beauty of the gnarled, silver-green olive tree has been extolled by poets over the centuries. An evergreen, the olive's tiny white flowers appear in late spring. There are two types of flowers: perfect, with both male and female parts, which develop into fruit; and male, which contain only pollen-producing parts. Olive trees can live for hundreds of years. The tough, decay-resistant wood is used to make furniture and a variety of tools.

Depending on the season, olives are harvested toward the end of November or, according to an old Tuscan proverb, never later than Santa Lucia's day on December 13. To prevent bruising, the harvest is still done by hand in most parts of Tuscany. The freshly picked olives are transferred from baskets to colorful canvas sheets and taken straight to the press. The best quality extra-virgin oil is cold-pressed and contains no chemicals or additives of any kind.

Newly pressed oil is a limpid golden green and has an extra, delicious bite in its full, rich flavor. The new season's oil appears in Tuscan shops in December (and in America by January). This is the ideal time to serve fettunta or Toasted bread with garlic and oil (see recipe, page 16).

Olive oil is graded according to the amount of oleic acid it contains. By Italian law, extra-virgin oil must contain less than 1 percent acidity. Extra-virgin oil is the basic fat used in Tuscan cuisine. Uncooked, it is used to dress salads, to preserve vegetables and fish, and to enliven a wide range of vegetable and antipasti dishes. Heated, it forms the basis of pasta sauces, stews, braised meats, roasts and many cakes. It is also used for deep-frying.

# Malfatti

## Spinach gnocchi

Bring a large saucepan of salted water to a boil. Add the spinach and cook for 10 minutes. ▪ Drain well, squeeze out excess moisture, and chop finely. ▪ Put the spinach in a large mixing bowl and add the ricotta cheese, the egg and egg yolk, half the parmesan, the nutmeg, if using, and salt and pepper. Combine these ingredients very thoroughly with a fork until smooth. ▪ Use a dessertspoon or tablespoon to shape little oval dumplings of the mixture, or roll into small balls between your floured palms, and then press to flatten slightly. Coat lightly with flour all over. ▪ Place the butter and sage leaves in a small saucepan and warm gently to melt the butter. Turn off the heat and leave to stand. ▪ Bring a very large saucepan of salted water to a gentle boil. Add a few drops of olive oil to prevent the dumplings from sticking to one another and then add the dumplings. They should simmer rather than boil. When they bob up to the surface, remove with a slotted spoon. Drain well and place in a heated serving dish. Drizzle with the sage-flavored butter ▪ Sprinkle with the remaining parmesan cheese and serve at once.

**Serves: 4**
**Preparation: 15 minutes**
**Cooking: 20 minutes**
**Recipe grading: fairly easy**

- 1½ lb/750 g trimmed, washed, and drained fresh spinach leaves
- 1 cup/250 g very fresh, drained ricotta
- 1 egg + 1 egg yolk
- scant 1 cup/100 g freshly grated parmesan cheese
- dash of grated nutmeg (optional)
- salt and freshly ground black pepper
- ⅔ cup/100 g all-purpose/plain flour
- 4 tablespoons butter
- 4 leaves fresh sage

Suggested wine: a young, dry red
(Rosso di Montalcino)

*Malfatti means, literally, "badly-made" and refers to the fact that the filling is the same one used for ravioli, but lacks the pasta covering. In some parts of Tuscany these dumplings are also known as strozzapreti (priestchokers!)*

Serves: 4–6
Preparation: 30 minutes + 5–6 hours'
    marinating
Cooking: 1¾ hours
Recipe grading: fairly easy

- 1 hare, well hung, cleaned and jointed
- 2 cups/500 ml full-bodied, dry red wine
- 1 onion, coarsely chopped
- 1 medium carrot, coarsely chopped
- 1 stalk celery, coarsely chopped
- 3 bay leaves
- sprig of rosemary
- large sprig of parsley
- 3 dried juniper berries
- 8 whole black peppercorns
- 1 onion, finely chopped
- 1 stalk celery, finely chopped
- 5 tablespoons extra-virgin olive oil
- about 2 tablespoons butter
- 1¼ lb/600 g store-bought pappardelle
- scant 1 cup/100 g freshly grated
    parmesan cheese

Suggested wine: a dry red
(Chianti dei Colli Aretini)

# Pappardelle sulla lepre
## Pappardelle with hare

Wash the pieces of hare thoroughly and dry with paper towels. Place in a large non-metallic bowl with the wine, the coarsely chopped onion, carrot and celery, the bay leaves, rosemary, parsley, juniper berries, and peppercorns. ▪ Leave for at least 5–6 hours, turning several times. Remove the hare from the marinade. Strain and reserve the liquid, discarding the vegetables and herbs. ▪ Sauté the finely chopped onion and celery in the oil in a large saucepan over a moderate heat for 3–4 minutes. ▪ Add the hare and cook over a slightly higher heat for about 5 minutes, turning the pieces to brown all over. ▪ Ladle some of the reserved marinade over the hare and bring to a boil. Cover and simmer over a low heat for about 1½ hours, turning the pieces occasionally and adding more marinade as necessary. ▪ Place the cooked hare in a covered dish to keep warm. ▪ Strain the cooking liquid, pressing the vegetables through a sieve (or use a food mill) and add to the liquid to add body. ▪ Select three meaty pieces of hare from the center section or "saddle," remove the meat from the bones and chop finely. ▪ Heat half the butter in a saucepan, add the cooking liquid and the chopped hare. Simmer for 8–10 minutes, stirring often. ▪ Bring a large saucepan of salted water to a boil, with a few drops of olive oil to prevent the pappardelle sticking to each other. Add the pappardelle and cook for about 8–10 minutes, or until al dente. ▪ Drain well and transfer to a heated serving dish. Top with the remaining butter, the hare sauce, and the parmesan cheese. ▪ Serve immediately.

*The remaining portions of hare on the bone can be served as the main course, after this dish.*

# Tuscan bread and pasta

In the Mediterranean world bread has always been a staple food and Tuscany is no exception to this rule. What is extraordinary about Tuscan bread is that it is totally without salt. Legend has it that this derives from around 1100 when Florence and Pisa were at war. Salt was imported to Florence through the port of Pisa and the Pisans blocked the salt trade in an effort to convince the Florentines to depose arms. Needless to say, the heroic Florentines simply ate their food, and baked their bread, without salt. According to a more prosaic tradition, salt was simply too expensive for most Tuscans and so they baked or bought their bread made from a simple and economical mixture of flour, yeast, and water. Whatever the origin of the custom, traditional Tuscan bread remains saltless to this day. Eaten with flavorful toppings, such as Chicken Liver Pâté (see recipe, page 15), and tasty cured meats, the saltless bread provides striking and satisfying contrast.

Dante Alighieri, Tuscany's most famous poet and author of the Divine Comedy, was exiled from his beloved Florence by political enemies. During his absence, he mourned his hometown with the phrase *"come è salato il pane altrui"* (how salty other people's bread is).

Bread is the main ingredient in several Tuscan soups and first courses. From a dish called *Panata* (a soup dating back to the 14th century made of grated two-day-old bread, eggs, cheese, and nutmeg), to *Ribollita* (Vegetable and bread soup—see recipe, page 31), *Pappa al pomodoro* (Tomato bread soup—see recipe, page 32), and *Panzanella* (Tuscan bread salad—see recipe, page 29). It is also used in a wide range of appetizers, including the many *Crostini* recipes (see pages 15, 22, 23) and a basket of bread is always served with the main course. After dinner, you will see Tuscans sipping the last of the red wine and munching on the last slice of bread.

Although pasta is less typical of Tuscany than many other regions of Italy, a number of specialties are linked to the region. Over 2,000 years ago the early inhabitants of Tuscany, the Etruscans, prepared large flat noodles with Saracen wheat and water (these are the ancestors of modern lasagna and pappardelle). Nowadays they are generally served with meat or game sauces (*Pappardelle sulla lepre*—see recipe, page 40). During the 14th century we know that lasagna was prepared to celebrate San Lorenzo on August 10 when it was offered free to passersby (a tradition that is still observed). Other pasta dishes that have become linked to Tuscany, include *Penne strascicate* (see recipe, page 50), *Tortelli di patate* (see recipe, page 44) from the Mugello area just north of Florence, and *Pici* (see recipe, page 45), from the Mount Amiata region in southern Tuscany.

Spaghetti and penne with tomato or meat sauces are basic fare in any Tuscan restaurant or trattoria. Although they did not originate in Tuscany, tortellini served in meat broth or with meat or tomato sauce are another basic dish that you will find almost everywhere.

Besides the regular Tuscan loaf, there is another type of flat bread which does contain salt and which is brushed with olive oil. Similar to the better-known focaccia, in Tuscany it is known as *Schiacciata all'olio*. Other special breads include a special Siennese loaf baked on All Saints Day which has raisins and nuts added to the basic dough. *Pan di ramerino* (Rosemary Bread Rolls—see recipe, page 106) are traditionally baked at Easter, while *Schiacciata con l'uva* (Black grape sweet bread—see recipe, page 104) is made in autumn as the new season's grapes ripen on the vines.

# Tortelli di patate

## Potato tortelli

Serves: 4

Preparation: 40 minutes

Cooking: about 10 minutes + 30 minutes for
  boiling the potatoes

Recipe grading: fairly easy

To make the pasta:

- 3⅓ cups/500 g durum wheat flour
  + ⅔ cup/100 g extra flour

- 4 large eggs

- ½ cup/125 ml milk

- salt

For the filling:

- 1½ lb/750 g floury potatoes, peeled

- 1 large egg

- scant 1 cup/100 g freshly grated
  parmesan cheese

- 6 tablespoons butter

- freshly grated nutmeg

- salt and freshly ground black pepper

Suggested wine: a dry white
(Pomino Il Benefizio)

Prepare the pasta as explained on page 47. ▪ Boil the potatoes until cooked but still firm. ▪ Drain thoroughly and put through a potato ricer or sieve into a large mixing bowl. ▪ Stir in the egg, half of the parmesan cheese, 2 tablespoons of butter, nutmeg, and salt and set aside. ▪ Cut the ball of pasta dough in half. Dust the work surface with flour and roll out into two sheets about ⅛–1⁄16 in/3–1 mm thick. ▪ Drop teaspoons of the potato mixture onto one sheet at regular intervals, about 1 in/2.5 cm apart, as if making ravioli. ▪ Place the other pasta sheet on top, run a finger gently between the mounds, then cut between them, sealing the edges of the tortelli with the prongs of a fork. ▪ Set aside in a single layer on a lightly floured cloth. ▪ Melt the remaining butter in a small saucepan. ▪ Bring a large saucepan of salted water to a boil, adding a few drops of oil to prevent the tortelli sticking to one another. Add the tortelli and cook for about 3–4 minutes. ▪ Remove them as they rise to the surface, using a slotted spoon. ▪ Transfer to a heated serving dish and drizzle with the melted butter, pepper, and the remaining parmesan. ▪ Serve hot.

*Tortelli di patate are also very good when served with tomato or meat sauce.*

# Pici al ragù

## Fresh pici pasta with meat sauce

Sift the flour and salt into a large mixing bowl and make a well in the center. Gradually add just enough of the water to make a very firm dough, working it in by hand until the dough is as smooth and elastic. ▪ On a floured work surface, roll the dough out to about ¾ in/2 cm thick and cut into strips. ▪ Roll each strip between your floured palms, slowly drawing it out until it is very thin and resembles untidy spaghetti. ▪ Spread the *pici* out on a lightly floured clean cloth. ▪ Sauté the onion, carrot, celery, and parsley in the oil in a heavy-bottomed saucepan for 5 minutes. ▪ Add the beef and sausage meat, squashing any lumps that form. ▪ Stir while cooking for 5 minutes before adding the mushrooms. ▪ Add the wine and cook over a higher heat, uncovered, for 5 minutes. ▪ Add the tomatoes and salt and pepper to taste. ▪ Reduce the heat, cover and simmer for 45 minutes, adding a little stock to moisten. ▪ Bring a large saucepan of salted water to a boil, add the *pici* and cook until tender. ▪ Drain well and transfer to a serving dish. Add the meat sauce and toss gently. ▪ Sprinkle with the parmesan and serve hot.

Serves: 4
Preparation: 50 minutes
Cooking: about 1 hour for the meat sauce +
  about 5 minutes for the pasta
Recipe grading: fairly easy

To make the pasta:
- 2½ cups/300 g durum wheat flour
- dash of salt
- 1 cup/250 ml hot water

For the sauce:
- 1 medium onion, finely chopped
- 1 medium carrot, finely chopped
- 1 small stalk celery, finely chopped
- 1½ tablespoons finely chopped parsley
- 6 tablespoons extra-virgin olive oil
- 2½ cups/300 g ground prime lean beef
- 1 fresh Italian pork sausage, skinned
- 1 cup/25 g dried porcini mushrooms, soaked for 20 minutes in warm water, well drained and coarsely chopped
- ½ cup/125 ml full-bodied dry red wine
- 1⅔ cups/400 g chopped canned Italian tomatoes
- 1 cup/250 ml meat stock (homemade or bouillon cube)
- salt and freshly ground black pepper
- scant 1 cup/100 g freshly grated parmesan cheese

Suggested wine: a dry red
(Rosso di Montalcino)

Serves: 6
Preparation: 35 minutes
Cooking: about 3½ hours
Recipe grading: fairly easy

- 1 lb/500 g freshly hulled/shelled borlotti or similar beans or 1 cup/250 g dried borlotti beans
- 1½ cups/300 g rice (Italian semifino, cristallo, or Carolina rice)
- ½ small Savoy cabbage
- 10 oz/300 g spinach leaves
- 4 oz/125 g leaves of Swiss chard, stalks removed
- ½ cup/60 g finely chopped fatty pancetta
- 2 cloves garlic, finely chopped
- 1½ tablespoons finely chopped parsley
- 1½ tablespoons finely chopped basil
- 6 tablespoons extra-virgin olive oil
- 1 onion, coarsely chopped
- 1 medium carrot, coarsely chopped
- 2 stalks celery, coarsely chopped
- 2 zucchini/courgettes, coarsely chopped
- 2 yellow potatoes, coarsely chopped
- salt and freshly ground black pepper
- 2 quarts/2 liters meat stock (homemade or bouillon cube)
- scant 1 cup/100 g freshly grated parmesan cheese

Suggested wine: a dry red
(Chianti dei Colli Pisani)

# Minestrone livornese

## Leghorn-style minestrone

Cover the beans with salted water and boil for about 15 minutes, or until tender. If using pre-soaked dried beans, drain, rinse and boil until tender, adding salt when they are nearly done. ▪ Wash all the green leaf vegetables well. Shred or cut into thin strips. ▪ Place first the cabbage, then the chard and spinach in a saucepan containing a little salted water and cook for 5–6 minutes. Drain when only just tender, drain, squeeze out excess moisture, and chop finely. ▪ Sauté the pancetta, garlic, parsley, and basil in the oil for 4–5 minutes. ▪ Add the raw vegetables followed by the beans and their cooking liquid, then the cooked, chopped vegetables, stirring to combine. ▪ Pour in the hot stock, season to taste, cover and simmer very gently for 2½ hours. ▪ Add the rice, stir well, and cook for 20 minutes more. ▪ Serve hot and with extra grated parmesan to sprinkle over the top.

# Ravioli del Casentino

## Casentino ravioli

Heap the flour up into a mound on a marble pastry slab or wooden board or work surface. Make a well in the center and break the eggs into it with a generous dash of salt. Using your hand (fingers together) as a "paddle", or a fork, stir the eggs and gradually incorporate the flour, working with your hands once most of the flour has been absorbed. Knead the dough, sprinkling it with extra flour to prevent it from sticking, until it is smooth and elastic. Shape into a ball and divide in half or in quarters. Cover with a cloth and set aside. ▪ Place the spinach in a large saucepan of salted, boiling water and cook for 8–10 minutes. ▪ Drain, squeeze out excess moisture, and chop finely. ▪ In a large mixing bowl, combine the spinach with the ricotta, the eggs and the egg yolk, parmesan, nutmeg, salt, and pepper. ▪ On a floured work surface, roll out each piece of dough to paper thin. ▪ Cut into 3 in/7.5 cm squares. Place 2 teaspoons of filling in the center of each and gather the edges together over it, pinching them firmly. ▪ Place in a single layer on a floured cloth and let stand for 2–3 hours. ▪ Bring a large saucepan of salted water to a boil with a few drops of oil to prevent the ravioli sticking to one another. Add the ravioli and cook until they rise to the surface. Remove with a slotted spoon and transfer to a heated serving dish.

Serves: 4
Preparation: 30 minutes + 2–3 hours' standing
Cooking: 1½ hours
Recipe grading: fairly easy

To make the pasta:
- 2⅔ cups/400 g durum wheat flour
- 3 large eggs
- salt

For the filling:
- 2¼ lb/1 kg spinach leaves, washed
- 2 cups/500 g fresh ricotta
- 2 eggs + 1 egg yolk
- 1¼ cups/150 g freshly grated parmesan cheese
- dash of grated nutmeg
- salt and freshly ground black pepper

Suggested wine: a dry red (Chianti Rufina)

*Serve the ravioli with tomato or meat sauce (see recipes pages 52–53).*

# Acqua cotta

## Maremma-style soup

Serves: 4
Preparation: 30 minutes
Cooking: about 1 hour
Recipe grading: fairly easy

- 5 tablespoons extra-virgin olive oil
- 2 onions, thinly sliced
- 2½ cups/300 g fresh or frozen peas
- 1¾ cups/200 g freshly hulled fava/broad beans
- 1 medium carrot, sliced
- 1 stalk celery, thinly sliced
- 1 crumbled dried chile pepper
- salt and freshly ground black pepper
- 12 oz/300 g trimmed young Swiss chard or spinach leaves, washed and shredded
- 1¼ cups/310 g firm-ripe tomatoes, skinned and chopped
- 1½ cups/1.5 liters boiling water
- 4 large eggs
- ½ cup/60 g freshly grated parmesan or pecorino cheese
- 4 slices firm-textured white bread, 2 days old
- 1 clove garlic

Suggested wine: a dry white
(Montecarlo Bianco)

Pour the oil into a large, heavy-bottomed saucepan. Add the onions, peas, fava beans, carrot, celery, chile pepper, and a dash of salt. ▪ Sauté for about 10 minutes, or until tender and lightly browned. ▪ Add the chard and tomatoes and simmer for 15 minutes. ▪ Pour in the boiling water and simmer gently for 40 minutes, adding more salt if necessary. ▪ Using a fork or balloon whisk, beat the eggs with salt, pepper, and the grated parmesan. ▪ Toast the bread and when golden brown, rub both sides of each slice with the garlic. ▪ Place a slice in each soup bowl or in individual straight-sided earthenware dishes, pour a quarter of the beaten egg mixture over each serving. Give the soup a final stir and then ladle into the bowls. ▪ Serve immediately.

*The name of this sustaining soup, once a peasant dish,
means "cooked water".*

**Serves:** 4
**Preparation:** 25 minutes
**Cooking:** 1¼ hours
**Recipe grading:** fairly easy

- 1 medium onion, finely chopped
- 1 small carrot, finely chopped
- 1 small stalk celery, finely chopped
- 1½ tablespoons finely chopped parsley
- 6 tablespoons extra-virgin olive oil
- 10 oz/300 g ground/minced lean beef
- ½ cup/125 ml full-bodied, dry red wine
- 1⅔ cups/400 g chopped canned Italian tomatoes
- salt and freshly ground black pepper
- 1 cup/250 ml meat stock (homemade or bouillon cube)
- 14 oz/400 g penne pasta
- 1¼ cups/150 g freshly grated parmesan cheese

Suggested wine: a young, dry red
(Chianti dei Colli Fiorentini)

# Penne strascicate

## Florentine-style penne

Sauté the onion, carrot, celery, and parsley in the oil in a deep nonstick skillet for 4–5 minutes. ▪ Add the meat, breaking up any lumps that may form as it cooks. ▪ Once it has browned, pour in the wine and stir for 4–5 minutes. ▪ Add the tomatoes and season with salt and pepper. Stir well and simmer for another 4–5 minutes. ▪ Add 2–3 tablespoons of the stock, cover and simmer for 40 minutes or longer, stirring in a little more stock at intervals to keep the sauce moist (but not sloppy). ▪ Bring a large saucepan of salted water to a boil and add the pasta. ▪ Cook until just al dente but still with plenty of 'bite'. ▪ Keep the meat sauce warm over a low heat, add the drained pasta, toss together and stir for 2–3 minutes so that the pasta is coated thoroughly with the rich sauce and has absorbed its flavors. ▪ Turn off the heat, stir in the parmesan, and serve at once.

# Basic sauces and meat stock

Tuscan cooking boasts a wide variety of basic sauces to serve with pasta, vegetables, fish, and meat. Like all Tuscan cooking, they tend to be simple and sober and to rely more on the freshness and quality of the ingredients used, rather than complicated preparation. Here we have gathered four sauces that lie at the very heart of Tuscan cooking. Master these simple sauces and they will serve you well in a wide range of dishes.

## Béchamel

Although this sauce is strongly identified with French cooking, its origins are Florentine. It is another of the many recipes that left the Tuscan capital's brilliant Renaissance court with Catherine de' Medici when she went to north to marry the future King of France.

4 tablespoons butter
4 tablespoons all-purpose/plain flour
2 cups/500 ml boiling milk
freshly grated nutmeg
salt

Melt the butter in a small heavy-bottomed pan over low heat. Stir in the flour and cook, stirring continuously, for 1–2 minutes. ▪ Pour in a little of the milk and stir well. Gradually add all the milk, stirring continuously so that no lumps form. Cook over low heat, stirring all the time, for about 5 minutes. ▪ Season with nutmeg and salt to taste. ▪ Béchamel sauce is used in many baked pasta and vegetable dishes. Use a quantity of Béchamel sauce to revive yesterday's leftover pasta, by stirring it into the pasta and then baking it all in a hot oven for 15 minutes.

## Basic tomato sauce
For four, to serve with pasta, rice, or meat

2 cloves garlic, finely chopped
1 medium carrot, finely chopped
1 medium onion, finely chopped
1 stalk celery, finely chopped
2 tablespoons finely chopped parsley
4 tablespoons extra-virgin olive oil
2 cups/500 g chopped fresh or canned tomatoes
salt and freshly ground black pepper
6 leaves fresh basil, torn

Sauté the garlic, carrot, onion, celery, and parsley in the oil for 4–5 minutes. ▪ Add the tomatoes, season with salt and pepper and simmer, uncovered, over low heat for at least 45 minutes, or until the sauce has reduced to the required density. ▪ Turn off the heat, stir in the basil, and serve. ▪ For a spicy sauce, add chile peppers to taste. ▪ In late summer, when tomatoes are cheap and plentiful, make a large quantity in a very large, heavy-bottomed pan. Preserve in sterilized glass jars for use throughout the winter. When making large quantities of the sauce, simmer for at least 1½ hours.

# Rich meat sauce

For eight, to serve with pasta, rice, or vegetable dishes

2 cloves garlic, finely chopped
1 medium carrot, finely chopped
1 medium onion, finely chopped
1 stalk celery, finely chopped
2 tablespoons finely chopped parsley
$^1/_2$ cup/60 g diced pancetta
4 tablespoons extra-virgin olive oil
8 oz/250 g ground veal or beef
4 oz/125 g chicken breast, coarsely chopped
4 oz/125 g chicken livers, finely chopped
1 oz/30 g dried porcini mushrooms, soaked in warm water for
    20 minutes, then finely chopped
$^1/_2$ cup/125 ml dry red wine
2 cups/500 g chopped fresh or canned tomatoes
salt and freshly ground black pepper

In a large heavy-bottomed saucepan, sauté the garlic, carrot, onion, celery, parsley, and pancetta in the oil over medium heat until the onion turns light gold. • Add the veal or beef, chicken breast, and livers and cook for 5–7 minutes, stirring all the time. • Add the mushrooms and cook for 5 minutes more. • Pour in the wine and cook until evaporated. • Add the tomatoes, season with salt and pepper, partially cover and simmer over low heat for at least 2 hours. The longer the sauce cooks, the tastier it will be, so don't be afraid of simmering for 3 or even 4 hours. Add a little hot stock or water if it becomes too dry.

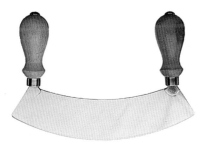

# Meat stock

Many of the recipes in this book call for a meat stock. You may use stock made with bouillon cube, although the results will be superior if you use homemade stock. Stock freezes very well, so make a large quantity, pour it into small containers (ice-cube trays are ideal) so that it can be used as required. Makes about $1^1/_2$ quarts/1.5 liters.

$2^1/_2$ lb/1 $^1/_4$ kg various cuts beef with bones (neck, shoulder, short
    ribs, brisket)
2 carrots
2 onions
1 large stalk celery
2 ripe tomatoes
2 cloves garlic
2 sprigs parsley
1 bay leaf
2 quarts/2 liters cold water

Put the meat, vegetables, and herbs into a large pot with the water. Cover and bring to the boil over medium heat. Season with salt and pepper. • Partially cover, and simmer over low heat for 3 hours. • Turn off heat and set aside to cool. • When the broth is cool, remove the vegetables and herbs, and skim off and discard the fat that will have formed on top.

# Minestra di farro

## Spelt and vegetable soup

If using dried beans, soak them overnight in cold water, drain and rinse. ▪ Soak the spelt in cold water for at least 4 hours. ▪ Cover the beans with cold water, add the garlic, sage, tomatoes (skins pierced with a fork), and a little salt (unless using dried beans). Cover and bring to a boil and simmer for about 25 minutes, or until tender (longer if dried beans are used, adding salt at the end). ▪ Remove and discard the garlic and sage. ▪ Purée half the beans in a food mill, reserving the cooking liquid. ▪ Heat the oil in a heavy-bottomed saucepan over a moderate heat and sauté the pancetta for 3 minutes with the crushed garlic. Discard the cloves as soon as they start to color. ▪ Add the remaining vegetables and the tomato purée, salt, pepper, and stock. Stir well, cover and simmer over a low to moderate heat for 30 minutes before adding the drained spelt. ▪ After another 20 minutes, add the two bean mixtures. Adjust the seasoning and simmer for a final 20 minutes. ▪ Drizzle each portion with 1 tablespoon of oil and serve hot.

Serves: 4
Preparation: 30 minutes + 4 hours' soaking for the spelt
Cooking: about 30 minutes for fresh beans, longer if dried + about 1¼ hours
Recipe grading: fairly easy

- 14 oz/400 g freshly hulled/shelled cannellini beans or 1 cup/200 g dried cannellini beans
- generous 1 cup/200 g spelt
- 2 cloves garlic, whole
- 1 small sprig sage
- 3 cherry tomatoes or small tomatoes
- salt and freshly ground black pepper
- 6 tablespoons extra-virgin olive oil + extra for serving with the soup
- 3½ oz/100 g finely chopped pancetta
- 2 cloves garlic, lightly bruised
- 1 onion, very thinly sliced
- 1 leek, thinly sliced
- 1 stalk celery, thinly sliced
- 1 carrot, peeled and diced
- 5 oz/150 g young spinach or Swiss chard leaves, washed and shredded
- ½ small, dark green cabbage, washed and shredded
- 3 tablespoons tomato purée
- 1½ cups/1½ liters stock (homemade or bouillon cube)

Suggested wine: a young, dry red (Chianti Rufina)

*Spelt is a cereal grain which has been grown in the Mediterranean since the dawn of farming. It is now available from good wholefood stores.*

# Spaghetti allo scoglio

## Seafood spaghetti

Soak the mussels and clams for at least an hour to purge them of sand. Scrub them under running water after pulling the beards off the mussels. ▪ In a large skillet, sauté 1 clove garlic in 2 tablespoons oil over a moderate heat. Add the mussels and clams with half the wine, cover tightly and cook for 8–10 minutes or until they are open, shaking the pan now and then. ▪ Discard any shells which do not open. Put aside a few of the best ones for garnishing and detach the rest from their shells. ▪ Slice the body sacs of the squid and cuttlefish into rings and strips. ▪ Heat the remaining oil in a large nonstick skillet and sauté the chopped garlic, parsley, and chile pepper for 3–4 minutes. ▪ Add the squid and cuttlefish, season with salt and pepper, and stir for 2–3 minutes. Pour in the remaining wine, cover and cook for 12 minutes. ▪ Add the shrimp tails and a little more salt if needed and cook for another 3 minutes before adding the clams and mussels. ▪ Simmer for a final 3 minutes, then turn off the heat. ▪ While the sauce is cooking, bring a large saucepan of salted water to a boil, add the spaghetti and cook until it is tender but still al dente. Combine with the hot seafood sauce and stir over a gentle heat for about 2 minutes. ▪ Serve immediately, garnished with the reserved clams and mussels in their shells.

Serves: 4
Preparation: 40 minutes + 1 hour to soak
Cooking: 1 hour
Recipe grading: fairly easy

- 1 lb/500 g mussels
- 2 dozen (about 1 lb/500 g) very small littleneck clams
- 1 clove garlic
- 8 tablespoons extra-virgin olive oil
- 1 cup/250 ml dry white wine
- 14 oz/400 g prepared squid
- 14 oz/400 g prepared cuttlefish (or substitute more squid)
- about 10 oz/300 g Pacific shrimp tails/ large Mediterranean prawn tails, washed
- 3 cloves garlic, finely chopped
- 2–3 tablespoons finely chopped parsley
- 2 crumbled dried chile peppers
- salt and freshly ground black pepper
- 12 oz/350 g spaghetti

Suggested wine: a dry, spicy white (Alicante)

# Secondi piatti

Almost all main courses are based on meat or fish. Some of the tastiest dishes make use of variety meats, such as tripe or liver. Along the coast, fish and seafood are the most common fare. *Cacciucco*, or Mixed fish stew from Livorno, must be the richest of all the fish-based dishes in Tuscany. Further inland, chicken, beef, and lamb are cooked simply by roasting, grilling, or braising with olive oil and a handful of local herbs. The recipe for Duck with orange, dating from the Renaissance, recalls Tuscany's days of glory.

# Peposo

## Spicy braised veal

Pour the oil into a heavy-bottomed saucepan (traditionally a flameproof earthenware casserole dish is used) and sauté the onion, garlic, carrots, celery, and chile peppers for 5 minutes. ▪ Trim any gristle or fat from the meat and cut into 1 in/2.5 cm cubes. ▪ Coarsely crush the peppercorns using a pestle and mortar or place them in a strong paper bag and crush with a rolling pin. ▪ Add the whole garlic and the meat to the saucepan. Season with salt, add the peppercorns, and cook for about 8 minutes, or until the meat is browned all over. ▪ Add the tomatoes, stir well, and cook for 12 minutes. ▪ Pour in the wine. Lower the heat, cover and simmer for 2 hours, stirring occasionally, until the meat is very tender. ▪ Serve very hot.

Serves: 6
Preparation: 20 minutes
Cooking: 2½ hours
Recipe grading: fairly easy

- 5 tablespoons extra-virgin olive oil
- 1 onion, finely chopped
- 3 cloves garlic, finely chopped
- 2 small carrots, finely chopped
- 2 small stalks celery, finely chopped
- 2 crumbled dried chile peppers
- 2¾ lb/1.3 kg cubed meat from veal hind shanks/hind shin of veal
- 5 teaspoons whole black peppercorns
- 5 cloves garlic, whole
- salt
- 2½ cups/625 g chopped canned Italian tomatoes
- 1⅔ cups/400 ml full-bodied, dry red wine

Suggested wine: a dry red
(Chianti Classico)

59

# Paparo all'arancia

## Duck with orange

Serves: 4
Preparation: 25 minutes
Cooking: 1½ hours
Recipe grading: fairly easy

- 1 oven-ready duck, weighing 2½ lb/1.2 kg
- 2 cloves garlic, whole
- sprig of rosemary
- salt and freshly ground black pepper
- 3 oranges (organic: not treated with any fungicide)
- 5 tablespoons extra-virgin olive oil
- 1 onion, coarsely chopped
- 1 carrot, coarsely chopped
- 1 stalk celery, coarsely chopped
- ½ cup/125 ml dry white wine
- ½ cup/100 g sugar
- 1½ tablespoons water
- 1 tablespoon lemon juice

Suggested wine: a dry red
(Vino Nobile di Montepulciano)

Wash and dry the duck and place the garlic, rosemary, salt, pepper, and the zest of 1 orange into the cavity. ▪ Pour half the oil into a large roasting pan. Add the duck and sprinkle with more pepper. Arrange the onion, carrot, and celery around the duck and drizzle with the remaining oil. Roast in a preheated oven at 375°F/190°C/gas 5 for about 1½ hours. ▪ Ten minutes into the roasting time, pour the wine over the duck. ▪ Meanwhile, peel the zest off the remaining 2 oranges and cut it into very thin strips. Place in a small saucepan with cold water, bring to a boil, and drain. Repeat the process twice to remove bitterness. ▪ In a small, nonstick saucepan, heat the sugar, water, and lemon juice over a moderate heat until the sugar melts and caramelizes to a pale golden brown. Add the zest strips, stir over a low heat for 2 minutes, and set aside. ▪ Thirty minutes into the roasting time, squeeze the juice from 2 oranges over the duck. ▪ When the duck is done (test by inserting a sharp knife into the thigh, if the juices run clear the duck is well done), remove the garlic, rosemary, and orange zest from the cavity. ▪ Transfer the duck to a casserole with the cooking juices and vegetables and spoon the caramelized orange zest over the top. Place over a moderate heat for 5 minutes, turning the duck once or twice. ▪ Serve hot.

*Despite French claims to this recipe, it actually originated in the Florentine court of the Medici family during the Renaissance. When Catherine de' Medici went to France to marry the future King Henry II, in the 16th century, she took this and many other secrets of Tuscan cooking with her.*

# Scottiglia

## Mixed meat stew

**Serves:** 6
**Preparation:** 25 minutes
**Cooking:** 1¼ hours
**Recipe grading:** fairly easy

- 5 tablespoons extra-virgin olive oil
- 2 cloves garlic, finely chopped
- 1 medium onion, finely chopped
- 1 small carrot, finely chopped
- 1 small stalk celery, finely chopped
- 1½ tablespoons finely chopped parsley
- 1 tablespoon finely chopped basil
- 2 crumbled dried chile peppers
- about 3 lb/1.3 kg assorted meat, poultry, and game (veal, pork, rabbit, guinea fowl) trimmed and cut in small pieces
- ½ cup/125 ml full-bodied, dry red wine
- 3 tablespoons tomato purée
- salt and freshly ground black pepper
- scant 1 quart/1 liter hot stock (homemade or bouillon cube)
- 6 fairly thin slices firm-textured white or brown bread, 2 days old
- 1 clove garlic, whole

Suggested wine: a dry red
(Chianti dei Colli Fiorentini)

Pour the oil into a heavy-bottomed saucepan and sauté the garlic, onion, carrot, celery, parsley, basil, and chile peppers. ▪ After 5 minutes, add the meat, poultry, and game and cook over a slightly higher heat for 8 minutes. ▪ Pour in the wine, increase the heat, and cook, uncovered, for about 7 minutes to reduce the liquid. ▪ Add the tomato purée, season with salt and pepper, and stir well. ▪ Pour in the stock. Lower the heat, cover and simmer for about 1 hour, stirring occasionally. There should be plenty of liquid when the dish is cooked; it should be halfway between a hearty soup and a casserole. ▪ Cut each piece of bread in half and toast. Rub the toast with the remaining garlic, place in heated soup bowls, and ladle in the stew. ▪ Leave to stand for 2–3 minutes before serving so that the bread can absorb some of the liquid.

# Francesina

## Boiled beef with onions

If you have to cook the beef first, put it in a large saucepan with cold water to cover. Add the onion, carrot, celery, parsley, tomatoes, and sea salt and bring slowly to a boil. Simmer gently for about 1 hour until the beef is very tender. Leave to cool in the cooking liquid to make it easier to cut when cold. ▪ Sauté the sliced onions in the oil in a large heavy-bottomed saucepan over a moderate heat for 2–3 minutes. ▪ Add half the stock, partially cover and cook for 10 minutes, or until reduced. ▪ Chop the meat into small pieces or thin slices. ▪ Add the meat to the onions, season with salt and pepper, and stir for 3–4 minutes. ▪ Stir in the tomatoes and season with a little more salt. Stir again, cover and simmer over a low heat for about 15 minutes. If necessary, moisten with some of the remaining stock. ▪ Serve hot.

Serves: 4
Preparation: 15 minutes
Cooking: 30 minutes + 1 hour for boiling
   the beef
Recipe grading: easy

- 1½ lb/750 g leftover boiled beef (brisket, rump roast, or bottom round/brisket, topside or silverside)
- 1 onion, cut in half
- 1 carrot, cut in 3–4 pieces
- 1 stalk celery, cut in 3–4 pieces
- sprig of parsley
- 4 ripe tomatoes, pricked with a fork
- 1 tablespoon coarse sea salt
- 3 large onions, very thinly sliced
- 4 tablespoons extra-virgin olive oil
- 1 cup/250 ml beef stock (homemade or bouillon cube)
- salt and freshly ground black pepper
- 1⅔ cups/400 g canned Italian tomatoes, sieved

Suggested wine: a dry red
(Chianti Classico)

*This dish is a delicious way of using up the beef from* Bollito Misto *(Mixed Boiled Meats), which is usually cooked in large quantities. If you are cooking the meat especially for this dish, it is best if cooked the day before.* Francesina *is equally good reheated.*

# Cacciucco

## Mixed fish stew

To make the fish stock, pour the water into a large, deep saucepan and add the onion, carrot, celery, parsley, and bay leaf. Cover and bring to a boil. ▪ Add the hake and sea robin. Bring back to a boil and reduce the heat. Cover and simmer for 20 minutes. ▪ Strain the stock into a large bowl. Push the flesh of the fish through a sieve or flake it finely and add to the bowl with the stock. ▪ Heat the oil in a large heavy-bottomed saucepan and sauté the chopped onion, garlic, parsley, and chile peppers for 5 minutes. ▪ Chop the octopus in pieces about 1 in/2.5 cm square. Separate the tentacles from the body of the cuttlefish (if not already done). Cut the squids' body sacs in half. ▪ Add the octopus, cuttlefish, and squid to the pan and cook for 5 minutes. ▪ Pour in the wine and reduce over a slightly higher heat. ▪ Stir in the tomatoes and season with salt and pepper. Cover and simmer for 20 minutes. ▪ Add the fish stock, dogfish or shark, and shrimp. Cover and cook for 10 minutes, stirring gently at intervals. ▪ Toast the bread and rub the slices all over with the whole clove of garlic. ▪ Place a slice in each soup bowl, ladle the seafood stew over the top, and leave to stand briefly before serving.

Serves: 6
Preparation: 50 minutes
Cooking: 1¼ hours
Recipe grading: fairly easy

- 1 quart/1 liter salted water
- 1 onion, cut in half
- 1 carrot, cut lengthwise in half
- 1 stalk celery, cut in half
- small bunch of parsley
- 1 bay leaf
- 8 oz/250 g filleted hake
- 8 oz/250 g sea robin/gurnard, cleaned
- 4 tablespoons extra-virgin olive oil
- ½ onion, finely chopped
- 4 cloves garlic, finely chopped
- 3 tablespoons finely chopped parsley
- 2 crumbled dried chile peppers
- 8 oz/250 g each of baby octopus, small cuttlefish, and small squid (ask your fish vendor to prepare by removing the stomach, bony parts, and the ink sacs)
- 1 cup/250 ml dry white wine
- 1⅔ cups/400 g canned tomatoes
- salt and freshly ground black pepper
- 8 oz/250 g smooth dogfish or shark/ smooth hound or shark, cleaned and cut in pieces
- 8 oz/250 g shrimp/prawns, heads removed but not peeled
- 4 slices firm-textured, white bread
- 1 clove garlic, whole

Suggested wine: a dry red (Sassicaia) or a dry white (Bianco di Nugola)

# Tuscan wine

For centuries Tuscan wine was synonymous with Chianti, and the classic straw-wrapped flasks sprang to mind whenever the name was heard abroad. Unfortunately, the name, and the flask, also became associated with much that was lacklustre (and worse) in red wines. All this has changed over the last thirty years and Tuscan winemakers are now among the most innovative in Italy. Dating from the

times of the Chianti League in the 13th century, the name originally referred to the area north of Siena (the southern part of today's Chianti Classico zone), but as the wine became more popular this century it was extended south below Siena, east to Arezzo, and north and west towards Florence and Pisa. Chianti wines are traditionally made from a combination of Sangiovese, Canaiolo, Malvasia, and Trebbiano grapes. Although Chianti is still the most widely produced wine, some of the older wines, such as *Vernaccia di San Gimignano* and *Vino Nobile di Montepulciano*, have been revived and modernized, while relative newcomers, including *Brunello di Montalcino* and table wines such as *Sassicaia*, have won awards and acclaim in Italy and internationally. Tuscany's traditional dessert wine—*Vin Santo*, or Holy Wine—is still produced, and enjoyed, while a recent trend has seen a huge increase in the number of *Vin Novellos*, very young, new season's wine, on sale from early November after harvest.

The Castello di Brolio in the province of Siena is part of the Ricasoli family estates. In the first half of the 18th century Baron Bettino Ricasoli improved Chianti wines by laying down strict guidelines. Winemaking in Tuscany has always been linked to the regions' illustrious families. Three of the big names in Tuscan viticulture today, Ricasoli, Frescobaldi, and Antinori, date back over 600 years.

*Brunello di Montalcino* is Tuscany's most famous, and arguably Italy's best, red wine. In Tuscan terms, it is a relatively new wine, since it was first made in the 1880s by Ferruccio Biondi-Santi. Centered on the tiny town of Montalcino, the Brunello-producing region is very small and the wines themselves expensive. A Brunello has to be aged for at least five years, and many need far longer to reach their full potential. Recently, winegrowers have begun producing *Vino Rosso di Montalcino*, which can

be a very good, younger alternative to *Brunello*. Faced with some real competition, in recent years the neighboring hilltop town of Montepulciano has greatly improved its traditional red, *Vino Nobile di Montepulciano.*

Although Tuscany is traditionally associated with red wines, some very respectable whites are grown as well. *Vernaccia di San Gimignano*, which has been grown near the medieval town of San Gimignano since at least 1286, is perhaps the best-known. Other traditional whites include *Bianco Vergine Valdichiana, Bianco di Pitigliano, Montecarlo, Bianco Pisano di San Torpè*, and wines from the island of Elba. Winemakers are now developing a host of non-traditional whites for modern palettes.

While the great red wines are aged in wooden and stainless steel barrels in underground cellars, Tuscany's most famous dessert wine—*Vin Santo*—is aged in casks in special lofts where it is exposed to extremes of temperature. *Vin Santo* ranges from very sweet to very dry; all are acceptable and the degree of dryness preferred is left to personal taste. *Vin Santo* is traditionally served with *Biscottini di Prato* (see recipe, page 108). Other Tuscan dessert wines, now almost unobtainable, include sweet red *Aleatico* and golden *Moscato* from the island of Elba, and *Moscadeletto of Montalcino.*

# Fagioli con salsicce

## Italian sausages and beans

Serves: 4

Preparation: 5 minutes + 12 hours soaking if dried beans are used

Cooking: 40 minutes + time to cook the beans

Recipe grading: easy

- 8 medium Italian pork sausages
- ½ cup/125 ml hot water
- 5 tablespoons extra-virgin olive oil
- 2 cloves garlic, finely chopped
- 4 leaves fresh sage
- 2 cups/500 g canned Italian tomatoes, sieved
- salt and freshly ground black pepper
- 1½ lb/750 g fresh cannellini beans, precooked, or 2 cups/350 g dried cannellini beans, soaked and precooked

Suggested wine: a dry red (Chianti dei Colli Fiorentini)

Pierce the sausages in 3 or 4 places and put into a nonstick skillet. Add the hot water and cook over a fairly high heat for about 10–12 minutes, turning frequently. ▪ Pour the oil into a large, nonstick skillet and add the garlic. Cook over a low heat with the sage, tomatoes, and salt and pepper for 5 minutes. ▪ Increase the heat and cook for 10 minutes. ▪ Add the beans and sausages. Cover and cook over a moderate heat for 15 minutes, stirring occasionally. ▪ Serve very hot.

*This traditional Florentine dish makes a hearty meal in itself. If short of time, use two cans of high quality Cannellini (or white kidney or great northern beans).*

# Seppie in zimino

## Cuttlefish casserole

Chop the cuttlefish into small pieces. ▪ Wash the spinach very thoroughly and boil in a little salted water for about 10 minutes. ▪ Drain well, squeeze out all excess moisture, and chop coarsely. ▪ Pour the oil into a large, heavy-bottomed saucepan and sauté the onion, garlic, carrot, celery, parsley, and chile peppers for 4–5 minutes. ▪ Stir in the cuttlefish. Season with salt and pepper and pour in the wine. Cook, uncovered, for 5–6 minutes to reduce. ▪ Add the spinach and cook for 3–4 minutes before adding the tomatoes. Taste and add more salt if necessary, mix well, cover and leave to simmer for 30 minutes, stirring occasionally. ▪ Serve hot.

Serves: 4
Preparation: 25 minutes
Cooking: 1 hour
Recipe grading: fairly easy

- ▪ 2 lb/1 kg small cuttlefish (ask your fish vendor to prepare these by removing the stomachs and bony parts)
- ▪ 2 lb/1 kg fresh spinach
- ▪ 5 tablespoons extra-virgin olive oil
- ▪ 1 onion, finely chopped
- ▪ 2 cloves garlic, finely chopped
- ▪ 1 small carrot, finely chopped
- ▪ 1 small stalk celery, finely chopped
- ▪ 1½ tablespoons finely chopped parsley
- ▪ 2 crumbled dried chile peppers
- ▪ salt and freshly ground black pepper
- ▪ ½ cup/125 ml dry white wine
- ▪ 2 cups/500 g canned Italian tomatoes

Suggested wine: a dry white
(Vernaccia di San Gimignano)

*If you can't get cuttlefish, use small tender squid in its place. In this case make sure that your fish vendor also removes the ink sacs.*

# Trippa alla fiorentina

## Florentine-style tripe

Rinse the tripe thoroughly under cold running water and drain and dry with a clean cloth. Cut into thin strips with kitchen scissors or a very sharp knife. ▪ Sauté the onion, carrot, and celery in the oil in a heavy-bottomed flameproof casserole for 5 minutes. ▪ Add the tripe and season with salt and pepper. Continue cooking for 3–4 minutes, stirring continuously. ▪ Add the wine and cook over a higher heat, uncovered, for 5–6 minutes to reduce. ▪ Mix in the tomatoes, checking the seasoning. Cover and leave to simmer for 30 minutes, stirring occasionally. If necessary, reduce the amount of liquid by cooking uncovered over a higher heat for a few minutes. ▪ Serve very hot with the cheese served separately.

Serves: 4
Preparation: 20 minutes
Cooking: 45 minutes
Recipe grading: easy

- 2 lb/1 kg ready-to-cook calf's honeycomb tripe
- 1 large onion, finely chopped
- 1 large carrot, finely chopped
- 1 stalk celery, finely chopped
- 4 tablespoons extra-virgin olive oil
- salt and freshly ground black pepper
- ½ cup/125 ml dry white wine
- 1⅔ cups/400 g canned Italian tomatoes, sieved
- scant 1 cup/100 g freshly grated parmesan cheese

Suggested wine: a dry red (Pomino)

*Mobile tripe vendors still sell
tripe sandwiches or plastic containers
full of delicious tripe on many
Florentine street corners.*

Serves: 6
Preparation: 10 minutes + 2 hours
   to marinate
Cooking: 1 hour
Recipe grading: easy

- 2 lb/1 kg leg or shoulder of lamb
- 3 cloves garlic, each sliced into three
- 1 tablespoon chopped rosemary
- ½ cup/125 ml white wine vinegar
- salt and freshly ground black pepper
- ½ cup/125 ml extra-virgin olive oil

Suggested wine: a dry red
(Brunello di Montalcino)

# Agnello al forno

## Tuscan roast lamb

Using a small, pointed knife, make deep slits in the meat and push a garlic slice and some rosemary into each incision. ▪ Mix the vinegar with the salt, pepper, remaining rosemary, and oil in a large deep bowl and add the meat. ▪ Leave to stand for 2 hours, turning the meat several times in the marinade. ▪ Preheat the oven to 200°C/400°F/gas 6. ▪ Place the meat in a roasting pan, pour the marinade over the top, and roast for about 1 hour (depending on whether the lamb is to be pale pink in the center or well done), basting at intervals. ▪ Serve with roast potatoes.

Serves: 4
Preparation: 20 minutes
Cooking: 1¼ hours for veal,
   1¾–2 hours for beef
Recipe grading: easy

- 2 lb/1 kg shank or shoulder/shin or shoulder of veal, or beef chuck, round or shank/beef chuck or shin
- ½ cup/75 g all-purpose/plain flour
- 2 cloves garlic, finely chopped
- 1 tablespoon finely chopped sage
- 1 tablespoon finely chopped rosemary
- 5 tablespoons extra-virgin olive oil
- 4 canned Italian tomatoes
- salt and freshly ground black pepper
- 1 cup/250 ml dry red wine
- 1 cup/250 ml stock (homemade or bouillon cube)

Suggested wine: a dry red
(Chianti Rufina)

# Spezzatino toscano

## Tuscan casserole

Trim the meat and cut into 1 in/2½ cm cubes. Lightly coat all over with flour, shaking off the excess. ▪ Sauté the garlic, sage, and rosemary in the oil in a heavy-bottomed saucepan for 3–4 minutes. ▪ Add the meat and brown the pieces all over for 5–6 minutes. ▪ Add the tomatoes and salt and pepper and cook for another 5 minutes. ▪ Pour in the wine, cover and simmer for 1 hour (longer for beef) until tender, if necessary adding some of the stock to moisten. Taste and add more salt if desired. ▪ Serve piping hot.

*Country-style potatoes make a delicious accompaniment to this classic Tuscan casserole. To prepare: sauté a finely sliced onion in a little olive oil, then add 1 can of drained, chopped tomatoes and 1 lb/500 g of boiled or steamed potatoes, cut into fairly small pieces. Stir over a moderate heat for 5 minutes before stirring.*

# Fegato alla salvia

## Calf's liver with sage

Lightly flour the liver, shaking off any excess. ▪ Heat the oil with the garlic and sage over a moderate heat in a large nonstick skillet. When the oil starts to sizzle around the garlic, raise the heat to moderately high. Add the liver and cook quickly to ensure tenderness, turning once. ▪ Sprinkle with a little salt and pepper when well-browned and remove from the heat. ▪ Serve at once with puréed potatoes, or boiled or steamed spinach, briefly sautéed in garlic-flavored oil.

Serves: 4
Preparation: 5 minutes
Cooking: 10 minutes
Recipe grading: easy

- 1¼ lb/600 g calf's liver, thinly sliced
- ½ cup/75 g all-purpose/plain flour
- 4 tablespoons extra-virgin olive oil
- 3 cloves garlic
- 6 leaves fresh sage
- salt and freshly ground black pepper

Suggested wine: a young dry red
(Rosso di Montepulciano)

*This simple, elegant dish, also known as Fegato alla fiorentina (Sautéed Calf's Liver, Florentine-Style), originally comes from the Tuscan capital, although it is becoming more and more difficult to find in the city's trattorias and restaurants.*

# Cooking in Renaissance Florence

The Renaissance is synonymous with the rebirth of the arts and the revival of Classical Greek and Roman ideas and values. It is also synonymous with the Tuscan capital city of Florence, where it began and where so many of its greatest artists lived and worked. Under the guidance of the Medici family, Florence became a major center of European cultural and intellectual life and remained so for over three hundred years. Among the arts fostered by the Medici, cooking and "the art of entertaining" occupied an important place. The Medici and other noble Florentine families held sumptuous banquets where guests feasted on staggering quantities of extravagant foods. One such dinner, on the occasion of the marriage (by proxy!) of Marie de' Medici with Henry IV of France, took place in the Palazzo Vecchio on October 5, 1600.

Giambologna and Piero Tacca created the most expensively ephemeral statues in history, made of sugar: the cost of the raw material alone amounted to some 1,700 gold florins. Emilio de' Cavalieri's music accompanied the whole banquet which was served in five "services" or "removes": the first was a cold buffet with 24 different courses, including wild boar molds and jellies with live fish encased in them. The second, known as a "kitchen" service, comprised 9 courses of hot dishes, among them pies which the pastrycooks had decorated with the family crest; this was followed by two more hot "services" of 18 and 10 courses respectively, including game and various meat dishes. The banquet ended with a final "service" of fruit, cheeses, and desserts.

Meat and game were usually the main dishes served at banquets. The meat was generally cooked with a variety of spices and with fruit. The fruit helped to mask the taste of meat that quickly went bad because it could not be kept cold, while spices, so rare and difficult to come by, were proof of the host's wealth and power.

Many of the Medici court artists were connoisseurs of fine cooking: the letters of Bronzino, Pontorno, Andrea del Sarto, and Cellini contain many references to suppers and banquets, listing dishes they had particularly enjoyed: artichoke frittatas, eggs and asparagus, roast lamb, and pea soup are among the many mentioned by name.

With the assistance of artists such as Bernardo Buontalenti, the Medici family's banquets evolved into what can truly be described as a "theater of marvels," famed for mechanical devices which caused entire banqueting tables to vanish, only to be replaced by others, ready laid and decorated for the next stage of the banquet. Buontalenti also used "*ghiacciaie*" or underground stores of ice (and from which a street in Florence, Via delle Ghiacciaie, takes its name) to ensure that even in the hottest summer weather his master, Francis I, could indulge his love of drinks made with crushed ice, an early form of flavored water-ices.

Another member of the Medici family—Catherine de' Medici (above)—left her native Florence for France when she was only fourteen years old, with her recipe books and her retinue of cooks, to marry Henry de Valois, the future King of France. Catherine introduced the French to many Tuscan delicacies, including duck with sweet oranges, *crespelle* (crêpes), an early form of Béchamel made with olive oil, the art of frying, and the use of olive oil, spinach, peas, and artichokes.

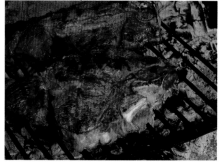

**Serves:** 2
**Preparation:** 1 minute
**Cooking:** about 10 minutes
**Recipe grading:** easy

- a 1½ lb/800 g T-bone steak from a young steer, at least 1½ in/4 cm thick
- salt and freshly ground black pepper

Suggested wine: a dry red
(Brunello di Montalcino)

# Bistecca alla fiorentina
## Florentine beef steak

Season the steak well with pepper. ▪ Place on a grill about 4 in/10 cm above the glowing embers of a wood fire. ▪ After 4–5 minutes the steak will come away easily from the grill. Sprinkle the seared surface with a little salt, turn and cook the other side, sprinkling again with salt and a little more pepper. ▪ When cooked, the steak should be well-browned and sealed on the outside, rare and juicy inside. ▪ Serve at once.

*A grilled Florentine T-bone steak is the ultimate treat for steak-lovers. In Italy the steak is cut from Tuscan-bred Chianina beef and hung for at least 6 days. Traditionally it is cooked over the embers of a charcoal or wood-burning grill and eaten very rare. The steaks are also very good barbecued. Ask your butcher for a steak which has been well-hung to ensure plenty of flavor and tenderness.*

# Pollo ai semi di finocchio

## Chicken with fennel seeds

Serves: 4
Preparation: 20 minutes
Cooking: 1 hour
Recipe grading: easy

Wash the chicken inside and out and dry with paper towels. ▪ Mix the pancetta, garlic, herbs, and fennel seeds with a good pinch each of salt and pepper and place in the cavity. Use a trussing needle and thread to sew up the opening. ▪ Pour half the olive oil into a roasting pan and add the chicken. Drizzle with the remaining oil and sprinkle with salt and pepper. ▪ Roast for 1 hour or until the juices run clear when a knife is inserted deep into the thigh. ▪ Serve hot, accompanied by a mixed green salad.

- a young, oven-ready roasting chicken, about 3½ lb/1.5 kg
- scant ½ cup/100 g diced pancetta
- 2 cloves garlic, finely chopped
- 1 heaped teaspoon finely chopped sage
- 1 heaped teaspoon finely chopped rosemary
- 1 tablespoon finely chopped parsley
- 1 level teaspoon fennel seeds
- 5 tablespoons extra-virgin olive oil
- salt and freshly ground black pepper

Suggested wine: a young dry red (Chianti Putto)

# Frittata di bietole

## Swiss chard frittata

Serves: 4
Preparation: 5 minutes
Cooking: 20 minutes
Recipe grading: fairly easy

Bring a little salted water to a boil and cook the Swiss chard over a moderate heat for about 10 minutes. ▪ Drain well, squeeze out excess moisture, and chop coarsely. ▪ Break the eggs into a bowl. Beat briefly with a fork and season with salt and pepper. Stir in the cheese, followed by the prosciutto and cooked Swiss chard. ▪ Heat the oil in a fairly large nonstick skillet over a moderate heat. When it is hot, pour in the egg mixture and cook for about 5 minutes, until the eggs have set and the underside is lightly browned. ▪ To turn the frittata, place a large plate over it, turn both upside down and then slide the egg mixture back into the pan, browned side up. Cook for 3–4 minutes more. ▪ Turn the cooked frittata out onto a heated serving dish. ▪ Serve at once with green or red chicory/Belgian endive or radicchio.

- 1 lb/500 g trimmed tender young Swiss chard, well-washed
- 6 large eggs
- salt and freshly ground black pepper
- ½ cup/60 g freshly grated parmesan cheese
- ½ cup/60 g diced prosciutto/Parma ham
- 4 tablespoons extra-virgin olive oil

Suggested wine: a young, dry rosé (Bolgheri)

*Replace the Swiss chard with the same amount of spinach to make an equally delicious frittata.*

# Verdure

Like all traditional cuisines, until recently Tuscan vegetable cooking was strongly seasonal. Spring was the season for fava beans and pecorino cheese, summer was a vegetable-lovers paradise when zucchini, peppers, eggplant, tomatoes, green beans, peas, and many others vied with each other for a place on the table. Fall and winter brought artichokes and fennel bulbs. All this has changed in the last ten years since most vegetables have become available at affordable prices throughout the year.

# Fagiolini alla fiorentina

## Florentine string beans

Cook the beans in salted, boiling water until they are tender but still crisp. ▪ Drain and set aside. ▪ Heat the oil in a skillet over a moderate heat and sauté the garlic and onion for 3–4 minutes. ▪ Add the fennel seeds and tomatoes. Season with salt. Simmer for 3–4 minutes before adding the cooked beans. ▪ Season with pepper and mix carefully. Cover and cook for about 12 minutes. If the mixture dries out too much during cooking, moisten with the water. ▪ Serve hot.

Serves: 4
Preparation: 15 minutes
Cooking: 35 minutes
Recipe grading: easy

- 1¼ lb/625 g string/French beans, washed, topped, and tailed
- 4 tablespoons extra-virgin olive oil
- 1 clove garlic, finely chopped
- 1 onion or shallot, very thinly sliced
- 1 teaspoon crushed fennel seeds
- 2 large ripe tomatoes, skinned, seeded, and diced
- salt and freshly ground black pepper
- 1–2 tablespoons hot water

Wine: a light, dry white
(Bianco Pisano di San Torpè)

Serves: 4
Preparation: 15 minutes
Cooking: 25 minutes
Recipe grading: easy

- 4 cups/500 g freshly hulled fava beans/
  broad beans (about 5 lb/2½ kg of
  fresh bean pods)
- scant ½ cup/100 g diced pancetta
- 2 cloves garlic, bruised
- 1 onion, thinly sliced
- 4 tablespoons extra-virgin olive oil
- 1½ tablespoons finely chopped parsley
- salt and freshly ground black pepper
- generous 1 cup/250 ml hot chicken or
  vegetable stock (homemade or
  bouillon cube)

Suggested wine: a dry white
(Vernaccia di San Gimignano)

# Stufato di fave

## Fava bean stew

Put the beans in a bowl and cover with cold water to prevent their skins from toughening. ▪ Sauté the pancetta, garlic, and onion in the oil in a large skillet over a moderate heat for 5–6 minutes. ▪ Remove the garlic and add the drained beans, parsley, salt, pepper, and stock. Cover and simmer over a moderate heat for about 20 minutes, or until the beans are very tender. ▪ Reduce any remaining stock by increasing the heat with the lid removed. ▪ Serve hot.

*This stew is equally good when
made with frozen beans.*

# Fiori di zucca fritti

## Fried zucchini flowers

Remove the pistil (the bright yellow center) and calyx (the green leaflets at the base) from each flower. Wash quickly and gently pat dry with paper towels. ▪ Sift the flour into a mixing bowl and make a well in the center. Add the salt and 1 tablespoon each of oil and water. ▪ Gradually mix into the flour, adding enough extra water to make a batter with a thick pouring consistency that will cling to the flowers. ▪ Heat the oil in a large skillet until very hot. ▪ Dip the flowers in the batter and fry until golden brown on both sides. ▪ Drain on paper towels. Fry all the flowers in the same way. ▪ Serve immediately.

Serves: 4
Preparation: 10 minutes
Cooking: 25 minutes
Recipe grading: fairly easy

- 14 oz/400 g very fresh zucchini/ courgette flowers
- ⅔ cup/100 g all-purpose/plain flour
- ½ teaspoon salt
- 1 tablespoon + scant 1 cup/200 ml extra-virgin olive oil
- 1–2 tablespoons cold water

Wine: a dry white (Elba Bianco)

*Replace the water with the same quantity of beer. The batter will be much crisper, with its own special taste.*

Serves: 4
Preparation: 15 minutes + 10–15 minutes'
    standing
Cooking: 30 minutes
Recipe grading: fairly easy

- 8 very young globe artichokes
- juice of 1 lemon
- 1 clove garlic, finely chopped
- 1½ tablespoons finely chopped parsley
- ¾ cup/90 g diced pancetta
- 1 cup/60 g fresh bread crumbs
- 6 tablespoons extra-virgin olive oil
- salt and freshly ground black pepper

Suggested wine: a dry white
(Montecarlo Bianco)

# Carciofi ripieni

## Filled artichokes

Prepare the artichokes by cutting off the tops and removing the tough outer leaves. Cut the stalk at the base so that they will stand upright on their own. Peel the stems and place them in a bowl of cold water with the artichokes and lemon juice. Set aside for 10–15 minutes. ▪ Chop the stems finely and place in a bowl with the garlic, parsley, pancetta, and bread crumbs. Add 2 tablespoons of oil and mix well. ▪ Drain the artichokes and pat dry with paper towels. ▪ Open each artichoke and push a little of the bread crumb mixture firmly down to the base of each leaf. ▪ Pack the filled artichokes upright in a flameproof pan only just large enough for them. Add the remaining oil and enough water to come halfway up the artichokes. ▪ Bring to a gentle boil, cover tightly and simmer for 25–30 minutes. Test by removing one of the lowest, outermost leaves; if it is tender, they are done. ▪ Continue cooking, uncovered, over a high heat until all the cooking liquid has evaporated. ▪ Serve hot, warm, or cold.

# Fagioli in fiasco

## Beans cooked in a flask

Feed the beans into the flask. Pour in the oil, add the garlic, sage, tomatoes, salt, and pepper, then top up with the water. ▪ Cork up the flask tightly and place the bulbous end deep among the barely glowing embers of a wood fire to cook gently for several hours. These flasks used to be left in the embers last thing at night. By the morning the beans were cooked. Tip the beans out of the flask. Discard the garlic and sage and serve, with an extra drizzle of olive oil, salt, and freshly ground black pepper.

Serves: 4
Preparation: 10 minutes
Cooking: at least 3 hours
Recipe grading: easy

- 1½ lb/750 g freshly hulled cannellini beans or 2 cups/350 g dried cannellini beans, soaked for 12 hours
- ½ cup/125 ml extra-virgin olive oil
- 2 cloves garlic, whole
- 4 leaves fresh sage
- 2 cherry tomatoes, pricked with a fork
- salt and freshly ground black pepper
- water, sufficient to fill the flask to three-quarters

Suggested wine: a young, dry red
(Chianti dei Colli Fiorentini)

*This is a traditional Florentine recipe which may appeal to the adventurous cook as an enjoyable experiment. You will need an empty, straw-wrapped Tuscan wine bottle and its cork. Remove the straw, leaving a glass flask. In the modern version of this recipe the beans are cooked in a special earthenware container like the one shown here. If you do try this recipe, be sure to place the bottle in the dying embers and not in the flames. If you put it in the flames it may well explode.*

# Feast days: keeping traditions alive

Like most people, Tuscans can usually think of a good reason to throw a party. Rural feast days, known as *sagre*, often have very old, pagan origins and are usually held to give thanks for nature's bounty. Christian festivals, such as those held to celebrate the town or village Patron Saint's Day, occur alongside celebrations to

commemorate important political or local events. Each of these events is associated with an array of typical dishes. In Tuscany Christmas is popularly known as *ceppo*, the equivalent of the English "Yuletide," a shared reference to the custom of burning a large log of wood, the Yule Log, on Christmas Eve while work started in the kitchen to prepare the capon for the main meal next day.

The Palio (shown left in an historic painting), held twice a year in June and August, is the most famous celebration in Siena. Tourists come from all over the world to watch the horses from the various *quartieri* of the city race around the beautiful shell-shaped piazza. But Christmas is a special time too, with an abundance of seasonal specialties, from the legendary *Panforte*, made from a centuries-old recipe with candied fruits, almonds, honey, sugar, and spice (see recipe, page 114), to *Cavallucci* (see recipe, page 117), made with honey, sugar, flour, candied fruits, and pepper, so-called because they were given to the stable boys (called "*cavallari*" in Italian) employed in country inns, and *Ricciarelli* (see recipe, page 116), another very old recipe for diamond shaped sweetmeats made with almonds and sugar.

For *Berlingaccio* (Fat Thursday, the last before Lent), synonymous with over-indulgence and to be repented of the following Ash Wednesday, it was customary to slaughter the fattened pig which would not only replenish the family larder with various cuts of meat but also provided excellent fare for the feast day: blood puddings and pork fat used to prepare *Schiacciata alla fiorentina* and *Cenci* (see recipe, page 112), the traditional Florentine cakes and sweets of Carnevale.

At New Year and Epiphany in Viareggio little witch-shaped-cookies are made with flour, eggs, sugar, anise, milk, and rum. The sweet dough is rolled out into a thin sheet and stamped out with special pastry cutters to represent a seasonal visitor from popular folklore, a kindly old witch (the Befana).

Throughout the year, but particularly in the summer months, the villages and hilltop towns of Tuscany celebrate historical events and customs with parades, medieval flag-throwing, archery or jousting competitions as well as a host of food and wine festivals and events. The magic of walking into a medieval village such as San Quirico d'Orcia on a hot summer's night to find the whole village feasting at a long table stretching down the main street is unforgettable.

Easter in Florence is celebrated every year with the *Scoppio del Carro* (Explosion of the Carriage) on Easter Sunday in Piazza Duomo. A good explosion bodes well for the fall harvest.

Serves: 4
Preparation: 30 minutes + time to make the
  meat sauce
Cooking: 45 minutes
Recipe grading: fairly easy

- 1 quantity meat sauce (see recipes on pages 45, 50, or 53)
- 2 whole, tender celery bunches with plenty of heart, washed
- 5 oz/150 g chicken livers
- 2 tablespoons butter
- 2 tablespoons + scant 1 cup/200 ml extra-virgin olive oil
- 1 onion, finely chopped
- 1 clove garlic, finely chopped
- 1¼ cups/150 g diced prosciutto/ Parma ham
- 7 oz/200 g ground/minced lean veal
- ½ cup/125 ml dry white wine
- ⅓ cup/50 g all-purpose/plain flour
- 2 eggs, beaten
- ¾ cup/90 g dry bread crumbs
- salt and freshly ground black pepper
- 1 cup/125 g freshly grated parmesan cheese

Suggested wine: a dry, fruity red
(Chianti Mantalbano)

# Sedani alla pratese

## Filled celery stalks

Prepare the meat sauce. ▪ Boil the celery in a large pan of salted water for 5 minutes. Drain and cool. ▪ Trim any connective tissue and discolored parts from the chicken livers and chop finely. ▪ Heat the butter with the 2 tablespoons of oil in a nonstick skillet. When foaming, add the onion and garlic and sauté for 3–4 minutes. ▪ Add the chicken livers and prosciutto and cook for a few minutes. ▪ Add the veal, breaking up any lumps. ▪ Season with salt and pepper. Stir and cook for 4–5 minutes. ▪ Pour in the wine and cover and cook over a low heat for 20 minutes. ▪ Cut the celery stalks into 3 in/7.5 cm lengths and pack each one with the chicken liver stuffing. ▪ Coat each piece of celery with flour, dip in the egg, and coat with bread crumbs. ▪ Heat the remaining oil in a large nonstick skillet and fry 3–4 of the sticks until golden brown on both sides. ▪ Drain on paper towels. Repeat until all the stalks are fried. ▪ Place a layer of celery sticks in a warm ovenproof dish. Spoon some meat sauce and any remaining stuffing over the top and sprinkle with a little cheese. Repeat until all the celery, meat sauce, and cheese are used up, finishing with a layer of cheese. ▪ Bake in a preheated oven at 425°C/220°C/gas 7 until the cheese turns golden brown. ▪ Serve at once.

Serves: 4
Preparation: 10 minutes + 10–15 minutes'
　　standing
Cooking: 15 minutes
Recipe grading: fairly easy

- 8 baby globe artichokes or 16 frozen
  artichoke hearts, thawed
- juice of 1 lemon
- ⅓ cup/50 g all-purpose/plain flour
- ½ cup/125 ml extra-virgin olive oil
- 5 large eggs
- salt and freshly ground black pepper

Suggested wine: a young, dry white
(Bianco Vergine Valdichiana)

# Tortino di carciofi

## Italian artichoke omelet

If using fresh artichokes, cut off the tops and remove the tough outer leaves. Cut the stalk at the base leaving ¾ in/2 cm of the stem attached. Wash, cut into quarters, and place in a bowl of cold water with the lemon juice for 10–15 minutes (this will stop them turning black). ▪ Drain well and pat dry. ▪ Coat the artichoke pieces or defrosted hearts with flour, shaking off any excess. ▪ Heat all but 2 tablespoons of the oil in a large, nonstick skillet over a high heat until very hot. ▪ Fry the artichokes for about 8 minutes, turning them several times so that they cook evenly. When they are lightly browned, drain on paper towels. ▪ Tip out the oil used for frying and replace with the remaining oil. Arrange the artichokes in the skillet and return to a moderately high heat. ▪ Beat the eggs lightly with the salt and pepper, then pour over the artichokes. Cook for 4–5 minutes. ▪ Turn the omelet carefully and cook for 4 minutes more. It should be firm and lightly browned on both sides. ▪ Turn out onto a heated serving dish and serve hot.

*Use frozen artichoke hearts unless you can find tiny, very fresh artichoke buds.*

# Piselli alla Montaperti

## Peas with pancetta, garlic, and wine

Wash the peas in a colander under cold water. ▪ Sauté the onion or shallot, garlic, parsley, and pancetta together in the oil over a moderate heat for 2 minutes. ▪ Add the peas, season with salt and pepper, and stir. ▪ Pour in the wine, cover and simmer gently for 15–20 minutes, stirring occasionally. Moisten with a little stock as necessary. ▪ Serve hot.

Serves: 4
Preparation: 10 minutes + time for hulling/
 shelling the peas
Cooking: 25 minutes
Recipe grading: easy

- 5 cups/600 g hulled fresh peas or frozen petits pois
- 1 small white onion or shallot, very thinly sliced
- 1 clove garlic, finely chopped
- 1½ tablespoons finely chopped parsley
- 1 cup/120 g diced pancetta
- 4 tablespoons extra-virgin olive oil
- salt and freshly ground black pepper
- ½ cup/125 ml dry white wine
- scant ½ cup/100 ml stock (homemade or bouillon cube)

Suggested wine: a young, dry, lightly sparkling red (Vino Novello)

95

# Funghi trifolati

## Mushroom stew

Trim the ends off the mushroom stalks. Brush away any dirt and grit and wash quickly under cold running water. Pat dry with paper towels. ▪ Slice the caps into thin strips and dice the stalks. ▪ Sauté the garlic in the oil with the calamint over a low heat for 3–4 minutes. When the garlic starts to color, add the mushroom stalks. Season with salt and pepper and cook for 5 minutes. ▪ Add the caps and cook for another 5 minutes. If necessary, stir in enough hot water to keep the mushrooms moist. ▪ Finally, stir in the tomato purée and more seasoning, if needed. ▪ Simmer gently for 10–12 minutes. ▪ Serve hot.

Serves: 4
Preparation: 10 minutes
Cooking: 30 minutes
Recipe grading: easy

- 2 lb/1 kg fresh porcini mushrooms
- 3 cloves garlic, whole
- 4 tablespoons extra-virgin olive oil
- sprig of fresh calamint (or parsley or thyme)
- salt and freshly ground black pepper
- 1–2 tablespoons hot water
- scant 1 cup/200 ml tomato purée

Suggested wine: a dry white
(Vernaccia di San Gimignano)

*This same recipe can be made with a variety of wild mushrooms. Cooking times may vary according to the type of mushroom used. For a stronger mushroom flavor, omit the tomato pureé. These mushrooms make a delicious side dish and a wonderful sauce for fresh pasta.*

Serves: 4
Preparation: 25 minutes
Cooking: 1 hour
Recipe grading: fairly easy

---

- 8 large Bermuda or yellow onions/mild red, or Spanish onions
- 1 oz/25 g dried porcini mushrooms, soaked in about ½ cup/125 ml warm water
- 2 tablespoons extra-virgin olive oil
- 4 oz/125 g ground/minced lean veal
- 1 fresh Italian pork sausage
- 1 egg
- 1 tablespoon finely chopped parsley
- salt and freshly ground black pepper
- freshly grated nutmeg
- 2 tablespoons butter
- 6 tablespoons stock (homemade or bouillon cube)

---

Suggested wine: a young, dry red
(Chianti Classico)

# Cipolle alla grossetana

## Stuffed onions

Cut both ends off the onions. Put into a saucepan and cover with salted boiling water. Cook over a fairly high heat for 10 minutes. Drain. ▪ Carefully push the center out of each onion leaving the 2–3 outermost layers intact to be stuffed. Set aside. ▪ Finely chop the center sections. ▪ Drain the mushrooms well, pour the liquid through a fine sieve, and reserve. ▪ Chop the mushrooms finely and sauté in the oil in a small skillet for 3 minutes. ▪ Add the veal and sausage meat, using a fork to crush any lumps that may form. Cook for 10 minutes, moistening with the reserved mushroom liquid as necessary. ▪ Combine the chopped onion, egg, parsley, salt, pepper, and nutmeg in a large bowl with the meat mixture. Mix well and stuff the onions. ▪ Arrange the onions in a large, shallow ovenproof dish greased with the butter and pour a little stock over the top. ▪ Bake in a preheated oven at 400°F/200°C/gas 6 for 30 minutes, adding more stock at intervals, if necessary ▪ Serve hot.

# Dolci

In keeping with the rest of Tuscan cooking and with the Tuscan temperament itself, traditional sweets are simple and closely linked to natural products produced in the region: honey, hazelnuts, almonds, raisins, grapes, rosemary, and chestnuts are typical ingredients. Essential simplicity and style might be the best way to sum up a Tuscan dessert. Try finishing a four-course meal with a glass of Vin Santo and a handful of Prato cookies for dunking and ponderous munching.

100

# Zuccotto

## Ice cream trifle

Cut the cake in half horizontally, then divide it into 8–12 triangular wedges. ▪ Moisten the cake on both sides with Cointreau or rum and use to line a 1½ quart/1½ liter capacity mold. ▪ Beat the cream until stiff, adding the confectioners' sugar when almost ready. Fold in the grated chocolate, almonds, and candied fruits. ▪ Transfer half this mixture to a separate bowl. ▪ Melt the remaining chocolate in a double boiler (or a bowl over boiling water) and mix gently into one half of the cream. ▪ Spread the white cream over the sponge cake lining in the mold. Cover with foil and place in the freezer for 10–15 minutes. ▪ Remove the foil and spoon the chocolate cream into the mold, which should be completely full. ▪ Cover with foil and freeze for at least 3–4 hours before serving.

Serves: 4
Preparation: 15 minutes + 3–4 hours' freezing
Cooking: 10 minutes
Recipe grading: fairly easy

- 12 oz/375 g good-quality bought fatless sponge cake (Madeira type)
- ½ cup/125 ml Cointreau or rum
- 2 cups/500 ml light whipping cream
- ⅓ cup/50 g confectioners'/icing sugar
- 2 oz/60 g good quality semisweet/dark chocolate, grated
- 3 tablespoons peeled finely chopped almonds
- ¼ cup/50 g diced candied orange and citron peel
- 2½ oz/75 g semisweet/unsweetened dark chocolate, coarsely chopped

Suggested wine: a dry, sparkling white (Vernaccia di San Gimignano spumante)

# Frittelle di riso

## Lemon rice fritters

Cook the rice in the milk for about 1 hour, until the grains have almost disintegrated. ▪ Stir the butter into this very thick mixture and remove from the heat. ▪ Add the sugar and the zest. ▪ Stir in the eggs one at a time, then add the salt, flour, raisins, and rum. Stir thoroughly and chill for about 1 hour in the refrigerator. ▪ Heat the oil in a nonstick skillet until very hot. To test, drop a tiny piece of fritter into the oil. If bubbles form around it immediately, it is hot enough. ▪ Drop tablespoons of the fritter mixture into the hot oil. Fry 5–6 fritters together until they are golden brown all over. This should take about 4 minutes for each fritter. ▪ Drain on paper towels. Dust with the confectioners' sugar and transfer to a heated serving dish. ▪ Serve at once.

Serves: 4–6
Preparation: 20 minutes + 1 hour chilling
Cooking: 1¼ hours
Recipe grading: fairly easy

- 1 cup/200 g short-grain, pudding rice (or sticky rice)
- 2 cups/500 ml whole/full cream milk
- 1 tablespoon butter
- 3 tablespoons sugar
- grated zest of ½ lemon
- 2 eggs
- dash of salt
- ⅓ cup/50 g all-purpose/plain flour
- ⅓ cup/50 g golden raisins/sultanas, soaked in warm water for 15 minutes, drained and squeezed
- 3 tablespoons rum
- scant 1 cup/200 ml olive oil, for frying
- ⅔ cup/100 g confectioners'/icing sugar

Suggested wine: a medium or dry dessert wine (Vin Santo)

*These scrumptious fritters originally come from Siena where they were served on St. Joseph's Day (March 19).*

# Schiacciata con l'uva

## Black grape sweet bread

Serves: 6
Preparation: 25 minutes + 3 hours' rising
Cooking: 30 minutes
Recipe grading: fairly easy

- 1 tablespoon fresh baker's yeast or 1½ packets active dried yeast
- scant ½ cup/100 ml warm water
- 1⅔ cups/250 g unbleached or all-purpose white flour/strong white or plain flour
- ½ teaspoon salt
- scant ½ cup/100 ml extra-virgin olive oil
- ¾ cup/150 g superfine/caster sugar
- ⅓ cup/50 g all-purpose/plain flour
- 2 lb/1 kg unpeeled ripe, black grapes, seeded

Suggested wine: a slightly sweet, sparkling white (Moscadello di Montalcino)

Dissolve the yeast in the water and set aside for about 15 minutes. ▪ Sift the flour and salt into a large mixing bowl and make a well in the center. Add the frothy yeast liquid and gradually combine with the flour. ▪ Transfer to a floured work surface and knead briefly. ▪ Shape the dough into a ball, wrap loosely in a clean cloth, and leave to rise for 1 hour in a warm place. ▪ Knead again, gradually working in three-quarters of the oil, one-third of the sugar, and a little more salt. ▪ Shape into a ball, wrap in a cloth, and leave to rise for another hour. ▪ Use the remaining oil to grease a rectangular 11 x 16-in/28 x 40 cm baking pan. ▪ Divide the dough in half and press one half into the pan. ▪ Gently press just over half the grapes into the dough and sprinkle with half the remaining sugar. Roll the rest of the dough out into a rectangular shape and use it to cover the grapes. ▪ Press the remaining grapes into this top layer and sprinkle with the remaining sugar. ▪ Leave to stand at warm room temperature for 1 hour to rise, then bake in a preheated oven at 375°F/190°C/gas 5 for 30 minutes. ▪ Serve warm or cold.

*This delicious sweet grape bread appears in bakeries and cake shops from August as the new season's grapes mature.*

Serves: 6
Preparation: 25 minutes + 1½ hours
   rising time
Cooking: 25 minutes
Recipe grading: easy

- 1 tablespoon fresh baker's yeast or 1½ packets active dried yeast
- ⅔ cup/150 ml warm water
- small branch of fresh rosemary, washed and dried
- 4 tablespoons extra-virgin olive oil
- 2⅓ cups/350 g unbleached white/strong white flour + ⅓ cup/50 g extra flour
- ¼ cup/50 g superfine/caster sugar
- 1 teaspoon salt
- scant ½ cup/100 g Muscatel dried grapes (seeded) or seedless white raisins/golden sultanas, washed
- 1 egg, lightly beaten

Suggested wine: a slightly sweet, sparkling white (Moscadello di Montalcino)

# Pan di ramerino
## Rosemary bread rolls

Dissolve the yeast in the warm water and leave to stand for 15 minutes. ▪ Strip the leaves off the rosemary, reserving the smaller, younger ones. ▪ Place the larger leaves and the oil in a small saucepan and warm over a low heat for about 5 minutes. ▪ Strain the oil through a fine sieve into a small bowl, discarding the rosemary. ▪ Sift the flour into a large mixing bowl, make a well in the center, and add the frothy yeast liquid. Gradually incorporate the flour, sugar, rosemary-flavored oil, and salt. ▪ Transfer the dough to a floured work surface and knead well. ▪ Shape into a ball and place in a large bowl. Cover with a clean cloth and leave to rise for 1 hour. ▪ Work the raisins into the risen dough, together with the reserved rosemary, kneading to distribute them evenly. ▪ Divide the dough into 6 equal balls and flatten slightly. ▪ Space out on a nonstick baking sheet. Brush with egg, mark with a cross, and leave to rise again for 30 minutes. ▪ Bake in a preheated oven at 400°F/200°C/gas 6 for 20 minutes.

*These sweet bread rolls are an old Florentine recipe. They were traditionally served at Easter. Bakers set up stalls outside church doors, selling the rolls to churchgoers on their way home. It was sacrilege to waste even the tiniest crumb!*

# Castagnaccio

## Chestnut batter pudding

Sift the flour into a mixing bowl and make a well in the center. Pour in the water, 1 tablespoon of the oil, and salt. Stir thoroughly to obtain a thick, lumpfree, pouring batter. ▪ Stir in the drained raisins and the nuts and then pour into a baking pan greased with 2 tablespoons of the oil. ▪ Sprinkle with the rosemary leaves and drizzle with the remaining oil. ▪ Bake in a preheated oven at 400°F/200°C/gas 6 for about 30 minutes, or until a thin crunchy crust has formed. ▪ Serve hot or at room temperature.

Serves: 4
Preparation: 15 minutes
Cooking: 50 minutes
Recipe grading: fairly easy

- 2 cups/300 g sweet chestnut flour
- 1½ cups/375 ml water
- 6 tablespoons extra-virgin olive oil
- dash of salt
- ½ cup/90 g small seedless white raisins/small, golden sultanas, soaked in warm water for 15 minutes, drained and squeezed
- ⅓ cup/60 g pine nuts
- a few young, tender rosemary leaves

Suggested wine: a dry dessert wine
(Vin Santo)

*Use a larger pan if you prefer your castagnaccio thinner and more crunchy, or smaller if you like a creamier, softer texture under the crust.*

# Biscottini di Prato

## Prato cookies

Serves: 6
Preparation: 15 minutes
Cooking: about 40 minutes
Recipe grading: easy

- scant 2 cups/250 g sweet almonds, unpeeled
- 4 large eggs, separated
- 2½ cups/500 g sugar
- 3⅓ cups/500 g all-purpose/plain flour
- dash of salt
- 1 tablespoon butter
- 2 tablespoons all-purpose/plain flour

Suggested wine: a sweet, medium or dry dessert wine (Vin Santo)

Spread the almonds out in a shallow baking pan and roast at 400°F/200°C/gas 6 for 4–5 minutes. ▪ When cool enough to handle, skin and chop coarsely. ▪ Beat the egg yolks and sugar together in a mixing bowl until pale and fluffy. ▪ Stir in the flour, almonds, and salt gradually, using a fork and then combining by hand. ▪ Beat the egg whites in a large bowl until frothy and fold them into the mixture. ▪ Knead the mixture quickly but thoroughly on a floured work surface. ▪ Shape the dough into long cylinders about ½ in/1 cm in diameter. ▪ Transfer to a buttered and floured cookie sheet. ▪ Bake in a preheated oven at 375°F/190°C/gas 5 for 25 minutes. ▪ Remove from the oven and raise the temperature to 400°F/200°C/gas 6. ▪ Slice the cylinders diagonally into pieces 1½ in/4 cm long, and return them to the oven for 10 minutes more, or until pale golden brown.

*Be sure to roast the almonds. They will lack their distinctive flavor and texture if unroasted ground almonds are used. Served with a glass of Vin Santo (Holy wine) for dipping.*

# Brutti ma buoni

## Almond cookies

Use a deep bowl and electric beater to beat the egg whites until stiff but not 'dry'. ▪ Fold in the ground almonds and sugar. ▪ Transfer to a large bowl over a pan of simmering water. Cover and cook for 20 minutes. ▪ Use a tablespoon to scoop out egg-shaped spoonfuls and place them on a lightly buttered and floured cookie sheet. ▪ Bake in a preheated oven at 350°F/ 180°C/gas 4 for about 45 minutes, or until they are golden brown. ▪ Leave to cool before serving.

Serves: 6
Preparation: 15 minutes
Cooking: 1 hour and 10 minutes
Recipe grading: easy

- 6 large egg whites
- 1¼ lb/625 g ground almonds
- 2½ cups/500 g sugar
- 1 tablespoon butter
- 2 tablespoons all-purpose/plain flour

Suggested wine: a sweet, medium or dry dessert wine (Vin Santo)

*These can be served in their own with a sweet dessert wine such as* Vin Santo *or together with the Prato Cookies.*

# Ongoing traditions

While it is commonplace nowadays to find a Milanese risotto or a southern dish of pasta with broccoli on the menu of many restaurants in Tuscany, nevertheless Tuscan cooking retains its own clear identity with distinctive flavors and aromas linked to the region's culinary traditions and to its famous wines and olive oil. Furthermore, Tuscan cooks have recently rediscovered a host of dishes steeped in tradition, made with their original ingredients. For example, spelt (*farro*, in Italian), a cereal widely used by the Etruscans, has returned to many tables in traditional dishes such as Spelt and bean soup, or Spelt and vegetable soup. It is also used as a base for modern dishes, such as Spelt salad (below) with fresh vegetables. Traditional Tuscan cooking has always been typified by the use of absolutely fresh produce. Plenty of filling soups and nutritious "*minestre,*" not a lot of pasta, and beans in preference to rice, provide a diet that is low in fat, modest and digestible, based on ingredients that can easily be used up as leftovers, avoiding any waste. See *Panzanella* (see recipe, page 29), *Pappa al pomodoro* (see recipe, page 32), or *Francesina* (see recipe, page 63). The few desserts are good, plain fare: *Castagnaccio* (see recipe, page 107) or *Schiacciata all'uva* (see recipe, page 104), with one exception: Zuppa inglese or *Zuppa ducale* or "the Duke's trifle" created by Siennese cooks in honor of the Duke of Correggio (see recipe, next page).

## Zuppa inglese
For eight to ten people

5 large egg yolks
¾ cup/150 g sugar
⅓ cup/50 g all-purpose/plain flour
2 cups/500 ml milk
few drops of vanilla extract (essence)
3½ oz/100 g grated semisweet/dark chocolate
½ cup/125 ml Alchermes liqueur
½ cup/125 ml rum
4 tablespoons water
20 lady/sponge fingers
whipped cream, for decoration

Whisk the egg yolks and sugar until straw–colored and then stir in the flour. ▪ Heat the milk with the vanilla extract until fairly hot, but not boiling. ▪ Pour the milk into the egg mixture and then cook for 7–8 minutes in a heavy-bottomed saucepan over a low heat, stirring continuously to prevent lumps forming. ▪ Pour half the custard into a bowl and cover with plastic wrap touching the surface to prevent a skin forming. ▪ Melt the chocolate in a double boiler over barely simmering water. ▪ Return the remaining custard to the heat and stir in the melted chocolate. Cook for 2 minutes, stirring continuously. ▪ Pour the chocolate custard into a bowl and cover with plastic wrap touching the surface to prevent a skin forming. ▪ Set the custards aside to cool before using. ▪ Mix the Alchermes, rum, and water together in a bowl. ▪ Dip the ladyfingers into the water and liqueur mixture, then use one-third of them to line a 2-quart/2-liter glass bowl or soufflé dish. ▪ Pour the chocolate custard over the top, cover with another layer of dipped ladyfingers, and spread the plain custard on top. ▪ Finish with the remaining ladyfingers, cover with foil and refrigerate for about 12 hours. ▪ Just before serving, decorate with plenty of whipped cream and, if liked, a little more grated chocolate.

*Zuppa ducale* became famous in Florence during the 18th century as *"Zuppa inglese"*. It was renamed by the proprietor of the historic Caffé Doney (closed long ago) to reflect its great popularity with early members of the English expatriate community which has existed in Florence for more than two centuries. In Tuscany this wickedly rich trifle, made with lashings of egg custard and chocolate, is streaked crimson by the cochineal (made with crushed Kermes-oak insects) in the reputedly highly aphrodisiac Alchermes liqueur manufactured by the monks of St. Mark's monastery.

# Cenci

## Fried Carnival cookies with confectioners' sugar

Serves: 4
Preparation: 20 minutes + 30 minutes
    standing
Cooking: about 20 minutes
Recipe grading: easy

- 1²/₃ cups/250 g all-purpose/plain flour +
  ¹/₃ cup/50 g extra
- 2 tablespoons butter, softened
- 2 eggs
- ¹/₄ cup/50 g superfine/caster sugar
- 1¹/₂ tablespoons Vin Santo or other
  good quality sweet dessert wine
- dash of salt
- 1¹/₂ tablespoons grated orange zest
- 1¹/₄ cups/310 ml extra-virgin olive oil,
  for frying
- ¹/₃ cup/50 g confectioners'/icing sugar,
  sifted

Suggested wine: a sweet, medium or dry
dessert wine (Vin Santo)

Sift the flour onto a work surface and make a well in the center. Add the butter, eggs, sugar, dessert wine, salt, and orange zest. Gradually combine with the flour and knead well. The dough should be soft but hold its shape well. ▪ Cover with a clean cloth and leave to rest for 30 minutes. ▪ Roll out into a thin sheet using a lightly floured rolling pin. ▪ Cut into diamonds, rectangles, and into broad rectangular strips which can be tied loosely into a knot if wished. ▪ Heat the oil to very hot and fry a few at a time until pale golden brown all over. ▪ Remove with a slotted spoon and drain on paper towels. ▪ Serve at once, sprinkled with the confectioners' sugar.

*Cenci (which means "rags") are traditionally
served during Carnivale, the period leading up
to Lent before Easter.*

Serves: 6
Preparation: 30 minutes
Cooking: about 1 hour
Recipe grading: fairly easy

- scant 2 cups/250 g peeled whole almonds
- 1 cup/150 g walnuts
- ½ cup/100 g small, soft dried figs
- 1¼ cups/300 g best quality mixed candied peel (ideally orange, lemon, and melon), finely chopped
- 1 tablespoon ground spice mixture (cinnamon, cloves, coriander seeds, white peppercorns, and nutmeg)
- ⅓ cup/50 g unsweetened cocoa powder
- 1 cup/150 g confectioners'/icing sugar + extra to dust
- scant ⅓ cup/100 g clear, runny honey
- 1½ tablespoons all-purpose/plain flour
- confectioners' wafer papers or rice paper for lining the pan

Suggested wine: a sweet, medium or dry dessert wine (Vin Santo)

# Panforte

## Siennese dried fruit and nut cake

Spread the almonds and walnuts out on cookie sheets and bake at 400°F/200°C/gas 6 for 3–4 minutes. Leave to cool slightly and then chop very finely (ground almonds will not give the same texture). ▪ Mix the nuts in a large bowl with the finely chopped figs (remove the hard stalk end), the peel, the spices, and cocoa powder. ▪ Set aside while you dissolve the sugar in the honey in a double boiler over simmering water. After 8 minutes, test to see if it forms a thread when you lift a spoonful above the pan. If not, continue cooking for a few minutes more. ▪ Remove from the heat and stir in the flour and the nuts and figs mixture. Put into a shallow layer cake pan with a removable base which has been buttered and lined with the wafers or rice paper. Smooth the surface, cover with a layer of wafers or rice paper. ▪ Bake in a preheated oven at 350°F/180°C/gas 4 for about 40 minutes. Leave to cool, dust with the extra confectioners' sugar and place on a serving dish.

Panforte *will keep for months if wrapped in foil.*

Serves: 4–6
Preparation: 25 minutes + 10 hours' resting
   for the dough
Cooking: 1 hour
Recipe grading: fairly easy

- scant 2 cups/250 g peeled whole almonds
- 1 cup/200 g superfine/caster sugar
- 1 cup/150 g confectioners'/icing sugar + extra for dusting
- scant ¼ cup/40 g finely chopped candied orange peel
- few drops almond extract/essence
- 1 large egg white, stiffly beaten
- confectioners' wafers or rice paper

Suggested wine: a sweet, medium or dry dessert wine (Vin Santo)

# Ricciarelli

## Marzipan petits fours

Spread the almonds out on a cookie sheet and bake in a preheated oven at 400°F/200°C/gas 6 for 3–4 minutes. ▪ Grind the almonds in a pestle and mortar and transfer to a mixing bowl. ▪ Stir in the sugars, orange peel, and almond extract. Carefully fold in the egg white. ▪ Shape the mixture into lozenges or squares and place on rice paper or wafers, trimming off the excess. Put on cookie sheets and let stand in a cool place for about 10 hours. ▪ Bake in a preheated oven at 300°F/150°C/gas 2 for about 1 hour, reducing the heat if they show signs of browning. They should remain quite soft. ▪ Remove from the oven and dust with sugar. ▪ Serve when they have cooled.

*Although the Ricciarelli keep well for a few days, they are at their best when freshly baked.*

# Cavallucci

## Siennese cookies with spices, honey, and nuts

Using a double boiler or a bowl over simmering water, heat the sugar and honey together. When a thread of honey forms when a spoonful is lifted above the bowl, remove from the heat. Gently fold in the flour together with the walnuts, peel, anise, and coriander. ▪ Flour your hands to stop the mixture sticking to them and break off pieces of the dough, rolling them into small cylinders. Cut them into slices about 1 in/2.5 cm thick and form into curved shapes. ▪ Put onto a buttered and floured cookie sheet and bake in a preheated oven at 325°F/170°C/gas 3 for about 1 hour.

Serves: 6
Preparation: 20 minutes
Cooking: 1¼ hours
Recipe grading: fairly easy

- 1¼ cups/250 g sugar
- generous ⅓ cup/100 g clear, runny honey
- 2⅓ cups/350 g all-purpose/plain flour + about ⅓ cup/50 g extra
- ½ cup/50 g chopped walnuts
- ¼ cup/50 g finely chopped candied orange and lemon peel
- 1 teaspoon freshly ground anise seeds
- freshly ground coriander seeds

Suggested wine: a sweet, medium or dry dessert wine (Vin Santo)

*Cavallucci will keep fresh and crisp for several days in a tightly sealed container.*

# Acknowledgments

The Publishers would like to thank Mastrociliegia, Fiesole (Florence) who kindly lent props for photography.

All photos by MARCO LANZA except:
GIULIANO CAPPELLI, FLORENCE: COVER (LANDSCAPE), BACK COVER (C, CR, B), 1, 2, 3, 5, 7B, 11T, 12T, 13B, 21B, 21CL, 32T, 35T, 36T, 36B, 37TL, 37TR, 48, 66T, 67T, 67TR; GIUSEPPE CARFAGNA, ROME: 90B, 91TR, 91B; FARABOLAFOTO, MILAN: 9T, 43B, 67CL; ADRIANO NARDI, FLORENCE: 90T, 91TL, 112; NIEDERSAECHSISCHES LANDESMUSEUM, LANDESGALERIE, HANNOVER, 76; ARCHIVIO SCALA, FLORENCE: 8, 77R